So Far from
DIXIE

So Far from Dixie

Burnham

2003 - Lanham

A/33

1st Ed. SIGNED of Five 30⁻

FB

So Far from
DIXIE

Confederates in Yankee Prisons

For Bill Wood —
with all best wishes —
Philip Burnham

6/04

PHILIP BURNHAM

Taylor Trade Publishing

Lanham • New York • Oxford

First Taylor Trade Publishing edition 2003

This Taylor Trade Publishing hardcover edition of *So Far from Dixie*
is an original publication. It is published
by arrangement with the author.

Portions of this book originally appeared in altered form in
MHQ: The Quarterly Journal of Military History in
Autumn 1997 (vol. 10, no. 1).

Quotations from the Berry Benson Papers in the Southern
Historical Collection by permission of Frances Benson Thompson.

Published by Taylor Trade Publishing
A Member of the Rowman & Littlefield Publishing Group
4501 Forbes Boulevard, Suite 200
Lanham, Maryland 20706

Distributed by National Book Network

Library of Congress Cataloging-in-Publication Data

Burnham, Philip.
   So far from Dixie : Confederates in Yankee prisons / Philip
Burnham.
      p. cm.
Includes bibliographical references and index.
   ISBN 1-58979-016-2 (alk. paper)
   1. United States—History—Civil War, 1861-1865—Prisoners and
prisons. 2. Prisoners of war—United States—History—19th century. 3.
Prisoners of war—Confederate States of America—History. I. Title.

E615 .B68 2003
973.7'72—dc21

                                                        2003005067

♾™ The paper used in this publication meets
the minimum requirements of American National
Standard for Information Sciences—Permanence
of Paper for Printed Library Materials,
ANSI/NISO Z39.48–1992.

Manufactured in the United States of America.

To the memory of my father,

Joseph Andrew Burnham,
an Ozark boy
who made good in the North

CONTENTS

ACKNOWLEDGMENTS

DURING a beautiful fall trip to Elmira, I had the good fortune to meet Mike Horigan, a native of the city who knows as much about the Union prison at Elmira as anyone on Earth. I'm grateful for his good advice, his straightforwardness, and his camaraderie when discussing our respective Elmira projects. I'd like to thank George Farr for being an enthusiastic guide to the city and an entertaining dinner companion. My thanks also to the kind assistance provided by the Chemung County Historical Society, particularly Amy Wilson and Constance Barone.

My research benefited greatly from the help of several archivists and librarians. In particular, I'd like to thank John White of the Southern Historical Collection at the University of North Carolina at Chapel Hill; L. Eileen Parris of the Virginia Historical Society; Judy Lilly of the Salina Public Library in Kansas; Greg Carroll of the Cultural Center in Charleston, West Virginia; Deborah May of the Nashville Public Library in Tennessee; and Teresa Roane of the Valentine Museum in Richmond, Virginia. I'm also grateful to the Museum of the Confederacy in Richmond, the Steele Memorial Library in Elmira, and the staffs of the Library of Congress and the National Archives in Washington.

My work was enriched by correspondence and conversations with surviving relatives of some of the men described in the book. I would like to thank Frances Benson Thompson for kindly granting permission to quote from the Benson family papers in Chapel Hill, Arthur DuPre for his willingness to suggest Benson family materials, Martha Stump Benson for her encouragement and advice about materials concerning John Rufus King, and Robert Clifton King for further materials concerning his forebear. Their willingness to share material with me made my task far more enjoyable and fulfilling.

I owe many more debts of a personal nature. My thanks to Robert Cowley, former editor of *MHQ* magazine, who published my original article on the camps and got me going on the subject. Stephen Power had the fine idea of turning the article into a book in the first place, Bret Witter gave excellent advice to help shape the manuscript, and Krista Stroever made several useful suggestions. Robert Cosgriff read a draft of the manuscript and provided valuable commentary on military matters. A special thanks goes to Sam Dorrance, who introduced me to Alexander Hoyt, the man who finally placed an orphaned manuscript with Michael Dorr at Taylor Trade Publishing. The book was very ably seen through production by Stephen Driver and copyedited by Cheryl Adam.

On a more personal side, my family deserves a special thanks, as always. They have supported my wanderings and my work whatever the occasion. The Teaching Company has lent valuable support and flexibility as an employer. And Robbi, true to form, kept my spirits up. I hope this book pleases them all.

MANY have seen the posed photographs of Union prisoners who had come back from the 1860s Georgia hellhole known as Andersonville: the hollow eyes, the wan visage, the slack posture and protruding bones, the image of standing corpses who paused to have a studio portrait taken somewhere on their way to an early grave. They are among the most shocking images of the American Civil War, presaging as they do the grisly documentary footage filmed when the Nazi camps were liberated in Europe eighty years later.

We do not see any such photos of the men who fought for the Confederacy and returned home from northern prisons. Nor do we ever hear their stories. This omission is hardly due to a lack of published narratives, scores of which are scattered in archives and libraries across the country. The silence can hardly be passed off as a mere footnote to history, since Confederate prisoners (over 200,000) were generally agreed to have outnumbered their Yankee brethren during the war. Of these, some 26,000 Rebels died in captivity, more than all U.S. battle deaths recorded in the Revolutionary War, the War of 1812, the Mexican War, and the Spanish-American War *combined*.

We suffer from a collective amnesia. Our condition may be best explained by the venerable dictum that the winner writes history. Indeed, captive Johnny Reb has been three times cursed in our memory: he was captured in battle, he fought on the losing side of the war, and he defended a slave regime regarded as morally repugnant. Having already been tainted by slavery, the southern soldier encamped in a northern barrack, shivering under a blanket in subzero temperatures and subsisting on a twice-daily ration of watery gruel, is not exactly the stuff of which legends are made.

Their confinement was plagued with deprivation, brutality, physical collapse, and even death. But these same circumstances made some of them stand out as remarkable, even heroic. It might have been the sharing of rations or a blanket. It might have been tending to the sick. It might have been the nervous, raw-boned energy of digging a secret tunnel to freedom. In the end, survival was achieved only through an uncanny mixture of self-interest and solidarity.

Nowhere was the battle for survival more desperate than in Elmira, the infamous Yankee prison in upstate New York. What follows is the story of Elmira—a kind of "Andersonville on ice"—as told by a few of the men who left it while they still drew breath.

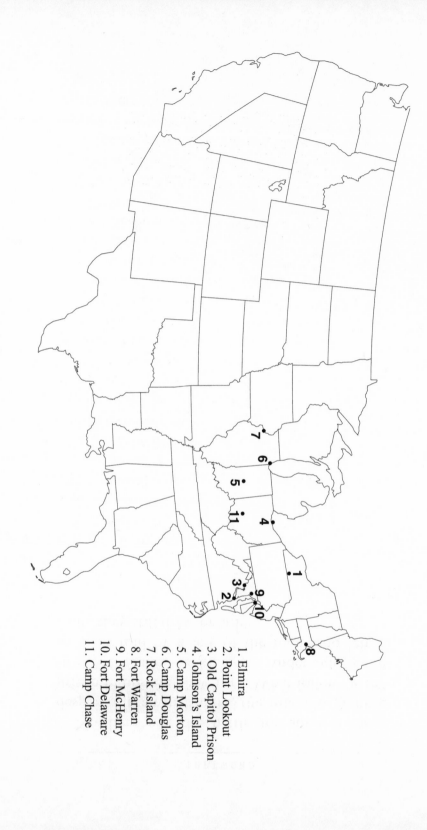

1. Elmira
2. Point Lookout
3. Old Capitol Prison
4. Johnson's Island
5. Camp Morton
6. Camp Douglas
7. Rock Island
8. Fort Warren
9. Fort McHenry
10. Fort Delaware
11. Camp Chase

T HE morning of June 9 dawned fair and warm. It was a Thursday like any other in early summer. The Thompson widow picked her way across the ruts in Market Street, on an urgent errand for molasses and yarn. A knot of merchants near the Exchange Building bickered over how soon the winter wheat would be in. On the river, the Peebles warehouse, stocked with prime bales of cotton (not to mention a rare consignment of apple brandy), opened for business—prices strictly negotiable. The magnolias were in full blossom. An infant giggled from an upstairs window on Bank Street. The honey locusts wrapped the streets in their heavy perfume. It was a day for a stroll, a visit to Aunt Rebecca's, a drowsy nap on the trellised front porch after dinner.

Except that it was 1864. Three years of civil war had aged the city of Petersburg, Virginia. The streets, picked clean of refuse, were now barren; even pigeons and cats had started to disappear. A visitor could have patrolled the downtown streets for a week without finding signs of a man under 50. (In the early years, young fellows who didn't enlist were likely as not to get a package by post containing a petticoat.) The stifling heat would soon be upon them—the women, children, and old men who remained in a city now as silent as the brooding cemetery of Blandford that bordered it on the east. She had been living a charmed life for years. The war had been, until now, a creaky train ride away, a folded message in a saddlebag crossing the next county.

Anthony Keiley was comfortably lodged in his downtown office, perusing newspaper reports of the latest Yankee invasion of Virginia. Then, at about 8 o'clock in the morning, the clamor began. The tolling started solemnly at the courthouse on Sycamore Street, then was taken up by the fire engines and whipped like a wild tale through the heart of town. Within minutes, every bell and carillon in the city took up the call until "all the available bell-metal in the corporation broke into chorus," the loyal citizen later wrote. It was as if the sky were about to fall on Petersburg, this thriving center of the tobacco and cotton trade founded in 1748 on a bend of the lazy Appomattox River.

Keiley knew it was no fire the bells were sounding—and feared it was no act of nature, either. He ran out into the street and collared a passerby. The news was grim: "Twenty thousand Yankee cavalry," the pedestrian cried, covering his ears from the din in the street and rushing toward the river, "two miles and closing!"

People were sprinting in a frenzy down Market Street. A riderless horse galloped by. Far away was the sound of thunder. It looked to Keiley like a scene out of the grimmest page of Revelations. *Twenty thousand Yankees?* The papers had borne no such warning. Why should he believe another rumor? Still, the incredible news gave him pause, since "the 'usual discount' of seventy-five per cent still left the tale uncomfortable to a degree." He ran inside to lock up his office and returned home as fast as his limp would carry him to "replenish my commissariat." Neither precaution, it turned out, was wasted: it would be many months before the ambitious lawyer would see his beloved Petersburg again.

You might say that Anthony Michael Keiley was spoiling for a fight. The sound of bells this June morning had dutifully aroused him, a veteran who enlisted as a private in Company E of the Virginia 12th Infantry in 1861, a week after Fort Sumter. He had been severely wounded in the right foot at Malvern Hill (Seven Days') in June 1862. Commissioned first lieutenant in early 1862, he returned to his unit after a period of convalescence with a command at the battle of Chancellorsville, Virginia. Soon after, he had been to Gettysburg and back, hobbling all of the way because of his wound. But he was no longer fit for marches. After seeking employment in the Confederate government (and personally imploring Jefferson Davis for a position), Keiley resigned his commission in late

1863 to attend to civilian duties. But he was restless. More than anyone, he knew that tending the home fires was not the proper work of a southern gallant.

In full civilian garb, without so much as a pistol stuck in his belt, Keiley set off from his house in the direction of the storm. At the south edge of town he found an unlikely assembly: a ragtag militia of some 125 old men and boys led by Fletcher Archer, a Mexican War veteran. The "parlor soldiers," or city troops, didn't look at first sight like they could hold back much more than a holiday parade. But they were the only obstacle, Colonel Archer reminded them, between the women of Petersburg and the advancing Union horde. The rumored 20,000 cavalry had melted into a mere 1,300 on the horizon by 11 o'clock, but no matter. The men of the Petersburg militia were going to be outmanned no matter how many Yankees poured in the breach.

Archer's Battalion had dug in behind earthworks along the Jerusalem Plank Road, the main thoroughfare south of the city, making a 600-yard front. When Keiley offered his services, all five feet eight-and-a-half inches of him, they issued him an antique smoothbore musket left by a comrade, a nervous fellow gone to town "on leave" that very morning. The men closed lines on the road and put up some fence rails in a slapdash *chevaux-de-frise.* Suddenly they heard music floating down from a cloud behind them. On Bragg's Hill, within eyesight, a Negro band struck up "Dixie" and "The Girl I Left behind Me" to provide the defenders some welcome moral support. A little before noon, the Yankee horsemen, unimpressed by the spectacle, were a half-mile away and approaching.

The first thing Archer's boys saw was a cloud of dust. A Yankee line of blue crossed the field at a canter. The battalion fired and "scattered the cavaliers like chaff," Keiley bragged, "three riderless horses being all of the expedition that entered our lines." Two other charges were quickly repulsed. The Rebs reloaded to give yet another volley, but their exhilaration was short-lived. They could see that the cavalry had dismounted and deployed along the road in a flanking maneuver.

The militia waited nervously. On came the enemy a fourth time. Armed with Spencer repeating carbines, a far cry from the muzzle-loading "arquebuses" issued to the militia, the Federals started to make short work of Archer's boys. After taking heavy fire, the colonel gave the order to retreat. Robert Martin, injured in the battle and quite deaf, misunderstood the order and ran forward instead, firing as he went. Captured by the Yankees, he was denied a trip across the field to say goodbye to his family.

The Yankee "foemen" came so fast that "the two nearest men to me were shot *in the back* while facing the line of original approach," Keiley remembered. Archer's men—Blanks and

Jones and Bannister and Staubley and Hardee and Bellingham—fell in the gathering smoke. To the Rebel rear, Confederate batteries charged down Sycamore Street to take a defensive position, and General P. G. T. Beauregard's regulars were digging in around the perimeter of action. The Federal assault, sweeping past the hindmost of Archer's men, soon met stiff resistance, and the cavalry pulled back to regroup. So it was that the grueling 10-month siege of Petersburg began. Keiley was convinced that his scruffy outfit, buying the regular army time to take up position, had saved the city from Lucifer's legions. The engagement lasted barely ninety minutes.

Keiley was nursing a wounded comrade when the enemy overran his trench. A "hatchet-faced member of the First District cavalry" ran up and thrust a carbine under his nose, spewing a train of curses. Probably for the first time in his life, Keiley surrendered without an argument. He looked at his comrades kneeling in the dust. The ragged pack of Rebs ranged from their teens to well over 50: clerks, farm boys, magistrates, tradesmen, doctors, schoolteachers, and even hospital patients and jailbirds. The Yankees stripped them of firearms. One Federal forgot to unload a captured weapon and blew a hole in his thigh, an ugly accident that gave the embittered Keiley a measure of "satisfaction." He had awoken that morning a reputable citizen and now, in the early afternoon, kneeled on the plank road, a helpless prisoner. The war had jumped from the newspapers to the city outskirts in less time than it would have taken a belle in Sunday dress to cross Market Street on a muddy day.

Keiley would have been loath to admit that he started life as a "Yankee." Born in New Jersey of Irish immigrants in 1832, he came to Petersburg with his family when he was still a boy. His mother was a fervent Catholic, his father a schoolteacher who lapsed into Methodism, creating an enduring family scandal. Anthony himself was an altar boy and Sunday school devotee, a background that contributed to a well-honed sense of moral indignation that he would soon have plenty of time to vent. He was stylish, opinionated, and almost brazenly literate: in 1852–1853, he enrolled at the University of Virginia and in 1859 was admitted to the state bar.

Three years of war had helped Keiley make sense of his life. Before Fort Sumter, he had sampled careers like a man tasting canapés at a buffet. By the age of 30, he had taught school, practiced law, and edited several newspapers, not to mention that he cultivated a chronic case of political ambition. In May 1863, he was elected to the Virginia House of Delegates and began to serve that fall, a position that didn't count for much when the war finally came to Petersburg. Keiley was hardly the first—or the last—member of a state delegation to be captured in the war. And the fact that he was carrying a blunderbuss on the Jerusalem Plank Road when he fell into Yankee hands was, for a politician, not a good omen as to where he might find himself come the next general election.

In 1860 he had been a Union man, one of a small minority in the South to support Stephen Douglas for president. But the election of Abraham Lincoln was an unacceptable affront. Keiley's politics were a mix of democratic bonhomie and aristocratic aloofness. He supported extending the franchise—at least to unpropertied white males. He railed against the laziness of slaves, yet had a lifelong commitment to relief of the "poor." A second-generation Irishman—and president of the local Hibernian Society—he had found success in a Protestant community otherwise closed to the immigrant rank and file. He exhibited all the enthusiasm—and scorn—of the grateful convert.

As such, he was the most unreconstructed of Southerners. "The North," Keiley asserted later, "in liberating four millions of blacks, enslaved eight millions of whites." He fancied himself something of a freeborn cavalier, a man reared on the commentaries of Caesar who had read about war and been to battle to test his worst suspicions. Some contemporaries described him as "poor," dismissing a very modest pedigree that was in every way obscured by his disposition. By the code of his day, he was an educated "gentleman" as capable of unraveling an extended metaphor as of handling an obsolete musket at the barricades. And even people who despised his politics couldn't resist him. The higher ranking a Yankee officer was, the more likely he would fall victim to Keiley's Irish charm in the months to come. That alone would be of immense service to Keiley at his ultimate destination in the North, a military camp known by its ill-fated inhabitants as "Helmira."

Not all Rebel soldiers came so confident and well bred. John Rufus King of the 25th Virginia Infantry couldn't quote any Latin, but he had a good head for numbers all the same. Like his father, he was a carpenter by trade: "I can use a saw and square much better than I can a pen," he admitted with typical modesty. Born in 1842 in Marion County, Virginia, King and his family moved to Upshur County, Virginia, in 1861 and were rare Confederate sympathizers in a pro-Union region in the mountains near Clarksburg, Virginia (later West Virginia). His brother Cyrus was injured by stoning early in the war for supporting the Cause. In July 1862, both brothers and their father were dragged before General William Rosecrans, a future congressman and minister to Mexico with a legendary temper, who forced them all to take an oath of loyalty to the Union. Such was proof, as King later put it, that even in Virginia "we were never safe at home."

King broke his oath on May 14, 1863, and enlisted in Company B of the 25th Virginia, a unit known as the "Upshur Grays." He was a fair-complexioned youth with auburn hair and blue eyes, measuring a lofty five feet ten inches. His unit soon joined the Army of Northern Virginia, and the young carpenter, though impressed with Commander Robert E. Lee's prowess, was not one to brag about his own. "I wish you could have seen me dodge the first shell," he said of his maiden battle near Winchester, Virginia, early in the Gettysburg campaign. "If a hole had been near I would have disappeared. I would like to impress on your minds that I had a fine brave heart, and a pair of legs that had a wonderful inclination towards carrying my body out of danger, but I succeeded in coaxing them to stay with the crowd." John King was as humble as Anthony Keiley was highfalutin.

The 25th Virginia, deploying as skirmishers and sharpshooters, arrived at Gettysburg on July 1 at the end of the battle's first day. Merely to survey the day's slaughter was a somber initiation: "Men's heads were torn from the bodies, legs and arms torn asunder and horses lying around mutilated," King wrote of the fighting near the railroad cut. He added, with typical reflection, "It took courage to face these things." And face them he did. The next day, he stormed Culp's Hill with the 25th under Richard Ewell's Second Corps and survived the ensuing carnage. The Yankee right gave way against the onslaught but recovered the ground by dusk. Though no one was counting then, almost 35,000 men had already fallen in two days of bitter fighting.

On July 3, George Pickett led his doomed charge into the sights of massed Yankee muskets and cannon. That same day, King had been pinned down in the Valley of Death, taking withering fire from the 20th Maine at Little Round Top. After his brother Cyrus and another comrade fell in the action, both badly wounded, he dragged them out of the crossfire to safety. General Lee fell back with his troops the next day, the wounded men on the field abandoned. "It is due to the hand of a Divine Providence that we were not both killed," wrote King, "for the cannon balls bored into the ground so close we thought sometimes we would be covered." But he had lost his brother as a prisoner to the enemy.

King's trip to the North was a passing good adventure. Traipsing through Chambersburg, Pennsylvania, on the way to battle, he had conversed with people who couldn't believe they were seeing Rebs in their own front yard. For once, he thought, the North was getting a taste of the war. Despite Lee's orders outlawing theft, General James Longstreet's men broke into various shops in town. ("I remember I did a fine job guarding a bed of onions, just long enough to pull all I wanted for my own use," wrote King.) The townsfolk and southern boys made small talk in the long midsummer light. Locals marveled at how the Johnnies looked just like their own boys—apparently they had been expecting ogres and trolls. "It seemed strange that anyone could know so little about the South," decided King, a testament both to rural isolation and the war hysteria that had gripped both sides.

A farm boy from a Virginia holler, King would fight in as many epic battles as Achilles did. He was back in northern Virginia near the Rapidan River on May 5–7, 1864, for the battle cum inferno called the "Wilderness." King watched helplessly as a classmate was killed at his side. Many others met what the Rebs called the "unseen death" at the Wilderness—the bullets hurtling from points unknown through the dense scrub and underbrush. Exploding ordnance set the woods ablaze, and scores of wounded men, unable to move, were left to die in the flames. The Yankees, with 2-to-1 superiority in numbers, stiffened under Lee's sustained attack, the first time they had stood fast on the bloody ground of Virginia.

With the fires of the Wilderness still burning, General Ulysses Grant wheeled southward toward Richmond with 100,000 men, Lee nipping at his heels. At Spotsylvania Court House, a key junction on the Richmond road, Lee took his stand. Nearby the town, the Upshur Grays were among those to build dense breastworks at Bloody Angle, a fortification that "was in the shape of a horseshoe and our Brigade occupied the toe." On May 10, the Yankees breached Bloody Angle at the high point of fighting and took 1,000 prisoners. At dusk, their attack stalled under an artillery barrage, and the Rebs repulsed them with heavy losses.

Picketing with the enemy continued. On the morning of May 12, the Yanks began massing before the tree line across an open field. In the mist slightly after dawn, the Union made another all-out charge. Fifteen thousand men advanced to split the Confederate left in the fog, running up and down the swells of the rolling fields as they approached the angle. Like phantoms emerging from the haze, the Federals suddenly overran the breastworks, crying, "Boys, surrender!" The furious fighting in King's sector was over in minutes. "They never fired again," he wrote with some surprise, "but stood looking at us good naturedly."

The look was deceptive. When Rebel John Keener of Company A refused to give up his rifle, a Yankee shot him, "and we saw him throw his arms across his breast and fall on his face." The other men of the regiment put down their arms and lined up by the breastworks. Some 4,000 Rebs had been captured. King couldn't get out of his mind the sickening sight of Keener being killed *after* the battle. But his own experience seems to have been a blessed one—in other sectors of the "Mule Shoe," the forward point of Confederate defenses, hand-to-hand fighting continued for hours.

The mob of graybacks was led through Union lines. They had to step over corpses piled two and three high, over 12,000 casualties, most of them Yankees, littering a square mile of ground. On the Rebel side, Lee had lost a third of his infantry commanders in some of the heaviest fighting in the war. Arriving in the Union rear, King was suddenly overcome by a fit of anger. He picked up a knife and began swinging it wildly, enraged to find himself a captive. He was halfway berserk when "a very young Yankee boy appeared who looked up into my face so kindly and lovingly and spoke so gentle to me that my foolish anger vanished." The Federals had lost a man for every prisoner they took, the boy reassured him—it had been a good fight. Calmed by the soothing words, King, for the first time, accepted his fate: he was on his way to purgatory, at least the military version of it. It was only later that he realized that he probably owed the boy his life.

Not far from King in the Spotsylvania trenches was Marcus Breckenridge Toney of Edgefield, Tennessee. Born in 1840, Toney was 20 years old when the war broke out. He was the son of a millwright who immigrated to Tennessee from Buckingham County, Virginia. Before the war, young Marcus was already something of a survivor. His three siblings died in childhood, and his parents had both passed away before he was 13. He went to school in Lynchburg, Virginia, near the old family home, shuttling back and forth between the two residences. His father owned slaves, and Marcus was raised by a black nanny in the absence of his mother; young Toney swore that the nanny had more affection for him than she did her own children.

Marcus was a strapping six feet tall, auburn-haired, and blue-eyed. A pious and well-to-do Methodist, Toney, like others in the spring of 1861, wasn't expecting a long war. By that time he held his own slaves in Virginia, the state of his birth, and more in Tennessee, proudly holding that slave and enslaver "were living as one great family in peace and harmony" throughout the South. His ire was raised by Harriet Beecher Stowe's spiteful depiction of his homeland in *Uncle Tom's Cabin*, a book he called "a libel upon the Southern people." He subscribed to states' rights and was willing to fight any damned Yankee to prove the soundness of the principle. As Toney wryly put it, "Our New England cousins first engaged in the African slave trade; but, finding their labor not profitable in that section, sold their slaves to the Southern people."

In April 1861, Toney signed a 12-month enlistment at Edgefield, located opposite Nashville, in Company B of the Rock City Guards (First Tennessee Infantry), no doubt sorry to have to say goodbye to "my negroes." Three days after Fort Sumter was fired on, he was drilling with his unit on the Edgefield town square, the regiment, 1,000 men strong, filling it from end to end. They were mustered in on May 10 and moved to Camp Cheatham, where the unit faced its first test: an epidemic of measles. "The doleful dirge of the dead march often touched our hearts," wrote Private Toney, who lamented this unromantic demise far from the field of battle. The Rock City Guards were afraid the war would be over before they ever made it to Virginia to prove their mettle. Worse than the danger of going to battle was the more depressing prospect of being left behind—or so they felt during the first year.

With the regimental band striking up "The Girl I Left behind Me," Toney and the First Tennessee marched to the Nashville and Chattanooga train depot in the summer of 1861. Climbing into ten boxcars, Toney wrote, the men were wedged "as thick as pins in a pincushion." They felt invincible as Spartans. The martial tradition of the South—General Washington at Trenton, Andy Jackson at New Orleans, and old William Henry Harrison at Tippecanoe—was all of theirs to defend. Toney believed, "We would have a battle in which one Southern man would whip five Yankees with cornstalks, England would intervene, peace would be declared, and we should return home finding all our servants smiling at our home-coming." He bragged, much as Keiley would, that "we left Nashville with as good a lot of boys as ever went to the front." Each of the men was given a New Testament by the regiment chaplain.

The First Tennessee rushed by rail to Virginia. In mid-July, they arrived for the battle of First Manassas—days late. Each soldier was loaded up like a mule: a rifle, Colt revolver, sword, and scabbard, with a knapsack and haversack slung over the shoulders and a hefty supply of cartridges for ballast. On a march to Warm Springs (southwest of Waynesboro, Virginia) in mid-August, Toney was overcome with heat exhaustion and ditched his sword, blanket, and revolver in the bushes. "I thought, probably, the war would end before the winter," he explained. The more superstitious among them threw away their cards and dice, ready for the judgment soon to befall them.

For the Rock City Guards, the Virginia campaign was little more than an extended parade maneuver. If Company B marched to the sound of the guns, they never found them smoking when they got there. Even so, the privations of the simple soldier—like finding potable water— were a part of the daily regimen. "How many wiggletails and tadpoles I have drunk will never be known," Toney mused of the streams and pools from which he had partaken. He remembered, on one occasion, how his company robbed a Kentucky man of a barrel of water, even as the poor farmer pleaded that his own family had nothing to drink. Company B stopped and emptied the barrel in a few minutes. "We felt sorry for him, but such is war."

In due time, the intense heat turned frigid. The winter of 1861–1862 brought heavy snow to northern Virginia. In below-zero temperatures, Toney recalled, "I ran picket for four hours around and around a big tree; I had to do it to keep from freezing," and he chewed on sassafras bushes for nourishment. Only an insulating snowfall managed to keep the sleeping men warm where they bivouacked. When the regiment returned to Tennessee after weeks of maneuvering, Toney wrote, "The fatalities of the campaign were three soldiers frozen to death," not the kind of circumstances they had planned to write home about to sweethearts, friends, and family.

But the First Tennessee remained alert, drilling daily on dress parade in Chattanooga. On April 1 they were loaded in boxcars again, and this time they shipped west toward the massing of armies near Corinth, Mississippi. As fate would have it, they missed another great battle. Arriving on the field on April 9, they met "a large number of wagons and all kinds of conveyances carrying our wounded to Corinth," this being the ghastly toll of Shiloh. A long row of Federal prisoners shuffled by. The Tennesseans slept in vacant Yankee tents that night and the next morning lined up for battle, which once again eluded them. By this time, they were more worried about being ignored by the gods of war than they were afraid of advancing into a blistering line of Union muskets.

So far, the men of the First Tennessee hadn't "seen the monkey show," as some southern boys called the shock of battle, but they got a glimpse of the performance soon enough. In the fall of 1862, the Rock City Guards entered onto what Toney called "the dark and bloody ground of Kentucky." On October 8, vastly inferior Confederate forces under Braxton Bragg attacked Union troops under Don Carlos Buell at Perryville. Company B, Rock City Guards, overran an eight-gun Union battery and charged another. "We had ten men killed in attempting to carry the colors," Toney wrote of the murderous enfilade from Bush's Indiana Battery, probably no exaggeration given the arch disgrace of losing a flag. "We lost some two hundred and fifty men in a short time." In hindsight, Toney wasn't enamored of the fact that the guards had bivouacked twice before the battle in cemeteries, using grave markers for pillows, what seemed a macabre reflection of things to come.

The battle raged thick and confused: "Our boys got so close to the battery that the smoke covered them," Toney recalled. Rare atmospheric conditions prevented the sound of cannon from being heard at nearby Yankee headquarters a couple of miles distant and delayed the dispatch of Union reinforcements. But nearly 8,000 total casualties wouldn't be enough to make for a decisive battle. Bragg withdrew to Chattanooga, and Buell went to Nashville, refusing repeated orders from Washington to pursue his opponent. Fourteen men from Company B were killed on the Perryville field, including one of Toney's friends, Robert Hamilton. A devout Christian, Toney made it his business to bury Hamilton along with 26 other men, using a breastplate from a Yankee corpse for a shovel.

Detailed as a nurse while the army retreated, Toney spent several sleepless nights listening to the cries of fallen men for water. But he was doomed to become a prisoner. Soon after the battle, he was taken by the Yankees and "paroled," meaning he gave his word not to take up arms until formally exchanged for a Union prisoner. The next four months he spent in a private residence with Confederate sympathizers near Danville, Kentucky, waiting for an exchange. It wasn't the kind of captivity the twentieth century would even recognize—a man bound by his word of honor rather than a line of menacing sentries and a coil of concertina wire.

Next, Toney was boarded at the National Hotel in Louisville for six weeks pending exchange. On April 4, 1863, he signed another parole and was finally swapped with a group of Rebs for a like number of Federals at City Point, Virginia, on the James River. Even then he was far from safe. Within a few days, Toney had survived a train wreck near Bristol in which a broken coupling pin caused his car to somersault several times near the Watauga River; the private from Edgefield escaped with barely a bruise. He had been absent from his unit for six months and experienced what amounted to a very liberal version of Yankee confinement.

Reporting to the First Tennessee in Shelbyville, Toney was back in the thick of the war before long, and his good luck continued. In June, a Federal cavalry raid at Tullahoma took the Rebs by surprise, and Toney hid out in a pig-pen, "bivouack[ing] in the dust with hogs and fleas" beneath a train depot. The Yankees rode off without finding him. That night, he found his way back to his unit, navigating by the stars.

After fighting at Chickamauga, Georgia, in the early fall, the regiment took an elevated position on nearby Missionary Ridge in November. "From the top of Lookout Mountain," Toney wrote, "it was a grand sight at night to see the campfires of [Joseph Hooker's] army." The high aesthetics of the experience didn't last long. On November 25, one day after a total lunar eclipse, the Rebs beat a Yankee charge back to Sherman Heights early in the day, only to flee the field when Grant, attacking from below, broke the Confederate center. The scrambling Rebels ran up the mountain, unable to fire down for fear of hitting their own men behind them. They retreated down the far slope and didn't stop for 30 miles, one of the most humiliating southern defeats of the war. They had, in the unforgiving lexicon of the boys in uniform, "showed the white feather."

The First Tennessee went into hibernation for the winter. Toney applied for a furlough—which was refused—in January 1864 to attend a relative's wedding in Virginia. (No matter—he erased the "dis" from "disapprove" and used it anyway.) The presence of family must have warmed him to his native state, for on February 4 he transferred to Company C of the 44th Virginia, an outfit in which a first cousin was soldiering, and walked ten miles through a foot of snow to join them. Like units all over the South, the 44th Virginia was in difficult straits: "By the first of May," Toney noted, "the meat was gone, and many of the soldiers were without shoes. . . . Three days' rations were three pones of corn bread without any sifting and minus salt."

On May 5 began the bloody struggle for the Wilderness. The 44th beat back several Union charges the first day on Palmer's Field. The 146th New York Zouaves, "as fine-looking a body of men as I ever saw," Toney remembered, advanced from a thicket and "were mowed down like grass before the sickle." Time and again the Virginia 44th "stood the gaff," the men aiming low to compensate for past cases of shooting in the trees. But the Yanks kept coming, so thick a mass of them that Toney counted over 1,000 Federals fallen on the field by day's end. On May 6, Toney's lieutenant took a ball above the heart and instantly died. Toney's cousin died soon after with a bullet to the head, and Toney buried him nearby "with a black-jack tree for his headstone." The Tennessee private saw how the pockets of the Federal corpses were turned inside out, picked clean by scavengers. The Rebs threw down their corn pone and took the Yankee rations of hardtack and bacon. But no one had time to dawdle.

The 44th Virginia sped to close off the Federal move on the capital. By May 12 at Spotsylvania Court House, Toney's regiment had dug in at the Bloody Angle, stabbing the earth with their bayonets and throwing it out in tin plates, not far from the Upshur Grays of John King. The collapse happened early that morning. A brigade of Yankees charged and overwhelmed the position, running across the swells of land like a dense blue wave. A burly Irishman walked up and waved a gun in front of Marcus Toney; "Why he did not shoot," the Reb wrote later, "I will never know." Ushered back through Yankee lines, thousands of prisoners found themselves in shock: "We were in a sorry plight to meet such an array of tinseled regalia," Toney wrote of the well-shod Yankees. "Many of our men were hatless, shoeless, and coatless and were covered with mud from the trenches." After surrendering on the field, he reported icily, several Rebs were shot or beaten to death.

The Federals hustled the prisoners off to the Belle Plain encampment, near Fredericksburg, Virginia, where they awaited transport to prison. While there, Toney made the acquaintance of the U.S. Christian Commission, a voluntary group founded by the Young Men's Christian Association (YMCA) that provided box lunches, hot coffee, and Bibles to soldiers in the field. The group didn't impress Toney with its generosity. "They did not minister to any of the Confederate prisoners," he griped. "I guess they thought we were an incorrigible set." Still, the Rebels drew healthy rations of bacon, sugar, and coffee, a feast compared with their usual fare. "I do not believe that, in January of 1864," remembered Toney, "there were more than five bags of coffee in Virginia."

For Private Toney, Private King, and discharged Lieutenant Keiley, confinement would prove to be a burden. Not so for Sergeant Berry Greenwood Benson of the First South Carolina Volunteers (whose own war credentials verged on the epic), for whom the very idea of captivity was unthinkable. Benson was the triggerman for a battery that fired on Fort Sumter during the war's first day. He was bruised by a bullet at Gaines' Mill at the start of the Seven Days'; fought at Second Manassas, Antietam, and Fredericksburg; and was wounded in the left leg at Chancellorsville, the only thing that kept him from following Lee to Gettysburg. (Eighteen of the 30 men in his company died at Second Manassas alone.) It had been no mistake that Benson enlisted in 1861 for the war's duration.

Young Benson was irrepressible. When he arrived in northern Virginia in June 1861 as a bright-eyed Carolina volunteer, he got it in his mind that he wanted to see the Potomac River. He wandered off from his unit to get an eyeful one day, only to be arrested as a straggler and thrown in the Rebel guardhouse. (While the guard was changing, he walked away unmolested.) The next year, he fell sick and struggled to keep up with his unit as they marched north to Antietam. Again, he was mistaken for a shirker and put in a Rebel pen near Harper's Ferry, Virginia. But it wasn't Benson's way to play "old soldier." He jumped the fence and caught up with his boys in time to trade murderous volleys with the Yanks at Antietam, a bullet leaving a black mark on his felt hat during retreat. Berry Benson was always getting nicked and buzzed and winged, but death couldn't seem to get any closer than a bare nudge.

He made corporal by early 1862 and sergeant by late the next year. A sharpshooter by the time of the Wilderness in 1864, Sergeant Benson soon became known for his nighttime scouts. During the Wilderness campaign, he went behind Union lines to gather intelligence for General Lee, a mission that nearly cost the scout his life. One night at Spotsylvania, Benson overheard a Yankee colonel give marching orders for the front. The South Carolinian stole a horse and returned to Confederate lines with the news, only to find that the enemy had already taken the Bloody Angle. The two armies struggled ferociously the next day. "There we fought with them," remembered Benson, "through blood and rain, for twenty hours, without food, or rest, or sleep, and only the muddy rain to drink." John King and Marcus Toney were among those taken in the melee.

It was a seesaw affair. The Rebels retook the angle and, for a time, hung on to the dubious prize. Late on the night of May 16, Benson volunteered to cross enemy lines again. Finding Federal pickets too numerous to avoid, he tried, in the darkness, to pass as a Union scout. He turned out to be a better soldier than actor. A brigade commander, Jacob Sweitzer, saw through his feeble attempt at a New York accent and had Benson arrested and placed under guard. It was a desperate situation. Benson knew full well he might be tried for espionage. The South Carolinian stayed on the alert, boasting of his own exploits until his guards revealed more about northern troop movements than prudence would have dictated. Benson, in his own words, was determined to "exchange myself" before dawn.

It didn't take long for an opportunity. In the darkness, he found a chance and wrested away a guard's rifle with a struggle. Benson ran down a hill and made a desperate beeline for a copse of pines. Before he could make the trees, the Yankees were thicker around him than flies on a cow's rump. They ran him to earth in a few seconds. Escorting him back to camp, a corporal scalded him under a torrent of verbal abuse, later reporting that Benson had struck him—a lie. Then the corporal had him bound to a tree, where Benson spent the rest of the night, figuring he would be tried as a spy the next day. The corporal added the indignity of confiscating Benson's pocketknife, which had belonged to his cousin Zack, who had died shortly before at the

Wilderness. That evening, the Union guards made it their pleasure to prod him with their bayonets.

The sergeant had violent dreams that night—of Indian captives roasting at the stake, of the execution of Major Andre, the Revolutionary spy. Shortly after dawn on May 17, the Yankees had the good manners to tell Benson to prepare for the worst. He knew what that meant: stringing him up by the branches of the nearest oak tree. The only question was how much rope the Federals would use once they decided they didn't want to spend any bullets on him. Benson figured he had only one chance left. Though he considered himself an indifferent talker, he would jaw his way out of a meeting with the gallows—or finish with a shout and a jerk.

Before noon, he was brought before an officer at General George Meade's headquarters. Secretly, he was afraid they would guess he was the same man who had stolen a horse a few nights before on his earlier scout. Benson pleaded with the colonel assigned to him, begging for leniency. He explained that he was taken as a scout, not as a spy, and that he was outside Union lines. The officer began to soften. Benson's plea may have caused the colonel to have a change of heart, perhaps endearing him to an enemy whose tongue had proved so much more able than his legs had the night before. The colonel said he would do what he could to influence the decision of the court. Then, abruptly, he took his leave.

The more Benson thought about it, the more he worried. What would they make of his attempt to escape? And what about the horse he had stolen from what looked to be the very same camp? Would anyone be able to identify him? That afternoon, a dejected Benson was escorted under guard to a group of captives gathered on a road. "I looked on everybody with suspicion, and imagined every horseman I saw approaching was bringing the summons for me to appear before the court." The men were preparing to march in a ragged column of twos—but to where?

Benson stayed alert for a last chance to skedaddle before the court-martial convened. Seeing a prisoner with a pocket watch nearby, he inquired as to the time. (He didn't know why; what difference did it make what time it was if he was going to hang?) No sooner did the two men fall to talking than Benson learned what his ears could barely credit: his fate had already been sealed. The stranger told him he had stood before the court that very morning on another charge and heard them dismiss Benson's case outright. Perhaps they had listened to the colonel after all.

The sergeant almost collapsed. He had been on the verge of trying to run away again, an act that probably would have gotten him killed, only to be saved by this chance encounter. Sergeant Berry Benson, all of 21 years old, was now officially a Union prisoner of war. But his newfound gratitude had limits. For such a free spirit, captivity would prove to be something of an intolerable blessing.

CHAPTER 1

"Fresh Fish"

IN the summer of 1864, thousands of Confederate prisoners were destined to spend their final months in a town that lay in the beautiful hill country of western New York. Carved by glaciers, a subject later of great interest to Berry Benson, it was a land inhabited by native people for over 10,000 years, the last two centuries by the fearsome Iroquois. The first white people probably didn't appear in the area until a century before the Civil War, and theirs was a peaceful beginning that would soon take a bloody turn. During the Revolution, the Continental Army left a path of scorched earth through the Chemung Valley in the Clinton–Sullivan campaign, burning Iroquois crops and villages in a convincing gesture that scattered the tribes from the region within twenty years.

Elmira (formerly Newtown) grew up in the valley in the years after the Revolution. By 1850 it was a prosperous burg—the turnpike had gone through, a bridge over the Chemung was built, and dams and locks were under construction on the river. The town had churches and banks, shoe factories and woolen mills, a women's seminary, a lecture auditorium, a boat-building yard, and a city hall. It was a major hub for the New York & Erie and Piedmont Central railways, making it a key rendezvous site for Union troops during the war. Elmira was a tough-as-leather river town, its perch on the Chemung Canal a link to Seneca Lake and the world beyond through the sweat-stained traffic in coal and gypsum, salt and lime and lumber. The bare-knuckled canal work was done by transients who were hardworking and harder playing, men with a taste for rotgut liquor and an ear for insufferable insults.

Elmira-on-the-Chemung was a paradox: a staunchly pro-Union settlement that just happened to be the seat of a county (Chemung) with strong Copperhead sentiments. In 1862, the town was home to four military barracks that could hold over 10,000 men. Thus did a town of barely 9,000 in 1860 more than double in size during the war, first as a state draft rendezvous post and then as a federal one, engendering what would become a tale of two cities. On the one hand, soldiers awaiting transport to the front in Virginia or assigned to duty in town were boarded in private homes on broad streets lined with elms and maples; on the other, Elmira near the tracks became a haven for vice and crime.

Pickpockets worked the busy Erie train station. Prostitutes and camp followers shadowed

the bars. Reports of murder were not at all uncommon on the pages of the local *Daily Advertiser*. There were, of course, the commonplace
tragedies that befell any town of the time: the
runaway horse, the disappeared husband, the
black man beaten senseless, the child drowned
in the river, the old woman mangled by a train.
And, in time of war, yet another misfortune was
added: the deserter's name announced in the
Advertiser's pages for all and sundry to ponder.
Even if their uniforms impressed the ladies and
they spent their wages downtown, the large
crowds of military men were not an unmixed
blessing in Elmira.

Barracks No. 3 (formerly Camp Rathbun)
fronted Water Street, about a mile west of downtown. It was built on low-lying ground near the
Chemung River, and a backwater called Foster's
Pond ran through the south end of camp.
Roughly rectangular in shape, the grounds were
enclosed in mid-1864 by a plank stockade about
12 feet high, a parapet running along the outside
for guards with roofed sentry boxes at intervals.
The stockade ran about 500 by 300 yards, en-
closing a space of 30-odd acres. A military report
from 1862 advised that it was a healthy environ-
ment, void of standing water and not a source of
malaria or other fevers. Like other camps in
town, Rathbun had been built to house and train
exclusively Union men. Before the war, the space
was used for the Chemung County fair, and part
of it had once been a racecourse.

In 1864, the grounds were dominated by 30 barracks, most built early in the war, that were about 90 feet long by 20 feet wide. Each was equipped with two rows of bunks, enough to house 100 men comfortably, and they were well ventilated with windows. Built with green lumber, they also warped in cold weather, causing a severe draft. By early 1864, authorities estimated that the barracks could comfortably hold 3,000 men, a number that would be steadily inflated. The two mess halls could each feed 1,000 men at a sitting, and the kitchen, equipped with steam engine and boilers, could spoon out hash for 5,000 residents a day. On the camp streets separating the rows of barracks, shade trees had been planted to give the grounds a cozy feel. Most conspicuously, the camp had no hospital.

As the war dragged on, towns like Elmira that were equipped with vacant barracks became likely depots for Confederate prisoners. Far to the south, as General Grant shadowed Lee's slow retreat across Virginia through the summer of 1864, the Rebels, harried by fierce fighting and meager rations, were surrendering in droves. In June, Washington decided that *10,000* prisoners must be accommodated in Elmira's Barracks No. 3, a prospect that foreboded severe overcrowding. To begin with, Foster's Pond and the proximity of the Chemung limited the building space available. "There should be ample room between the fences and the buildings," advised Lieutenant Colonel William Hoffman,

Union commissary general of prisoners, "that prisoners may not approach [the fence] unseen." As early as 1862, a report had already given out that the sinks (latrines) were "insufficient, incomplete, and filthy."

In the bigger picture, Barracks No. 3 would amount to little more than a small cog in the well-greased military engine housed far away in the nation's capital. The chain of command was calculated and long. An officer, the camp commandant, presided over the barracks who enforced rules, called inspections, and disciplined prisoners and guards. His performance was under review by the head of the Elmira Military Depot and Prison Camp, who was charged with overseeing all military installations in the city. But on any issue of substance, as soldiers on both sides would soon learn to their chagrin, these men needed to appeal to the commissary-general for prisoners at the Department of War, Pennsylvania Avenue, Washington, D.C. Any out-of-the-ordinary request—to build barracks, make sanitary improvements, expand cemetery facilities, or even permit a civilian to enter camp—needed to be routed through the commissary-general by telegraph or letter, and the post required three days to arrive in the capital. The most urgent request from Elmira could be tabled in Washington for months at a time, languishing in an office with a leather-topped secretary and high ceilings and perhaps even graced with a passing fair view of the Potomac.

Elmira was to be ambivalent about her new boarders. The prisoners would soon be seen shuffling through the streets to Barracks No. 3 with all the vigor of a failed fire drill, their mien sallow, their demeanor slack and depressed. Some, visibly covered with vermin, were a source of infection and disease. They were, as their numbers grew, a veritable Trojan horse in a city separated from them by nothing more than a slender wooden stockade. And they were the enemy. No one knew exactly if the next solemn parade might hold a man whose ball and powder had killed a brother at Gettysburg or a beloved son at Antietam, and here he was about to be fed by Mr. Lincoln on the charity of a government greenback.

Other Elmirans perceived opportunities. Copperheads saw friends, even kin, among the drab and dirty visitors. Preachers saw a willing audience for the Word. Masons recognized brothers of the third order in need of succor. Farmers and merchants knew lucrative government contracts when they saw them. It was as though an exotic if dingy circus had come to settle in their midst (on the old fairgrounds, no less), even if it had to be quarantined by the river. Not least, the prisoners were a welcome reminder that perhaps the fortunes of war were turning. If Jeff Davis was bleeding men this badly, the end of the slaughter might be near.

The first Confederates, a contingent of 400, arrived in Elmira on July 6, 1864, in transit from southern Maryland. Three weeks later, an official missive from the commissary-general provided important instructions: Depot Commander Lieutenant Colonel Seth Eastman was authorized to rent a plot of ground near the town cemetery to bury deceased prisoners of war. Somewhere in official Washington, it was decided that a half-acre would suffice for the depressing affair—an estimate that, like so much else in Barracks No. 3, proved inadequate. Before a year was out, they would need five times that much ground to house the pine coffins hauled out of Elmira prison.

In Transit

Anthony Keiley was among the first Rebels to reach Elmira. A Yankee by birth, he found his return to the North—"Doodledom," as he scornfully called it—a harsh homecoming. Following the skirmish near Petersburg, he and the survivors of Archer's Battalion were force-marched 26 miles, prodded "like cattle" by saber-wielding cavalrymen running them toward the Virginia coast. Still, he conceded, the trip could have been worse. A Federal officer, Lieutenant W. E. Bird, nephew of a prominent Petersburg citizen, shared "certain liquid comforts" with him on the march north and even gave him lodging in his tent the first night. In Victorian parlance, Keiley was getting tight with the enemy: "We had established a *rapport*," he exulted, "a canteen being the *medium*."

No doubt something of a curiosity, the Confederate politician was summoned to the tent of General Augustine Valentine Kautz, a veteran of the Indian wars and classmate of George Pickett at West Point—and the man whose troops had overwhelmed Archer's Battalion at Petersburg. At Kautz's invitation, Keiley agreed to discuss the war in gentlemanly fashion. He couldn't resist the temptation of asking Kautz why he hadn't captured Petersburg outright, to which the commander sheepishly replied that he wouldn't have been able to hold it anyway. Keiley ended up refusing a proffered cigar from the general, albeit politely, claiming he was not a man of any *small* vices.

The same day, Keiley was one of three prisoners chosen by lot to parley with the commanding officer, the notorious General Benjamin Butler. Known throughout the South as "Beast Butler" and the "monster of New Orleans" for his iron-fisted military rule of Louisiana, the general was anxious to joust with a few of the enemy far from the sound of siege guns—and perhaps glean some information about the Petersburg defenses. What also interested him was the continuing controversy over military captives. President Jefferson Davis's continued refusal to exchange captured slaves for Rebel prisoners had led to an impasse with the North over what to do with POWs, who were now multiplying faster than either side could provide for them.

Cowed neither by Butler's rank nor reputation, nor by his considerable girth, Keiley proved a worthy sparring opponent. Perhaps free black *soldiers* should be returned to the North, Keiley conceded with a shrug, but not *slaves*, who were mere property. Contraband had no business fighting in the first place, he informed the good general, citing ancient Roman law as a precedent—as only a schoolteacher-turned-lawyer could. When Butler, an attorney himself, tried fishing for intelligence about the Petersburg defenses, Keiley scoffed at him, offended by the "despotism in his lowering eyebrow." Only after Keiley had insulted the abilities of a number of Federal generals was the prisoner angrily dismissed.

The days of brandy and courtly debates were over. In mid-June, the Rebels were boarded on the riverboat *John Warren* under a "Negro guard," an intolerable state of affairs for a devoted Confederate. When the *Warren* pushed off for parts unknown, it was, as Keiley saw it, "the 'bluest' moment of my imprisonment." The boat shuttled to Newport News, Virginia, where the men were loaded on the *Louisiana* and packed away "in savory quarters" where horses had lately berthed.

Their destination: the western shore of Maryland. Their new home: Point Lookout prison, sunk on a spit of land straddling the Potomac River and the Chesapeake Bay, a tract of real estate, noted Keiley, "utterly innocent of tree, shrub, or any natural equivalent for the same." A resort for seaside vacationers before the war, Point Lookout had reopened for business after the battles of Gettysburg and Vicksburg in 1863. This time it was refitted as a major holding pen for Rebel prisoners, a gauntlet many ran as neophyte captives before being sorted for destinations further north when the Union began to fear that the borderlands camp was susceptible to enemy attack.

Keiley thought the place (known locally as "the point") poorly named. "Why this cape is so-called I am at a loss to imagine," he wrote, "as there is nothing in the prospect to make the most curious inhabitant 'look out' in any direction." The Yankees made the Rebs wait on the pier the night they arrived, and the next morning they searched them, fingering the linings of their coats for hidden currency and "turning the contents of our pockets on the ground, and then taking off all our clothing, except what was absolutely next the skin, *and part of that also.*"

Keiley was assigned to bunk in a tent affectionately known by its residents as the "Lyon's Den." It housed 18 men and measured 15 feet in diameter. Point Lookout, in fact, was the only large camp in the North where prisoners lived entirely in tents. (A few enterprising souls built wooden frame shacks from cracker boxes and papered the insides with old newspapers.) Creature comforts in the "pen" were few. Prisoners were allotted an armful of wood for cooking and heating—every five days. The drinking water was, Keiley wrote, so black that "a scum rises on the top of a vessel if it is left standing during the night, which reflects the prismatic colors as distinctly as the surface of a stagnant pool"; it was the immediate cause, he supposed, of his diarrhea. Food rations included "a half-pint of watery slop, by courtesy called 'soup.'"

The greatest danger was less tangible than a bowl of brackish gruel. It was the empty passage of time, the fear of drifting into severe depression—or worse—that ruined many a man in camp. Life in prison, wrote Keiley, had "all the stupidity of a tread-mill without its exercise" and no visible point of termination. Aside from swimming (under supervision), talking, eating, and sleeping, there was little to do. Daydreaming and dawdling became popular vocations—what might have been suitable pursuits in a holiday resort before the war. "From disregard of the formalities of life," wrote Keiley, "[prisoners] become indifferent to its duties." The gentleman from Petersburg went back over his Byron and Shakespeare, reciting favorite passages to fill the days. Sometimes rumors filled the breach—"Petersburg has fallen!" hissed a particularly malicious one—though Keiley remained dubious. Of camp commandant Major H. G. O. Weymouth, he wryly concluded: "He conducts this establishment on the '*laissez faire*' principle—in short, he lets it alone severely."

Boredom could be fatal. After a few days in the pen, "Men became reckless, because hopeless," remarked Keiley, "brutalized, because broken-spirited." One day he absentmindedly wandered close to the deadline—a shallow ditch adjacent to the interior prison wall that inmates crossed at their peril—and narrowly avoided being shot by a guard. Fearing that his own will to survive was disappearing, he volunteered for camp labor, getting a few hours of exercise each day and a chaw of tobacco. The first week, he remembered, passed like a year. "Another month here and I shall become a candidate for one of the piled-up pine boxes."

July 4 came and went. The first week of the month was unseasonably hot. After three weeks, Keiley was slipping into a funk. The camp sprouted gambling dens, underground "restaurants," and a black market in hardtack rations—hardly a place for a squire who knew the taste of Havelock roast beef and Lynnhaven oysters, and who could quote Plautus in the original. Though Keiley's griping about victuals had something of the ring of a well-fed tourist, he had earned his supercilious air. After all, he had spat on the notion that this was "a rich man's war and a poor man's fight," and he was a politician who preferred to come out and fight the Yankees in his own backyard rather than caucus with a bevy of lobbyists in a smoke-filled Richmond salon.

On July 9, his prayers to escape Point Lookout were answered—if Elmira, New

York, could be said to be the answer to any Confederate prayer during the war. On the "mensiversary" of his capture, Keiley and a few hundred other prisoners were packed into the narrow ship hold of the *El Cid* and bound for New York City, given a ration of bread and two ounces of fat to sustain them for 48 hours. The midsummer heat was suffocating, he remembered, "the sun melting the pitch in the seams over our heads. . . . There was a unanimous devotion of all Yankeedom to the devil." For the time being, "Daniel" had escaped the Lyon's Den.

A day or two later, the transport arrived in New York Harbor. A Yankee corporal named Bernstein shared his hardtack and coffee with the famished Keiley, who was blessed with his usual good fortune. On or about July 10, the prisoners disembarked in "the American Venice," as Keiley called New York, a small crowd watching them without expression. The enormous wealth and bustle of the city only caused the adopted Rebel to marvel at the resilience of the Confederacy in daring to take on "the endless tide of wheel and foot" on Broadway. At the train station, the prisoners were crammed on passenger and boxcars, the whistle screamed, and the locomotive, bound for western New York, left the ocean lapping at their backs. Curious crowds ogled them as they stopped at stations on the Erie Railroad route, although the onlookers were respectful for the most part, and some smuggled tobacco and food to the gaunt-looking Rebs.

On the next day, a Tuesday morning, the captives debarked at Elmira, the modest town of 9,000 people on the Chemung River, "a sort of fungus of the Erie Railroad" from what Keiley had heard. Near the Pennsylvania border, Elmira was a prominent stop on another "line" that Keiley had even less use for than the Erie—one that ran underground with the aid of nocturnal conductors, its passengers fleeing from points south of the Mason–Dixon. As Keiley glanced across town, he had no idea he was passing near a depot of the Underground Railroad—and would have scoffed if he had. But Elmira, he admitted finally, was "a pretty little city" whose "admiring citizens" escorted the captives through the center of town as they debarked.

A mile from the town center was Barracks No. 3. On July 12, Keiley and his troop, one of the first captive herds to arrive, found the plank stockade sheltering 30 barracks. The luck of the Irish held up again—the place was near empty. As Confederate battlefield losses persisted, a stream of prisoners soon turned into a flood of graybacks, and the Yankees would soon have to undertake a crash-building program to make room for them at Elmira. But for now Barracks No. 3, with about 1,000 men, was still little more than a village.

So the delegate from Virginia began his stint as a "fresh fish" in New York, prisoner no. 766, claiming a top bunk in barracks 21 near some Petersburg cronies. It was an experience no one could have prepared for. One inmate later described Elmira as "nearer Hades than I thought any place could be made by human cruelty." If so, it was a Hades that, like a faraway moon, burned hot and cold by turns. The New York summer that year was sweltering. For southern boys raised in the Tidewater, however, it was the prospects for the near future that seemed alarming: Elmira was far removed, Keiley wrote, "in the hyperborean regions of New York, where for at least four months of every year, anything short of a polar-bear would find locomotion impracticable." Even in July, winter glowered like a threat.

At first glance, Keiley seemed a fresh fish out of water. A scholar trained for years in Latin and French, capable of quoting Congreve and Horace in his sleep, he must have seemed a refined species on the marshy, pestilential ground of Barracks No. 3. But Keiley, if brazen, was no educated fool. He employed his manners and education with political acumen, soon ingratiating himself with camp authorities and using his bookkeeping talents (a skill honed from his lawyerly days) to record statistics for his Union warders in Elmira's new suburb on the Chemung.

For anyone inclined to pity them, Keiley and his mates were the lucky ones. Only a few days after they arrived, disaster struck near Elmira. A trainload of Rebel prisoners collided with a freight train near Shohola, Pennsylvania, on July 15—and 48 prisoners and 17 guards were killed. The Rebel corpses were buried four to a coffin, mutilation making many of them impossible to identify.

Some eighty prisoners wounded in the mishap were taken to Elmira and stowed in temporary hospitals. Their treatment didn't augur well for the future of Elmira's other guests. The Yankee doctors were undermanned and overmatched. "Many of [the injured] were in a horrible condition," noted Keiley, "and when I went to the hospital the following Monday I found the wounds of many still undressed, even the blood not washed from their limbs, to which, in many instances, the clothing adhered, glued by the clotted gore." Keiley—as was his wont—expressed his outrage to the authorities, even though Elmira sent many volunteers to care for the wounded. The lack of hospitals and basic provisions in Barracks No. 3 meant that many of the sick would be confined to the common wards in the months to come, which only increased the spread of infection.

There was one bit of welcome news in the disaster, at least so far as Keiley could discern: a handful of surviving Rebs managed to "flank out," escaping in the confusion of the wreck and disappearing into the darkness of west-central New York. It was a fate he envied, even if, to a man of his refinement, the method seemed most unreliable.

***

Sergeant Berry Benson preferred a pinch of opportunism to a hundred bushels of righteous indignation any day. Following his capture at Spotsylvania, his passage to Elmira had taken a number of diversions. He had slept on the ground at Fredericksburg, without shelter or blanket in the rain, before finding his lodgings vastly improved when he boarded in a stable at Belle Plain on the Rappahannock River—only to be submitted to a Union lecture on abolitionism as part of the rent. The next stage of the journey took him by steamer to Point Lookout on May 23—a welcome, if difficult, passage for a young man of 21 who had just talked his way out of being executed as a spy. Sergeant Benson found accommodations in the camp not at all to his liking, and he decided to do something more than just complain about it.

Point Lookout was crawling with rumors of escape. Benson heard of a prisoner who allegedly tunneled out the night before he arrived, but he doubted the sandy soil would have allowed it. Other inmates had patched together an assortment of cracker boxes and scrap lumber into a seaworthy vessel—a plan discovered before it could be put into effect. Still another tale told of a pair of prisoners who undertook a swimming match in the Chesapeake Bay within full view of the sentries—one of the Rebs just kept swimming down the coast and never came back. A man with a practical turn of mind, Benson took the last scenario for the most likely, duly admiring its simplicity and sheer nerve.

The sergeant didn't have time to acquaint himself with his new digs before opportunity came knocking—more precisely, pounding—on the door. On May 25, at sundown, Benson was watching the changing of the guard at the front gates. As he idly looked on, the incomprehensible happened: the new detail of Yankee guards somehow failed to close the front gate when they came on duty. Word began to spread through camp—"The front door of the barn is open!"—faster than the old rumor that Grant was dead. Normally, the prisoners were free to walk in and out during daylight hours to swim in the Chesapeake, the men watched by lines of sentries and prevented from swimming past a certain point, but the gates were closed and locked at dusk every day after the men returned inside. It was an absurd blunder that wouldn't go uncorrected for long.

Benson didn't wait for a footman with an invitation. The light dying in the west, he ambled through the gate toward one of three privies, squatting on stilts like railroad water tanks, stationed about 25 feet from the waterline. He walked up a ramp into the privy, slid down one of the wooden poles, and backed into the water, keeping the privy between himself and the sentinels' line of sight. He slid across the "deadline" of logs driven into the coast in the shallow water, the line swimmers weren't allowed to cross. (It was easier to swim in saltwater than fresh water, he quickly noticed.) It was as simple as that. The sergeant paddled away from the shore in the twilight, soon beyond the range of federal musket fire. Benson had spent barely 48 hours at the point.

He treaded water northward for a few miles along the coast. When he could no longer see the camp, he swam and walked in the darkness along the bay's edge, his feet lacerated by raccoon oysters. Over the next several days, he trekked 50 miles through unfamiliar bush and over dangerous roads before he could bring himself to beg a pair of shoes from a stranger. Benson made his way across Maryland's western shore and swam the Potomac River 14 miles below Washington, D.C., "with all my clothes on, and my shoes, also, my hat buttoned under my Confederate jacket, and three matches tied on the top of my head."

On the far side, Benson found himself once again in Virginia. The next day, near Mt. Vernon, the estate of George Washington, he was recaptured behind enemy lines. The Yankees jailed him as a "guerrilla" in nearby Alexandria, then transferred him to the Old Capitol prison in Washington. On June 5, Benson and other prisoners who marched down the street were greeted with the taunt of "Johnnies!" by the partisan residents of Capitol Hill. The front of the prison faced the east wing of the Capitol, now crowned with its new cast-iron dome, glimmering like alabaster in the summer light. Berry Benson had gone to an awful lot of trouble to summer in the splendid backyard of Uncle Sam.

The Old Capitol, which held some 600 prisoners by Benson's count, was outfitted with both a legion of enemy guards and an army of nasty bedbugs. The men, in fact, found it preferable to sleep on the floor than in the vermin-infested bunks. As for the cuisine, Benson grew to rather like the bean soup, but soon complained when the coffee ration was stopped a month later—on July 4. The prisoners could hear the guns from Jubal Early's attack on the Washington suburbs the next week, an event that made Benson antsy to get out. One of his first acts at the Old Capitol was to trade his gray jacket to another prisoner for a coat thinner than his own (not much of a problem in July), but one that bore no military markings in the way of color, braiding, or buttons.

Despite apparently lax security, escapes from the Old Capitol were rare. A couple of Rebs had once walked out the front door in the guise of carpenters, Benson learned. One prisoner blackened his face and masqueraded as a Negro cook, only to be discovered on his way across the threshold. Some men, planning a full-scale assault, eventually had to discard the idea as impractical. But Benson knew enough to be patient. He played sick to gain admittance to the second-floor hospital, hoping to get a good view of the local neighborhood from an upstairs window. Once there, he had to gulp down a mouthful of castor oil for what ailed him, a "cure" so offensive as to deter, for a few days anyway, any serious revisions to his itinerary.

Benson was moved to a ground-floor cell to bunk with William Fleming Baxter, son of the Virginia attorney general, who was an acquaintance of Keiley's. Wasting no time, the two began to cut a hole from the floor of their cramped quarters into the cellar below, a Capitol Hill encore of *The Count of Monte Cristo*. When, for no apparent reason, the men were suddenly moved upstairs, the plan was foiled. On July 23, after six weeks on the Hill, they were marched out of prison for transfer. As they walked away from their summer palace on First Street, Benson couldn't help but be impressed by the new Capitol dome towering above them: "I would occasionally turn, and look, but it never seemed to grow smaller; indeed it seemed to be following after, like the moon in a piece of water by which one is traveling."

Benson never forgave himself for what would happen—or didn't happen—next. The prisoners went by train to Baltimore. He thought first to scramble to freedom amidst the crowd of civilian gawkers at the Baltimore station—but hesitated. Then, on the train hurtling northward, he was about to say "goodbye" to his mates, standing at the edge of a moving car, when the train passed under a bridge—and again he lost his nerve. "I ought to have escaped on the way by jumping off the running train," he confessed later, "and if I had not been a coward I would have." He would be despondent about the lost opportunity for years: "It is a matter, not only of regret, but of unalloyed shame to me that I ever entered the gate of Elmira prison." He arrived on a Sunday, the 24th of July. The Elmira *Advertiser* noted two days later that the motley prisoners' "clothing was of all sorts that may have been worn since the days of Methusaleh." Benson's name was inscribed on the Elmira roll as prisoner no. 1948.

Berry Benson made for an unlikely coward. The moment he marched into Barracks No. 3, he was making a detailed mental map of the grounds for future reference. He noted the sentry catwalk surrounding the main yard, a tree that grew near a prison wall, and the backwash of the Chemung that ran through camp, guards only allowed on the bridge. He got used to the place quickly. Benson came to prefer the lower, southern end of the prison for sentimental reasons: "I liked to go over there; it was that much nearer home." Allowed on one occasion to bathe with fellow prisoners in the river outside camp, he contemplated running off, but the Yankee guards were too wary. It was the last time Benson would find himself alive outside Elmira prison—at least in a bathing party chaperoned by Yankee privates.

The sharpshooter from South Carolina met up with some old friends. He shared a bunk in his ward with William Baxter, his accomplice in the attempted break from the Old Capitol. The two slept on a hard pine plank with nothing but their coats to cover them. One day, Baxter was given a blanket by a fellow prisoner and old friend of his father's—Anthony Keiley, who was looking after the less fortunate who arrived in the wake of the Shohola debacle. Benson had to admire Keiley's devotion to the Cause, figuring it wasn't every legislator who chose to fight a line of drawn sabers rather than haggle with constituents up in arms over a tax increase or a new domestic tariff.

Within days, Berry Benson was plotting how to get his liberty. First, he planned to swim across the pool when it was dark, steal over to the wall, dig through the sand at the wall's base, and go under. He put off the scheme for two nights. But somebody else was also thinking about the darkness. The next day the commandant installed locomotive headlights on the camp walls, and the kerosene lamps illuminated the interior so brightly that "the prison by night was like a gaslit sidewalk," he later remembered. As on the train, another opportunity had been missed. Caution was a good thing, Benson knew, but too much of it could kill a man in Elmira, where the first prisoner names had already been scrawled under "deceased" in the official camp ledger.

The veteran of Fort Sumter was hardly fazed. In a brilliant stroke, he figured that he could *swim* out of Elmira, if only he could enter the pond without being seen, weight himself down with rocks, and "crawl all the way on the bottom" beneath the wall. Breathing would be a problem, but not an insurmountable one. "I stole a one-inch strip [of wood], and, starting this with my knife, I rived it carefully with my hands from end to end. Then I hollowed a trench in each piece, and, fitting the pieces together again, and winding strongly a cord round, I had a watertight tube to breathe through while crawling under the water. This tube I laid away in my bunk to wait an opportunity."

Ingenious though it was, the idea of the pine snorkel didn't draw breath for long. After closely inspecting the grounds for a few days, Benson arrived at a better plan. The soil was dark and firm, he could see, not porous and sandy like Point Lookout's. The best way to leave Elmira might well be to tunnel out. He knew he couldn't do that alone. There would be no way to escape without accomplices—and meticulous planning. The days of just walking away from prison were over. The caution that had doomed him on the train was perhaps his greatest ally now. Only something like the patience of Job, not the desperation of Jonah, would get him out of Elmira alive.

Other Elmiras

Courageous and high spirited, Sergeant Benson was far from the typical prisoner in the North. Most POWs felt the hand of a rude baptism— not by water or fire, but by mud and cold, disease and depression, brutality, homesickness, and death. "To go into a prison of war is in all respects to be born again," wrote Sidney Lanier in 1866, a celebrated poet who spent a grueling stretch as a prisoner at Point Lookout. "For of the men in all prisons of the late war," he added, "it might be said, as of births in the ordinary world—they came in and went out naked." Naked many virtually were in 1864, by which time the South, crippled by blockade and three years of war, could barely afford to clothe its own soldiers.

"Helmira" was only the most infamous of dozens of northern "bastilles" where hunger, exposure, brutality, and disease were epidemic. It is hard to account for the fact that Yankee prisons remain such a well-kept secret, whereas houses of horror like Andersonville and Libby Prison are the stuff of national legend. In fact, Union prisoners, of whom some 30,000 died in confinement, numbered over 200,000; by comparison, some 214,000 Rebels were taken prisoner, a much larger percentage of their total forces. In sum, 26,000 Rebels died in what was called "Yankee captivity"—six times the number of Confederate dead listed for the battle of

Gettysburg and twice that for the dead of Antietam, Chickamauga, Chancellorsville, Seven Days', Shiloh, and Second Manassas *combined*. Their story has been almost as neglected as the camps they died in.

In one sense, those who went to prison at all were lucky. POWs like Marcus Toney claimed to have seen combatants killed *after* they surrendered. The Federals were known to deal summarily with irregular cavalry outfits who terrorized settlements in the border states. A member of John Hunt Morgan's cavalry, Curtis Burke, reported that his men were sure to throw away looted items if capture was imminent, knowing that a sentence of death awaited them if they didn't. Union troops continued to execute captured irregulars until Confederates began returning the favor, at which time the two sides agreed to treat them as conventional prisoners. Morgan himself was captured by the Federals, surviving long enough to be stowed in the Ohio penitentiary in Columbus from which he fashioned a daring escape, leaving a clutch of red-faced captors in his wake.

Capture often meant display. Given the limited occasions for civic spectacle, many captives ran a peculiar kind of gauntlet in the public eye. Rebel infantryman John Copley reported his group of prisoners was assembled and exhibited on the capitol grounds in Nashville for five hours, the soldiers subjected to a jeremiad by Union loyalist Senator Andrew Johnson—and this in a state that *seceded* from the Union. (Copley noted that many of the men had relatives in the gawking crowd.) Such citizen assemblies tended to be well behaved in the North, as Keiley said they were in New York, though taunts were easily launched at defenseless and hungry strangers.

The men taken north were of all classes and types: deserters, volunteers, paid substitutes, the wounded, the war-weary, the malnourished, and the famished and half-dead, everyone from the cynically mercenary to green conscripts literally quaking with fear. With little ado, they were plundered of anything of value, including money, clothing, diaries, and boots—especially boots, a prize for men in an occupation that might ask them to march 20 miles in a day. (The Rebs were so poorly shod that they were well advised to sleep in their shoes, if they were lucky enough to have shoes at all.) Capture could be disorienting. Politician Lawrence Sangston of Baltimore awoke one night to find himself surrounded by police in his own house. J. B. Stamp of Alabama remembered surrendering to a Yankee sergeant at the Wilderness and "from his extreme bad English, for a moment, it was a question as to whether I had surrendered to Germany or the United States." Others like Keiley and Toney found the occasion terrifying, menaced by troopers waving guns as though the smallest excuse would be compelling enough reason to discharge them.

Much about the camps defies expectations. The number of military captives, for example, was swelled by political detainees with suspected Confederate sympathies who may have never picked up a gun—confined without trial or habeas corpus, an act the U.S. Supreme Court ruled illegal after the war. A member of the Maryland legislature, Sangston was hectored from his home in 1861 and spent the next several months committing a host of Yankee abominations to his prison diary. A proud patriot (and no mean ironist), Sangston wryly recorded on September 13, while impounded at Baltimore's Fort McHenry, that "this is the anniversary of the day on which the 'Star Spangled Banner' was written by the grandfather of one of the prisoners." A few months later, Sangston was paroled from Fort Warren in Boston, probably the most humane prison in the North with only twelve deaths recorded during the war.

Military celebrities joined yeomen in the Rebel ranks. Luminaries in stir included General Morgan, General Joseph Wheeler, General Basil Duke, and William Henry Fitzhugh Lee (son of Robert E.). And others, if lacking immediate credentials, were made heroes by later propagandists of the Cause. The "Immortal Six Hundred," captive Confederate officers employed as hostages during the siege of Charleston, were a rallying cry in the South long after the war ended because of their prolonged ill treatment at the hands of the callous Federals.

Prisoners were a surprisingly diverse lot. Keiley and Toney both made the acquaintance of a woman at Point Lookout who was captured in the guise of a Rebel artilleryman—and given quarters apart from her fellow captives. Camp Douglas in Chicago numbered five women among its inmates in 1862, who probably also disguised themselves to follow husbands, lovers, or brothers into confinement. The camp boasted an array of Mexican, Spanish, Cherokee, and "contraband" (black) males of all shades. Several of the latter, the property of other prisoners, eventually signed up to fight with the Federals. But not all blacks were so inclined: Private Isaac Wood, a bona fide combatant, agreed to be exchanged for a Yankee prisoner and returned south to finish out the war.

By the time Elmira opened for business in 1864, POW camps in the North had been operating for three years. Save for a three-month interlude toward the end of the war, they were administered by Lieutenant Colonel William H. Hoffman, a Federal officer taken prisoner in Texas *before* the war started—and paroled on the condition that he wouldn't take up arms against the South. Even if he didn't pick up a rifle for the war's duration, Hoffman did enough to make many a Rebel take his name in vain during the ensuing years. It was Hoffman who instituted, in 1864, a reduction of prisoner rations, a transparent revenge for the South's treatment of prisoners—and it was Hoffman who ordered that

the guard be increased should the prisoners revolt against the reduction. Point Lookout, in fact,
was officially known as "Camp Hoffman," though
the much-reviled name didn't stick with prisoners given a taste of his northern hospitality.

Of course, neither side wanted to be burdened with prisoners in the first place. Captives
had long been a strategic encumbrance of armies
in the field, which needed to feed, guard, and
quarantine them at great expense. As a result,
prison operations during the Civil War came to
hang on a delicate arrangement called the "cartel
of exchange," modeled on the United States–
British accord of the War of 1812, a conflict in
which reports of prisoner abuse had been common. Given limited resources, the South favored
a cartel that would permit the two sides to trade
prisoners on an equal basis. President Lincoln,
unwilling to recognize the Confederacy as a le-
gitimate entity, at first refused the very notion of
exchange. But when battles like the Seven Days'
brought thousands of captives into the Union
fold and swamped prisoner facilities across the
North, the commander in chief had a sudden
change of mind.

In the summer of 1862, the two sides agreed
to formal rules for repatriation. Within ten days
of capture, prisoners would be paroled and returned to their lines; once the men reached
home, local agents would make a formal tally of
their numbers. Prisoners were paroled on the
condition they wouldn't take up arms again un-

til an exchange of equal numbers, based on the cartel rules, was negotiated. The men were to be valued according to a calibrated scale: one general, for example, was worth 60 privates or common seamen in an official swap. It may have sounded more like a Victorian board game than the calculus for the first full-scale modern war, but for a time the plan worked.

Within days of capture, men were released on "parole" by signing their names to a promise that they wouldn't fight again until exchanged. When a sufficient number of men had gathered, they would be traded per the agreed values and permitted to rejoin their units in the field—just as happened to Marcus Toney. The oath, or parole, was a key concept of the cartel, a reminder that although the ordnance and tactics of war were rapidly changing, the code of honor that attended military engagements from Bull Run to Appomattox harked back to another century, if not another age.

What was simple in theory soon faltered. Within a year, the South announced it would not return black prisoners, retaining them as "contraband" (slaves) and declaring their white officers subject to execution. Fielding more and more black soldiers as the war progressed, the North was outraged. Secretary of War Edwin Stanton ordered further exchanges with the South abandoned in 1863, a decision that, if ostensibly based on principle, doomed thousands of POWs to death. The North's refusal to exchange with an enemy that regarded black soldiers as property coincided, it turned out, with its own pragmatic designs of winning the war.

Ulysses S. Grant, general-in-chief from early 1864, understood Stanton's resolve. Badly undermanned, Richmond stood to gain more from prisoner exchanges than did Washington. With superior numbers, the North could afford to have the cartel suspended—all prisoners frozen in military limbo—and watch the South founder for lack of recruits. Grant also feared that the existence of regular exchanges encouraged Federal soldiers to desert, seeking through capture and parole to find an easy way out of the war. So the prisoner cartel was left to collapse. Save for the severely sick and wounded, exchanges were abandoned from mid-1863 until early 1865, when the South, ready to conscript black soldiers itself, reversed course and agreed to exchange prisoners. In the interval, over a quarter of a million men languished in captivity on both sides, thousands never to return home again.

A media blitz made their confinement a public matter. Prisoners from Andersonville to Elmira became pawns in a newspaper campaign that stirred ideological passions on both sides of the Mason–Dixon. Newspapers in the North and South traded accusations about the other side's depraved treatment of captives: "The slaveholder is born to tyranny and reared to cruelty," cried the *New York Times* in 1864, commenting on woodcuts of photographs depicting sick Federal prisoners returned from the South. Charges in one paper that Richmond's Libby Prison fed mule meat to Yankees was met with indignation in the *Richmond Dispatch*, which uttered that mule meat was too good for men who had "essayed to bring starvation on the people who captured them, and they would have no right to complain if they were forced to that fate they designed for us."

If papers thrilled to recount the barbarities of the enemy, they also sought to emphasize the generous treatment accorded captives in their own house. "How different an example of humanity the North is setting," the *New York Times* boasted of prisoner treatment in 1862. Even an outbreak of smallpox at Rock Island (Illinois), Camp Chase (Ohio), and Fort Delaware (Delaware) didn't prevent federal Quartermaster-General Montgomery Meigs from telling the *Times* in 1863 that, so far as prisoners were concerned, "we are killing them by treating them as southern gentlemen until they die of gout." (Meigs, a native of Georgia whose engineering genius had helped raise the Capitol dome in Washington—and whose son died fighting in a Federal uniform—was unappeasable in his hatred of the Confederacy.) Northern apologies for prison conditions resembled nothing so much as the familiar excuses for slavery offered by Delta planters—victims were well fed, happy as clams, content to sing in confinement, and generally better off than their pathetic lives would have otherwise permitted.

For prisoners at Elmira and elsewhere, the consequences of the publicity war were dire. As tales circulated of new atrocities, Secretary of War Stanton forbade the construction of barracks at Point Lookout, issuing tents in August 1863 to hold what became a garrison of 20,000 captives. The U.S. Sanitary Commission visited the camp in November and concluded that, despite a high percentage of deaths, the prisoners were fortunate to be receiving as much food as the guards were.

A special committee made the prison rounds in 1864—the year Keiley and Benson were interned—only to reach a number of dubious conclusions. There were *no* deadlines in the northern camps, the committee offered in defense of the military—which was patently false. The prisoners had so much food that they were able to save rations to trade for luxuries, they contended, and were given ice water in the summer. Celebrated reformer Dorothea Dix (Keiley called her "the grand female dry-nurse of Yankee Doodle") testified that Point Lookout prisoners had been afforded excellent treatment and given better medical care than even their guards. Though such optimism was gratifying, nearly one in six prisoners who died in northern prisons perished at Point Lookout. "Thousands passed through that gate," John Rufus King dourly noted, "who never passed out alive again."

Whatever the media and official commissions may have done to encourage animosity—or conceal suffering—they were not the only culprits for degenerating conditions. Nothing less than supremely bad planning killed many a man—and boy—in the northern prisons, a fact for which Stanton bore considerable responsibility. Preparations in the South were also inadequate, although a comparative lack of provisions made poor conditions there more defensible. Unfortunately, both sides had vastly underestimated the scope of the war. Such was the prognosis for a quick victory that the Federals had been confident, in 1861, that Johnson's Island, Ohio, would be sufficient by itself to hold *all* POWs while the rebellion ran its course. But the number of prisoners General Grant took at Fort Donelson in early 1862 (15,000) was almost equal to the size of the *entire* U.S. Army on the eve of the war's outbreak. The military was unprepared for the buildup of enemy soldiers quartered within its lines and incapable of foraging or fending for themselves, a resentful "immigrant" population that would have done its mightiest to flee the land of abolitionists and bounty jumpers had the hated Abe Lincoln given them half a chance.

Only when it became clear that the South was a serious opponent did the Union recognize the enormity of its logistical problem. Dozens of POW camps had to be quickly outfitted. Masonry fortresses, fairgrounds, campsites, and

Union barracks were made over into makeshift quarters for Rebel occupants. "Elmire prison,— as I was informed,—was originally a camp of instruction," noted J. B. Stamp of the Third Alabama Infantry. And so it was—though built to "instruct" northern soldiers, not southern ones. Raised as an army barracks, the camp was designed to accommodate not more than a few thousand men before its transformation into a POW city almost three times that size.

Some camps could not have been more poorly planned. Improper drainage plagued sanitation at Elmira, which was unaccountably built on the swampy banks of the Chemung, a breeding ground for pestilence. To correct this problem, prisoners were detailed to dig drainage ditches from the latrine at Foster's Pond—only after months of waiting—and were paid with wages made possible by cutting rations for the entire camp. (Many of the workers eventually died of disease.) The removal of human waste proved a problem of Herculean scope—one Elmira surgeon estimated that an average of 7,000 prisoners discharged 2,600 gallons of urine *every day* into Foster's Pond. It was a testament to Berry Benson's audacity that, even to obtain something so noble as his freedom, he actually considered navigating such a cesspool as a human submarine. The idea probably didn't occur to everyone.

In the end, captivity might be made bearable by the leverage of two things: rank and money.

Captured Rebel officers were "lucky," if the word is used advisedly. Often culled from prisoner ranks to break down military organization, officers tended to receive better treatment as POWs. Coming from more privileged backgrounds as a rule, they were better prepared to purchase goods and services on the inside. Prisoners confined to Johnson's Island, a facility for officers in Lake Erie, found a barber, jeweler, baker, shoemaker, and tailor working out of the barracks. Debating groups, religious services, and a Rebel Thespian Society held sway for the more metaphysical minded. The men on the island, numbering about 12,000 during the course of the war, could buy uncensored newspapers— a rarity in northern camps—and inmates contributed to the local *Sandusky Register*. Since free time was abundant, sports were popular, and the prison baseball championship drew a crowd of several thousand people in 1864.

Despite its setting in the middle of Lake Erie resort country, however, Johnson's Island was no holiday. "When the weather got below zero, the scenery was scarcely compensation for the suffering," remembered one inmate. "We bury our own dead," remarked another, "and on such occasions, like our working parties, we are always attended by a sufficient guard." Even so, the death rate at Johnson's Island—some 220 men during its existence—was tiny compared with that of Fort Delaware, Point Lookout, or Elmira. In the prisons, as elsewhere, money and privilege bought favors denied to the great bulk of men.

When Elmira opened its gates in the summer of 1864, Anthony Keiley, Marcus Toney, John King, and Berry Benson reported under armed guard. Much of the war was already over. Gettysburg was a year in the past, Antietam two. Sherman and Grant were moving to turn military stalemate into total war—and victory. And although the South had not yet been broken, Appomattox was fewer than nine months away. A critical presidential election loomed in the months ahead, as did a string of Union victories from the fall of Atlanta to Petersburg. Given the steady northern advance, the months of captivity near the war's end would be hard ones for the men of the South. "Whenever there was any news favorable to the Federal side," wrote Toney, "it was bulletined on the inside [of barracks]; but of course the unfavorable we did not hear of." And from the summer of 1864 onward, the South had precious little to cheer about.

The bulk of prisoners at Elmira and elsewhere settled in for the war's duration. Everyone wanted to see his home and loved ones. But if a man had a good constitution (physical *and* mental), he stood a better chance of surviving the rigors of camp life than he did an assault at Devil's Den—unless he wintered at a place like Elmira. The bad news from the military front no doubt made the thought of escape less promising. But men like Anthony Keiley and

Berry Benson were resolved to leave. They were anxious to get home—too anxious, perhaps, for even the most daring escape meant returning to a South much nearer collapse than when they had left it. But they could not abide confinement. "I would attempt escape," Benson would write proudly after the war, "from a palace where I was feasted every day."

CHAPTER 2

The Fox and the Mole

ANTHONY Keiley, late of Petersburg, arrived at Elmira prison on a Tuesday. As was the practice of his social class, he wasted no time leaving a personal visiting card. Already suffering from a case of severely loosened bowels, he reported to the camp dispensary for a remedy—and perhaps a little free advice. Whatever the prognosis, he appears to have made a favorable impression. On a tip from the camp doctor, he sat down and composed, "in immaculate calligraphy," a letter to the prison commandant, Major Henry Colt, requesting immediate employment, a missive the good doctor delivered in person. Keiley knew that a man's fate could turn on the basis of a favor granted or denied, and there was no use looking for one in the barracks. If anyone grasped the importance of political patronage, the ambitious and self-assured delegate from Petersburg did.

His instincts proved uncanny. On the morrow, July 13, Colt summoned the Confederate politician to his tent, where he indulged him, as

Generals Kautz and Butler had, in "a free conversation on matters military, political and personal," no doubt impressed by a man who could
hold forth on Molière's farces and Napoleon's
campaigns with equal brio. Colt, who was of
the 104th New York Volunteers and the brother
of Samuel Colt, inventor of the famed revolver,
offered the well-spoken gentleman a position in
his adjutant's office. Keiley, recalling the mortal
dangers of camp tedium at Point Lookout, accepted. While most of the "fresh fish" were out
getting acquainted with the grounds of Barracks No. 3, the fox, in a manner of speaking,
had been hired on to keep the farmer's books. It
had taken Keiley the better part of a day to find
a job.

It wasn't an undertaking for the lazy or im-
precise. Keiley's first appointed task was to keep
the "Dooms-day Book," the ledger of every
prisoner entering Elmira. He recorded name,
prisoner number, regiment, ward, and circumstances of capture for every Confederate who
had so far taken up abode. He was paid for his
troubles, too, twice the rate of those who did
manual labor, receiving ten cents and two cups
of execrable coffee per diem.

On July 17, his third day on duty, 780 new
prisoners arrived from the South. Swamped
with names and numbers, Keiley surrendered
the Doomsday chores to a trio of Yankee ac-
countants, at which time the Virginia state delegate was appointed the unofficial man Friday of

Barracks No. 3. He now answered miscellaneous letters to the commandant, oversaw the sutler's accounts, paid for prisoner labor, and, the most grisly of tasks, compiled the morning report of men who had died the previous day. Ledger in hand, the lawyer found himself at the opposite end of the line from Saint Peter, holding the administrative keys of the camp as the prisoners made their unceremonious way to the boneyard wrapped in a pine coffin and a common prayer.

Keiley was given a personal room to bunk in for his trouble. With pocket money, he could afford to buy edible food and forget about the price of rats—"about four cents apiece—in greenbacks." But his rise to prison trusty left him feeling a twinge of guilt. "I had the happiness of being the means of making the stay of many [prisoners] less irksome, and their restraints less grievous to bear," he boasted, "without any compromise of their or my principles or position," he added, as though to defer any doubts. Keiley went so far as to claim a reputation for being the most rebellious inmate at Elmira. If so, his mutinous spirit never tempted him to scale a prison wall, or forge a pass, or paw through a cramped tunnel on his haunches. He considered himself a man of honor. The modern world, the way of contracts and loose morals and machinery and noisy curses, repelled him.

The son of immigrants, Keiley was set on a course by his parents to confirm their risky passage to America. And he had made his way up the social ladder by the sheer power of books and personal charm. His letter of introduction to Colt suggested how great a bond education forged between officers north and south. Keiley not only knew the camp officials by name, but his accounting of them, verging on the fraternal, also suggested his own penchant for the rubble of history: "[Captain C. C.] Barton was a good fellow," he wrote, "notwithstanding he considered Abe Lincoln a Chesterfield, and accounted Grant a compound, in about equal proportions, of King Solomon and Alexander the Great."

Whatever favors Keiley cadged from the officers, he was subject to the whim of nature as much as anyone. A plum camp job couldn't keep him from suffering diarrhea for months on end, an ailment so messy that the priggish Victorian could hardly bring himself to call it by name in his camp journal. The affliction was nothing to take lightly: that summer, the Elmira *Advertiser* averred matter-of-factly that the ailment was proving "rather fatal" to Rebel prisoners, the symptoms of dehydration spelling the end for more men during the war than minié balls ever would.

Keiley offered aid and comfort to his brethren, like the blanket he gave to William Baxter, acts of noblesse oblige often quashed in Barracks No. 3. There were obstacles to good works at Helmira, and none was apparently more prominent than Major Eugene Francis

Sanger. The hospital chief (and a "brute" in Keiley's estimation), Sanger, by some accounts,
failed to provide even minimum attention to
those under his care. His capacity for prognosis
proved limited. He refused to enter "fever" as
the cause of death for any patient, distorting the
facts of what caused many a demise at Elmira,
or so Keiley believed—the foul miasma emanat-
ing from Foster's Pond. (Most "experts," like
Keiley, little guessed that malaria and yellow
fever were transmitted by mosquitoes, not by
pestilential vapors.) Sanger's "systematic inhumanity to the sick," as Keiley put it, was apparently a response to rumors of Andersonville
atrocities. "I do not doubt that many of those
who died [at Elmira] perished from actual starvation," concluded Keiley, a bitter irony since he
believed himself to be "in a country where food
was cheap and abundant."

The work of physicians during the war was
everywhere dubious. Sterilization was unknown.
Infection was rampant. Doctors gave opium to
stop the bowels, blue mass of mercury and chalk
to loosen them. For pneumonia, they prescribed
bleeding or whiskey. Indeed, whiskey, or "pop
skull" as many Rebs knew it, was probably the
most effective common antidote that doctors
had to offer from their black bags. The clumsy
surgical utensils of the trade—saws, pliers,
drills, and drivers—looked more like the tools of
a streetcar mechanic than those of a devotee of
Hippocrates. Many men on both sides, with

some justification, believed that the "sawbones" killed more than they saved, more the result of benighted professional ignorance than personal incompetence.

The only thing worse than seeing southern boys locked up under such conditions was knowing that the Yankees were watching them suffer for sport. "Our curiosity has been excited for some days past," Keiley wrote in late July, "by noticing a wooden structure, consisting of two large platforms, one above the other, which has been going up across the road that bounds one face of our prison." It was, in fact, a 25-foot observation tower (soon to be joined by a second and much taller one), the result of enterprising Elmirans who realized they had a first-rate live attraction on their hands. The original entrepreneurs charged fifteen cents a head, recalled Keiley, to ascend the tower and gawk at the yard full of *misérables* below—what the *Advertiser* called a "living, moving panorama." The towers were particularly popular with Elmira ladies, Keiley complained, wondering why "Barnum has not taken the prisoners off the hands of Abe, divided them into companies, and carried them in caravans through the country" since the whole prospect "proposes to turn our pen into a menagerie."

Marcus Toney of Edgefield remembered the second observatory, recalling the price of admission as a dime and that customers, supplied with spyglasses, "scrutinized the camp with much curiosity." (He claimed that Horace Greeley, *New York Tribune* publisher, made a visit one day.) John King recalled of the second tower, which had three floors, that the price of admission climbed with the view. When private capitalism got a little out of hand in September with refreshment stands in the streets, the observatories were confiscated by the army. Though the second one was soon destroyed, the original tower remained standing throughout the war, long after the Johnnies had worn off as a casual novelty. Elmira, as a matter of fact, wasn't the only Yankee prison to inspire spectacles of the sort. A businessman erected a 25-foot tower outside Camp Douglas in Illinois and charged Chicagoans ten cents to ascend and ogle the enemy from the lofty height. In Sandusky, Ohio, operators advertised excursion boat tours that circled Johnson's Island in hopes of catching a glimpse of some imprisoned Johnnies playing baseball or doing the laundry. The camp sutler (Mr. Johnson himself) refused to sell any provisions to prisoners unless they first purchased a souvenir lithograph of the island at three dollars apiece, Johnson knowing a captive audience when he saw one.

The Elmira summer dragged on. On the night of July 31, A. P. Potts, an older member of Keiley's Ward 21, was shot by a guard after ignoring an order. On August 2, news of Jubal Early's probe into Pennsylvania buoyed the prisoners, a sign of uplifting, if short-lived, hope. On the 18th, news reached camp that Commissary-General

Hoffman had issued an order preventing the sutlers from retailing any more food or clothing to "healthy" prisoners. It was a dire signal that the coming winter might prove unbearable. Before sundown on the 21st, a popular young prisoner succumbed to a fever and died. The commandant supplied him with a metal coffin, and Keiley and others escorted the body to the main gate before it was buried in "the potter's field, where the prisoners are accorded their stinted share of 'God's Acre.'"

Keiley, a dutifully pious man, found himself in excellent company. Bibles and religious tracts were common in the Rebel camps, and revivals became increasingly popular as the war dragged on. He attended Sunday afternoon services in camp, which had been started in late July by Major Colt for the edification of prisoners. Thomas K. Beecher, brother of Harriet Beecher Stowe, came and delivered a sermon that turned out to be "practical and sensible," to Keiley's surprise. But some Yankee preaching was intolerable. On August 14, an abolitionist sermon by a Reverend Bainbridge so disgusted the men that several offended Rebs attempted to leave the audience, only to be threatened with the guardhouse. "The clerical world in Puritandom has not changed altogether from the happy days of Quaker whipping and Papist hanging," Keiley observed, always glad to tweak the noses of the Founding Fathers, at least those who hailed from New England.

Dressed in the sentiments of a high-church cavalier, Keiley was something of a Puritan himself. Northern newspapers with "obscene pictures" circulated among the men, he decried, contributing to "the debauchery of the people." Prostitution, divorce, adultery, and "crimes of violence traceable to lust" were rampant in the North, he alleged, a trend that only reinforced his conviction that the abolitionist cause was tragically compromised. Keiley claimed to have heard more "vulgarity of speech" from Yankee soldiers during a few months in the North than he had in three years' service in the Army of Northern Virginia. For a man who had seen action at Gettysburg and heard his share of harangues in the back rooms of the Virginia statehouse, his sensibilities were remarkably delicate.

One matter on which he was not so delicate was "the Negro question," a subject that earned his every invective short of the profane. The sight of a black man in uniform sparked fierce emotions among most Rebels, none more so than Keiley. The Yankees tried to exploit that bad blood. Captured Confederates were often paraded before Negro troops to hear bitter shouts of "Bottom rail on top!"—a common refrain hurled by black soldiers at their former masters. (Not all of them proved to be vindictive. At Point Lookout, a prisoner was gratified to be given $10 by one of the Negro guards—who turned out to be his former slave.)

Keiley first met Negro guards at Point Lookout (a company of freed slaves), an outfit that, brazen in its impudence and foul language, led him to conclude "their conduct is as black as their skin." And this was one of his more temperate remarks on the subject. Keiley found only one man of color in camp worthy of any respect: Old Dick, a servant at a Petersburg hotel who had been drafted as a cook for the Gettysburg campaign, then fell into Yankee hands. "Dick had been importuned, time and again, to renounce the Confederate cause, come out of prison and accept work and good wages outside," wrote Keiley fondly, "but he resisted with Roman fortitude." (For the classically trained Keiley, anything Roman was good.) That Dick was a "Jeff Davis man" gave him a special place forever in Keiley's heart.

Keiley found another "good" Negro at Elmira—perhaps to redeem his faith in the black race or simply to prove to later northern readers he wasn't a purebred racist. "Bonus" was a Kentucky slave captured by Yankees who became an orderly for Major Colt. He nonetheless had a decided preference for southern gentlemen and did Keiley many a small favor, even if "the army had spoiled him pretty effectually." But the lawyer saw him as little more than a minstrel clown—"his boots were as glossy as his cheeks"—and related at some length Bonus's intention to get "married" at Elmira, although he already had two other wives. Bonus was later convicted for stealing a revolver and banished to the front.

For all his rantings on "the sable race," Keiley hit a nerve. "The Northern people, and I speak from long acquaintance with them, care much less for Negroes than we," he proposed cheekily. Though a meager apology for the metaphysics of Negro-hating, it had a grain of truth. "It is the free states which have made the most odiously discriminating laws against the free blacks; and it is only in a free state that such bloody outbreaks against the Negroes as have characterized Chicago and New York could possibly occur." His reference to the draft riots was a bitter reminder that many of the white-skinned men who stood guard over him had serious doubts themselves about the fighting abilities and intelligence of black men—"Congoes," Keiley derisively called them—who had joined the Union army by the thousands.

By the end of August, conditions had deteriorated. New prisoners shuffled through the main gate every week, a sign of mounting Rebel reverses, and the camp census topped 9,000. The Yankees were confiscating all parcels from the outside. Two prisoners were caught in a tunnel trying to escape on the 27th. Their punishment: solitary confinement in the guardhouse, or "dungeon." On the 31st, the day George McClellan was nominated by the Democratic Convention in Chicago, a new order circulated forbidding Yankee officers from reading newspapers aloud in camp. By mid-September, scurvy was spreading through the prison, striking almost 2,000 Rebs. With no news from the front, little daily exercise, and an absence of fresh fruit and vegetables, many of the Elmira boarders seemed doomed.

Keiley's nerves began to fray. On September 21, he recorded 29 deaths *in a single day*. He scribbled in his log with the bland air of a bureaucrat: "Air pure, location healthy, no epidemic." Then he added, as though to rip away a mask he couldn't bear to wear in the privacy of his own thoughts, "the men are being deliberately murdered by the surgeon, especially by either the ignorance or the malice of the chief."

It seemed that Dr. Sanger and his confederates were on the loose. The stupidity of the doctors, Keiley alleged, was scandalous. One prescribed a rigorous styptic for inflammation of the bowels, the kind of diagnosis that kept many ward chiefs from sending anything but emergency cases to the sick ward. On his way to the hospital on the 21st, Keiley found 18 men scattered in his path, lying in various states of eternal repose. "Eleven more were added to the list by half-past eight o'-clock," he wrote, a normally allusive man surrendering to the blunt precision of numbers. Little did he suspect at the time that it was more Washington than Sanger that had turned an indifferent eye to Elmira, oblivious to a number of requests the surgeons had already made.

Of course, it wasn't the doctors' fault that Barracks No. 3 had no hospital when it opened to prisoners in July 1864. By early September, six wards for the ailing had been hastily constructed, by which time there were already 9,000 men in camp. Two more hospital wards and some converted barracks were soon added, but still it was normal to confine many of the sick prisoners with their "healthy" companions in barracks, a deadly strategy when smallpox struck in the winter. Walter Addison of Stewart's Horse Artillery was one prisoner who believed that the failure to adequately quarantine diseases was a deliberate attempt to decimate the Confederate ranks—and Keiley's opinion wasn't much kinder.

Oblivious to Elmira, the world turned. Atlanta finally fell. Early was drubbed at Winchester. Sheridan swept through the Shenandoah in late September. (And Maximilian, it was whispered in barracks, was emperor of all Mexico.) In the meantime, most men only waited to see if the next day's gruel would have chunks of beef or mule meat. "To us the book of events was sealed," Keiley wrote. "Occasionally, by a bribe, we would achieve the reading of a newspaper, and hear, in such partial phrase as prejudice affords, the story of the great tragedy our comrades were playing." The big picture was painted by propaganda and rumor. News of friends under fire and the siege that Grant had laid down around "our little city" was sparse, agonizingly so.

One of the few remedies for the deadly mix of anxiety and ennui was the donation by a New

York benefactor, in early September, of 300 volumes to establish a prison library. Even "infantile toy-books and dilapidated geographies," Keiley granted, were a welcome sight for men whose brains had begun to shrivel. The personal news from home, when it arrived at all, was no more inspiring. The last three letters he received, mysteriously nicked by the censor, were shorn of everything but a signature.

The lack of news only made Keiley more eager to return. The business of running the government beckoned. And he was imprisoned in the North on shaky grounds. Keiley could hardly be considered a bona fide combatant when all he had done was pick up an antique firestick in defense of his city, no less than any honorable Spartan would have done. But it could not have escaped him either that his imprisonment might prove more valuable one day than anything he had done in the war, even the ball he took in the foot at Malvern Hill. Here was the penultimate act of public service—he had suffered the deprivations of Helmira, the next best thing to being carried off the *champs de bataille* on his shield.

Already in his thirties, Keiley could pass for middle-aged, a decade older than many of the boys in Barracks No. 3. He had seen something of the North (New York City in 1860), which made him a worldly traveler compared to men who might not have ventured ten miles from home before the war. Despite his sardonic exterior he was a closet sentimentalist, intent on perfuming the worst of prison circumstances not attributable to the Yankees with a gallant flourish. He offered that "a fairer summer never blessed the eye" than the warmest months of 1864 at Elmira—which had actually been a brutal spell of drought for local farmers.

The man was more Victorian in his sentiments than Gladstone. A ferocious critic of his foes, he was subject to bouts of misty sentimentality when discussing his adopted homeland. Keiley could preach against the manners of the "profane devils" in the North, while offering of the South that "a more varied collection of heroes never blessed the eyes of man." His strong moral opinions on everything from Jacobean tragedy to the intricacies of French idiom saved him at the Point and Elmira—his absorbent mind, stuffed full of books and their myriad details, helped him retain a last defense against depression, something of an Epicurean with stoic sensibilities set down in a cold-climed Yankee slough of despond.

But the reverie was over by September's end. The thermometer dropped suddenly, and men sleeping in tents "began to suffer severely," Keiley complained. The hospital woes multiplied. Prisoners were vaccinated with a venereal virus, extracted from men suffering from the disease, and the new patients developed painful sores, some the size of a man's fist. Like Reverend Bainbridge, it seemed, those who would "save" the Rebs were proving to be as disagreeable as the rifle-toting sentinels, some of them black, who glared down at them from the catwalks like rebel angels.

Anthony Keiley had reached a turning point: he must either get out of Elmira or risk staying on until all his hard work in Richmond was rendered worthless. A few unbearable weeks at Point Lookout had led to more than two *months* at Elmira—with no reprieve in sight. Only the "generosity" of the enemy made the ordeal bearable, a bitter admission that the Yankees were giving him bed and board when his rightful place was in Richmond making policy against his hoteliers. The war was being won—or lost—hundreds of miles away, and Keiley was contributing nothing to the effort by tending to the poor ghosts bunked down in the Elmira infirmary.

He had once before talked his way into Major Colt's graces. Why not again? The man, he reminded himself, was a gentleman, susceptible, as the species should be, to all manner of reason. Keiley's garrulous Irish charm was about to be tested a second time. Before another epidemic struck. Before Sanger could get to him. Before winter came. It was time to get out of Elmira.

Notes from Underground

There was little doubt in Berry Benson's mind that he would be headed south from Elmira before the first frost. He had started making plans for freedom early. "I went barefoot both for comfort, it being summer," he related, "and to save my shoes for the long tramp south, when I should escape." Soon after arriving in camp, he met up with two old Georgia classmates, John Perrin and Coon Bohler, Elmira being a kind of informal school reunion for many prisoners. After "holding confab" the first few days in the "bullpen," as the prison was called, they hit upon a plan.

The trio pledged themselves to a private project: an 80-foot tunnel under a vacant house adjacent to their quarters in the northeast corner of camp. The space between their building and the next was screened from observation by an alley-like fence. Of course, they wanted to keep the tunnel a secret; the fewer who knew about it, the less was the chance for betrayal. By night, they crept out of their barracks through a makeshift window with leather hinges, an opening they had cut out next to a friend's bunk, and then crawled beneath the house. The digging was slow and laborious. The conspirators decided to take two other men into their confidence, the five of them bravely pushing on, depositing the dirt from the tunnel beneath the house and inching forward like a company of prudent worms.

The secret didn't keep. A certain Sergeant Joe Womack in a nearby ward had started another "business" under Hospital No. 1. One of his accomplices—also working for Benson—had told him of Berry's tunnel. So at Womack's behest, Benson threw in his hat with the others, but perhaps did not completely believe in their conviction—Womack, after all, was still wearing *his* shoes. The new burrow only needed about 16 feet to clear the camp wall, so Benson and mates took up digging for a cause whose success appeared imminent. There was no point in competition. Once a tunnel was successfully run, they knew, all others would be quickly discovered and destroyed by the vengeful Yankees.

After a few days, they had dug halfway to the exterior camp wall from beneath Hospital No. 1 when disaster struck. Part of the tunnel caved. Though no one was hurt, it marked a bad omen. Some men suspected sabotage. Were the Yankees watching? Was there a second tunnel nearby? Were they competing against their own men? Benson made a move to check under Hospital No. 2, and what he discovered must have made his heart sink even further: here was another tunnel, even closer to completion than their own. Womack's boys had been flanked on their right by another team in gray.

In late summer Benson joined forces with these men under Hospital No. 2, convincing them of his value as a tunneler. He was young, strong, and determined to flee the camp with a resolve matched by few others. But he feared that too many men were party to the plan. During the weeks to come, there was one man that

Benson noticed lurking around the hospital. He was a tall, quiet fellow wearing a long frock coat. He had, on his left hand, an inch-long fingernail on his pinkie. Benson didn't know why, but he felt sure the mysterious man was involved with the escape, and he marked him as closely as he could. Not long after, one night in Womack's tunnel, they found a crowbar and a bayonet mysteriously abandoned. Something beyond their ken was about to happen.

The tunnelers made their way forward. In less than a week, they were done. But the conspiracy had become common knowledge. "The last night came, the night to finish the tunnel," Benson wrote. "Scores of men also told other scores of men. So many collected in the dusk about the hospital, I became alarmed. It would be a dull sentry that would not suspect."

The risk of discovery didn't stop them—they had already wagered too much. "I went under," remembered Benson, taking a lit candle that was quickly extinguished by the lack of air. "Many men were there, lying down. More were coming. I crawled to the tunnel. . . . I went in and dug, panting for breath. . . . So it went on till after midnight. All the space under the building seemed filled with men. I could see none, see nothing, but I heard the shufflings, the cautious whisperings; men waiting, hungry for home." It seemed like even more souls than were packed on the Erie boxcar that had dumped them in Elmira a month before.

A sentry walked by on the parapet above. Benson could hear him from the tunnel. "'Three o'clock and all's well!'" he crowed in the darkness.

Not for long. The digger who broke through to the surface only minutes later realized their blunder: they had come up several feet short of the wall. As word was passed back down the line, the tunnel nearly emptied of men. Someone had to go out and stake a patch of grass on the hole they'd cut, or the Yankees would discover it the next day. Patches of red streaked across the sky in the east. Daybreak was coming.

Then a small, though momentous, thing occurred in the burrow below. A man crawled into the tunnel to tell a partner that the escape would have to wait until the next night. Neither of them saw Benson in the dark. Benson could only hear their conversation (it was too black to see even a raised hand), dripping sweat as he crouched on all fours, feeling as if he would soon perish for lack of air. There was another tunnel, the invisible man told his companion, if this one failed. "'Now tonight there'll be a crowd here again, and we may get parted in the darkness, be sure you keep 'longside of me,'" Benson overheard him say. "Pute, you'll know me by this." Then there was a silence, a long spell of quiet that seemed every bit as deep as the tunnel under Hospital No. 2. Benson couldn't make out in the darkness what the invisible man showed him. A scar? A kerchief? A knife?

Sergeant Benson turned the words over, very slowly: "*Be sure you keep 'longside of me.*" Then, in a flash, he understood. "Among the few gifts I have is intuition," he later wrote, "and when the man said, in the dark, in the black dark, 'You'll know me by this,' instantly I knew what he did. He reached out his left hand to the other man, to feel that long finger nail." Benson was sure it was the quiet man he had seen loitering by the hospital. But who was he—and could he be trusted?

The next day, the Yankees discovered and destroyed the tunnels under Hospitals No. 1 and No. 2. (Though the men didn't know it, their warders had a spy posing as a prisoner who looked for tunnels night and day.) The Federals smirked at the ruined handiwork of what they half-admiringly called the "engineer corps." For those who had believed they were only a few days from home, the sight of the caved-in lairs was agonizing. But too many of the boys had been in cahoots. Now Benson knew there was *another* tunnel, and this time he pledged to keep it to himself. If his intuition were right, he knew the man who could tell him where it was—at least he knew what he looked like. Finding him was another matter, for looking for a stranger among 10,000 men on the Elmira grounds might be like trying to find a penny in a bale of cotton. "Three days I looked everywhere for the long jeans coat, and never saw the tail of it."

On the fourth day, Benson found his quarry. There he was, sauntering toward the pond as though taking an evening constitutional on the Charleston battery. The "Chinese fingernail" on his left hand was visible from a distance. His coattails swung back and forth as he walked, swaying in the rhythm of a High Street dandy. Benson followed him across the yard. The man ambled down to Foster's Pond and, carefully parting his coattails behind him, took a seat by the water. Looking around nonchalantly, he commenced his business. What Benson saw next convinced him of his utter worthiness as a partner in the engineer corps. The stranger pulled a coat pocket forward, casually held it over the pond, and, from what Benson could see from an angle behind him, a series of concentric circles were soon swelling outward in the filthy backwash. He was dumping dirt in the pond. He *had* to be a tunneler.

Benson knew better than to run up to him. He calmly strolled over to have a word: "'You'd better be careful.'"

"'Careful about what?'"

"'If you are not careful, some of these men will see you.'"

"'See me? Why should I care?'"

"'Why, you are digging a tunnel,'" Benson replied, "'and if you are not careful, you'll be caught.'" The man tensed. He didn't know if he was talking to an angel, an impudent fool, or a plant who would soon peach on him to the Yankees.

"'See here, I'm all right,'" Benson reassured him. "'Now go ahead and empty your pockets; I'll stand here behind you.'"

Benson screened the man from the mess of soldiers on the north side of the pond. Once he decided Benson wasn't going to blow on him, the man finished his errand and stood up. They took measure of each other. As they walked away from the pond, Benson recounted the story of the night in the tunnel—how he'd seen the fingernail and heard the promise to "Pute," how he'd scoured the camp for days to find him. They stopped. The fellow had no choice. A snitch, he concluded, would never have been so patient as this. "'Come at eleven o'clock to the third tent in the second row from the fence," he said gravely. Then he added: "'I'll let the boys know; we'll initiate you.'" With that, Benson later recalled, began a lifelong friendship with the mysterious stranger from Alabama—Washington Brown Traweek of the Jeff Davis Artillery, also taken in the field at Spotsylvania.

Later that night, Benson reported for duty. He found himself in tent No. 3 in the midst of a full-fledged cabal. "The boys were all there. All eyes turned curiously on me as I came in. They had heard the story. I knelt down. They knelt down around me. Scruggs put the Testament in my hand. I kissed it, and swore to be faithful and industrious, and I swore to tell no man, not even my brother, were he there in the prison with me, or give the slightest hint, without the consent of all." The only reason Traweek surrendered the secret of the tunnel, Benson knew, was that he had been caught red-handed at the pond. They could afford no more such mistakes.

The men shook hands. It was all as solemn as a Masonic rite. Someone lifted up a blanket on the ground, took up a plank underneath, and there before him, cut into the earth, gaped the mouth of their earthly salvation. Benson had found the tunnel of his dreams. And these were practical—even desperate—men, not given by nature to unnecessary pomp and ceremony: "In ten minutes I had got my shirt and trousers wrong side out and was at work in the tunnel."

The number of conspirators gradually grew to a dozen, sworn to secrecy upon pain of violence: Traweek, J. W. Crawford, Gilmer "Hickory" Jackson, William Templin, S. Cecrops Malone, John Fox Maull, John P. "Pute" Putegnat, John P. "Parson" Scruggs, Glenn Shelton, and Benson. (Two others, unnamed, eventually dropped out.) Traweek's boys all knew that the penalty for being discovered was days, if not weeks, of solitary confinement, perhaps the death knell for men already enfeebled by the severe Elmira regime. For all they knew, they were betting their lives on the tunnel.

No one else could know. Though Benson and his kind hated to admit it, the prison was filled with snitches and thieves. Dishonest prisoners played the margins of camp life: gamblers, informers, and shysters looking for a weak mark.

They took rations from the mouths of the sick. They smuggled liquor out of the hospital. They "borrowed" blankets from shivering comrades. Some informed to the commandant for special favors. Deserters among them had no compunctions about trying to enlist with the enemy, if only to save themselves. It was no surprise that a community of some 10,000 men gathered at random from the ranks of society would hold its share of scalawags. The self-righteous Keiley had climbed too high on the camp ladder to really notice them. Benson, on the other hand, was too sequestered in the subterranean regions to fret about them for long.

This tunnel was an intricate piece of handiwork. The conspirators had stolen a spade from a contractor and started excavating several weeks earlier on the night of August 24. They dug a hole beneath the tent about three feet in diameter, which they covered with a wood plank taken from in front of the hospital. They bore a shaft four feet down until they had enough room for a man to work with his head below ground. Then they covered the hole with planking while the digger labored, an accomplice following him down as the tunnel progressed. The second man down took the dirt swept back to him and, using strips of a shirt torn into "bags," filled them and passed them up to a third man casually stretched along the plank. They dug at the rate of about one-and-a-half feet a day. The dark-colored earth and rocks were dumped in rat holes and sinks, or were taken across to Foster's Pond and sunk in the sand by a man wearing a jacket or cape. (Such had been Traweek's mission when Benson nabbed him.) Any friend not privy to their plans was temporarily stalled when trying to enter the tent and told that one of the occupants was bathing or dressing.

The pond or "pool" where they buried the evidence of their work was, as Benson called it, putrefying. The first prisoners to arrive at Elmira, he heard, had actually caught fish in it. The Yankees had finally thrown chemicals in to purify the sinkhole after it became an open latrine, poisoning many of the fish. Benson believed some men grew ill from eating the catch that remained, a fact that led to his own simple rule for any culinary materials gathered in camp: "I never tried fish or vegetables, doubtful or undoubtful." It would take several months of bitter complaints from the commandant—and Dr. Sanger himself—before Washington would agree, in late October, to dig a sluice to the pond. Using prison labor to drain its foul contents, the project took another two months to complete.

Beginning from under tent No. 3, the tunnel would need more than 60 feet to clear the wall. The cabal soon discarded the spade as too noisy and replaced it with a crude knife fashioned from a file. They also decided to work in broad daylight rather than in darkness, a plan less likely to draw suspicion from the guards with the constant traffic of people coming and going. On days when their ward sergeant passed on warning of official inspections, they did nothing at all. There were plenty of other hazards besides. Sometimes a man would get stuck crawling back out of the tunnel, and the others would have to pull him by the ankles. There wasn't enough air in the shaft to keep a candle burning, so they worked in darkness no matter how bright it was outside. A few of the men couldn't even bear the thought of going down—they preferred to carry and hide the dirt instead of digging it. When a tunneler came off-duty, he turned his clothes inside out to hide the telltale signs of clay. Sometimes Shelton would lead a prayer meeting for an hour or two after his shift came off work. The conspirators labored on, conscientious as a colony of field mice.

Considering the circumstances, the tunnelers were well provisioned. One of the conspirators, J. P. Scruggs, was a sergeant in the sick ward and could claim extra soup and bread every day. (Benson had a friend who shared vegetables with him that he received from acquaintances in the North.) They needed their sustenance to maintain mental powers every bit as much as the straining muscles in their arms and backs.

Groping in the dark, they were hard put to know exactly where they were. It was anyone's guess how far they had to go. One day, they gauged the length of the tunnel from the inside by measuring it with a piece of string. Then, above ground, they tied the string to a rock and nonchalantly threw it toward the wall to measure their progress. It was their first clear confirmation of success. They were, the experiment told them, within reach of the stockade in a couple weeks.

Benson was one of the few diggers. He knew the cost of the job better than anyone, unseen to those who considered him a cheerful volunteer. A violent headache would smite him less than a minute after he went under. When a man could take no more of it, he would yell "Back out" and begin to make his way butt-first out of a narrow den about 15 inches high by 20 inches wide. (Fox Maull vomited every time he went down and had to be reassigned to dirt-disposal duty.) Feeling the tread of feet and horses' hooves above them, the tunnelers dug in constant fear of a cave-in—they could even hear the guards walking their rounds on the fence overhead. Knowing the sting of falling dirt, Benson always dug with his eyes closed.

He would never forget the fear he felt descending into the darkness: "I go into the tunnel, dreading it—we all dreaded going in—I crawl a little way—there is not enough air, I breathe quicker—a little further my mouth comes open, I begin to pant, my tongue thrusts out, I breathe like a bellows. But there is no air. My lungs seem to collapse. I seize the knife and dig. The exertion doubles the agony and the need for oxygen. As I strike with the knife, tongue protruding, I pant like a dog. Then comes the headache, the fearful, merciless headache, a multiplied agony. Once—I never can forget it—sick at stomach, head bursting, striking recklessly forward with the knife, I moaned 'I cannot stand this any longer. . . . I will go back in this prison and rot.' And I struck on." There was a terrible irony to their labors: the further the men dug, the less air they had to breathe in the burrow.

All of Benson's life turned around his fellow moles. Unlike Keiley, he avoided contact with the guards, wishing to remain as anonymous as possible in the event of a break. He had even less to do with the world outside the camp. Ever since his escape from Point Lookout, he had been afraid of being discovered for taking "French leave" and suffering the typical punishment—hanging by the thumbs. (Benson had already run into a friend from Point Lookout who returned some of the personal items he had hurriedly left behind after his escape in May.) There were few people he trusted, even Rebs, with the Point Lookout story. So the sergeant never wrote his own family while at Elmira, afraid a censor might catch an untoward word about his earlier flight. Nor could budding rumors of a prisoner exchange deter him, a contingency that his friend Baxter—not a member of the tunnel conspiracy—was hoping would land him back in Virginia soon. Benson told a friend he'd sooner jump off a train and walk home than ride a blue-belly boxcar to Dixie: "I felt that I wouldn't be able to look the boys of the First in the face."

Most of the men who knew him called him "South C'lina," typical of the state nicknames that littered the camp. There were other sobriquets as well. Father Grant, Buttons, Judge Bogan, Gator, City of Glasgow—a man's name was an important belonging in a place where no one had many other possessions to speak of. Benson was happy not to have his name in common usage anyway, given the constant worry that he might be traced back to the Point Lookout furlough. With any luck, he hoped, he may not have been in the Maryland camp long enough for his name to be properly recorded.

At Elmira, however, a man was never completely invisible. One day at mess, Benson went up to speak with a prisoner in line, and a Yankee officer came up and struck the sergeant. Young Benson recoiled but held his tongue, knowing he could be shot if he dared pass the officer even a single lick. He went back to his quarters visibly trembling, the only time in his life he ever felt truly angry, he later claimed. The incident made him feel, he said with embarrassment, like a woman. It was not an indignity that someone of Anthony Keiley's standing, for example, would have likely ever had to suffer.

The tunnel became an obsession. In his "spare time," Benson consulted a copy of Sir Walter Scott's *Monastery*, given to him by one of the prisoners. He would sit outside the tent with a book, pretending to read as he casually dropped rocks from the tunnel into a rat hole. Sometimes, cramped in the confines of his own tent, he couldn't concentrate on the words for longer than a few minutes. Whenever he picked up the book, his mind only filled with thoughts of the tunnel—would one of the boys end up a "bad" egg, would someone peach, would the Yankees stumble on the secret, would someone suffocate in the hole? To make things worse, the weather was getting colder. Benson was issued no blanket and no clothing, making the occasional nights they did work in the "A" tent increasingly chilly.

They lived in perpetual fear of being discovered. They knew that Major Colt suspected something. One day, in mid-September, an informer peached on Traweek, who was promptly arrested and put in solitary confinement, accused with attempted escape. The Yankees put him in a sweatbox, a coffin-shaped contraption that stood on prominent display near headquarters. They could squeeze the air out of the box by turning a crank and create immense discomfort. It was an excruciating torture. A few minutes could feel like hours, a few hours like days. Finally moved from the box to solitary, Traweek was lucky about one thing, at least. Members of the "engineer corps" were spoiled by their guardhouse warders in deference to their courage—they were given no menial cleaning tasks like sweeping up.

The Yankees finally got Traweek to confess he was guilty, though only to digging one of the older tunnels. Colt offered to let him out of the cell if he would show the tunnel and give up the names of his accomplices. A former plantation overseer endowed with a healthy temper, Traweek cursed him with a blue streak. So as the tunnel progressed, Wash gathered dust in solitary—in the "dungeon," as his mates called it. Benson thought the bare quarters resembled something like a set of Chinese boxes, "for the cell was to the guardhouse what the guardhouse was to the prison." His mates worried that Traweek might not be out by the time they finished, in which case they would consider doing no less than storming the guardhouse. All agreed that they wouldn't leave Elmira without him.

Just in case this tunnel failed, Benson wasn't finished plotting. Some men talked about kidnapping an apple farmer who came to camp to sell his crop, then dressing someone in his clothes to leave the compound in disguise. But to men who had seen the monkey show at Chancellorsville or clashed in the mud and rain at Bloody Angle, this seemed too puny a stunt. So in between digging shifts, Benson and two other sergeants hatched a plan to storm the walls of Barracks No. 3 in three columns. Prisoners, armed with tools and rocks, would overpower the guards, liberate the camp, filter out and establish control of Elmira city, then head south before the Yankees could regroup. (Benson and another prisoner built a ladder for the assault.) As escape plans go, it was audacious. It was valiant. It was heroic. . . . And it was hopeless. After contemplating the heavy losses that would ensue, they discarded the notion. "It was only the enormous weight of the longing for freedom that could have brought us to consider seriously such a scheme." But Benson had good reason to be worried. As a latecomer to the congregation, he was going to be one of the last men out—by that time, he knew, the escape might already have been discovered.

They kept on digging without Traweek. In late September came a break in the tension. Colt, not a hard-hearted man by most accounts, released the prisoner after three weeks. Since the Reb stoutly refused to swear he wouldn't try another escape, Colt archly advised him to be more cautious the next time he did (sounding as though he really meant it), to which Traweek countered that he was too depressed to consider it for the moment. "We welcomed [Traweek] with open arms and silent cheers," Benson recalled. And the overseer from Alabama proved to be a pretty good dissembler about his depression.

Near the end of September, the tunnelers decided to run a test—Benson's idea. One night they banged on the top of the tunnel's end with a piece of tin while one of their number stood in the yard above, listening. When he came back down in the tunnel, it was to tell them of a shocking mistake. In spite of the tunnel's length, it turned out, they were still short of the wall: "As we lay on the left side, to have free use of the right arm," Benson explained, "punching forward we had punched too much in front, and so had curved to the right. . . . We had gone far out of our way in a wide curve, because we were normal in right-handedness." The bent arc of the tunnel had turned away many yards short of the stockade. "Now we had learned our lesson; we would dig with our left hands, too."

Benson and the others figured they were 18 feet short of the wall. Though hardened escape artists by this time, they found the daily descent wasn't getting easier: "It was next thing to death by suffocation to go into it," Benson recalled. They worked at widening the tunnel, enough so that a man could crouch on his haunches and, using an old raisin box pulled by a cord, shuttle dirt back and forth in the box after the prearranged signal of three taps. It was then that they hit on the idea of building a vertical ventilation shaft, or "ventilator." By digging through to the surface and disguising the top, they could suck in the air from a hole three fingers wide as they worked at the tunnel's far end, a device that also allowed them to verify their position. By day, men stood around the top of the shaft on the surface to keep the Yankees from stumbling on it.

In early fall, Benson and his comrades sounded the long-awaited words: they were at the skirt of the wall. It was a Thursday. The calendar leaf showed the 6th of October. The crew, eleven in number (one, according to Benson, would drop out at the last minute), would go out based on the order in which they had joined the team; Benson was ninth in line. The men made ready for the last day of digging, hoping for complete darkness that night. "At midnight, as though in answer to an unspoken prayer," Benson remembered, "came black clouds, with rain and thunder." But they weren't finished yet. Traweek, gasping for air as he dug the last foot, hit a post in the wall. Yelling encouragement underneath, Benson crawled forward to help him. At the last minute, the earth from the ceiling began to cave—then stopped just as suddenly.

As Benson slid forward, Traweek, exhausted, crawled back. The two friends became stuck fast in mid-tunnel. Grunting and gasping for air, they tried to dislodge themselves from the accidental embrace. For Traweek, becoming desperate, it was a bad echo of the sweatbox. "A button gives way, or something," recalled Benson, and finally he managed to crawl forward past Traweek. He had come with only one purpose. "I pass the post. I dig hard. I pant for breath."

It was up to Benson. The moment they had been dreaming of for six weeks was at hand. He tried to block out the headache. "I turn on my back. I work my fingers up through the clay. The dirt falls down in my face. My closed eyes are filled with dirt and gravel. All my face is covered with dirt. I work my fingers. What is that so cold? I draw out my hand—oh-h!—oh-h! the cold sweet air! It streams down in my face. It is like ice water poured from a vessel. I breathe! I breathe!"

Benson crawls back down the tunnel and tells Traweek to go up and have a swallow of air. Wash can hardly believe him.

"There is no more to do," Benson exults, grabbing his hand. "The tunnel is finished." The time has finally come.

On the night of October 6, Anthony Keiley was fast asleep, perhaps dreaming of victory parades in Petersburg. Major Henry Colt, turning in his bed, probably didn't expect Traweek to be back in the tunneling business again so soon. The guard called out the hour of one o'clock. It started to thunder. A stream of men sat poised, ready to emerge from a small crack in the earth. Like a contrary compass they waver wildly, then take sudden aim for Dixie.

CHAPTER 3

Escape from Elmira

ANTHONY Keiley brooded and schemed through the chilly autumn. Berry Benson braced himself in his gopher hole for a fond farewell to New York. Meanwhile, unbeknownst to either of them, a headstrong man-child had arrived in a hurry in the vicinity of Barracks No. 3. It might be said that Frank Wilkeson's coming to Elmira was an accident of fate. If so, it was a miserable accident. By the time he got to the Federal prison on the Chemung in the fall of 1864, he had already suffered, in the North, many of the indignities and rank abuses heaped on prisoners like Benson and Keiley. And Frank Wilkeson was a *Union* man.

A second lieutenant in the Fourth U.S. Artillery when he came to Elmira, Wilkeson's wartime travails could have upstaged the legendary exploits of Davy Crockett. Indeed, what the young man experienced in the year before coming to Elmira would have been enough to make a decorated veteran blush. The POW camp in the Chemung Valley would be the easiest tour of duty Wilkeson ever knew, and even then, he would be lucky to escape the place a few hours ahead of an impending court-martial.

Wilkeson proved to be one of the most perceptive enlisted men who ever took up pen and paper—on either side of the war. He soldiered, one might say, at an impressionable age. Barely in his teens when the conflict broke out, he experienced his first battle, one suspects, not long after puberty. It took him another 20 years to publish an account of the war, as though the grim seed planted in his youth needed decades before it could bear fruit—and before he could understand what it meant. When he did, the result was compelling. His account of the war is chiding, sardonic, impassioned, and harrowing by turns. Not once did he avert his gaze from the ugly slaughter he volunteered—against all odds—to experience, and defeated all odds to survive.

Who was Wilkeson? He was too young, too brazen, too blunt, too cynical, too naïve, and too rash of manner to be typical of anything or anyone. He broke ranks and consorted with the enemy. He robbed corpses and ignored orders. He volunteered for difficult duty and fought in battles where he had no business even being. He hated taking orders from officer "fools"—but not as much as he despised the fools themselves. Wilkeson was constitutionally unable to countenance authority of any kind—a trait developed with diligent exercise. "Most of this war history has been written to repair damaged or wholly ruined military reputations," he later wrote of the high command, perhaps thinking to revive his own name in putting the record straight. He was a "rebel" in every sense except the color of his uniform.

Yes, he knew military life from the roost of a privileged lieutenant. But like Benson and Keiley, Wilkeson also experienced the war from a rat's-eye view, knowing what it was to bribe or cadge a warder for a cup of slop spiked with rotten beef. By the time he arrived at Elmira, he had already guessed at its worst secrets, this at an age when most boys were busy toting schoolbooks or harvesting wheat in the fields. He was a born witness, of the rare sorts that are devoted to and discerning of the melee before them, incapable of the affected aloofness of the innocent bystander.

Frank Wilkeson was just shy of 16 years old when he ran away from his father's farm near Canaan, New York, in the Hudson Valley. His grandfather had been mayor of Buffalo; his father, a journalist, was a war correspondent for the Army of the Potomac. It was the winter of 1863–1864. Frank had seen two years of war without a Reb getting so much as within a week's march of upstate New York—and the prospect that it would ever happen was fading fast. More compelling, his brother Bayard had died at Gettysburg on July 1. The 15-year-old tramped into Albany, where he planned to enlist in the 11th New York Battery. It was, for the era, about as romantic an errand as a boy running away to join the circus. Wilkeson had decided to go and "see the elephant" for himself, the awful prospect of glimpsing battle, even if he had to fiddle with his age to get a glimpse of the dread creature.

He reported to a camp on the outskirts of town. No sooner had the ink dried on his enlistment papers, soon after his sixteenth birthday, than young Frank found himself being bodily escorted to the pokey. The charge was worse than anything he could have imagined: Wilkeson had been mistaken for a bounty jumper. The jumper, one of those despicable creatures Keiley reviled as the soul of Yankeedom, enlisted in one locale, claimed the bounty paid by the municipality filling a conscript quota, then deserted and reenlisted elsewhere, pocketing the cash. Bounty jumping was the moral antithesis of double jeopardy: a man was paid hundreds of dollars—more than once—without so much as putting life or limb in danger. For a boy who had run away to get a taste of war, the mistake could not have been more astonishing.

That Wilkeson was lily-clean of such designs hardly mattered. Without fanfare, Frank was escorted to the penitentiary outside Albany, whose gates were the portal to a world turned upside down. The pen was filled with nearly 1,000 Union conscripts under heavy guard—both guards and guarded ostensibly serving the same army. "Irreclaimable blackguards, thieves, and ruffians gathered in a boisterous circle around me and called me foul names," Wilkeson remembered of his inauguration. "I was robbed while in these barracks of all I possessed—a pipe, a piece of tobacco and a knife." Wilkeson was convinced that he was the only one of the mob who *hadn't* joined for the greenbacks. When a sympathetic major in command gave him a temporary pass out of the compound, his fellow inmates offered him a large sum for the piece of paper—and stomped him when he refused to give it up.

The pecking order wasn't what it was on a Hudson Valley farm: "A recruit's social standing in the barracks was determined by the acts of villany [*sic*] he had performed," noted Wilkeson. "The social standing of a hard-faced, crafty pickpocket, who had jumped the bounty in say half a dozen cities, was assured." The most craven soul held forth with his fellows in rapt attention and gained the best bunk in the room and front of the line for rations. The whole ragged lot made Fagin's gang seem like a flock of mewling babes. "Almost to a man they were bullies and cowards, and almost to a man they belonged to the criminal classes." Even when an uncle from Albany, hearing of his plight, obtained a discharge for him, the stubborn boy refused to leave, afraid that this might be his only chance to make it to the front. Wilkeson had become something even lower than a prisoner, finding himself among captives despised for their cowardice. It was not exactly an auspicious introduction to Mr. Lincoln's army.

Early one morning the guards came to roust them. The intent all along had been to hold the jumpers until their bounties were paid to them—and then ferry them as a group to the front. Though expecting a bonus of at least $400, some of the men didn't treasure the thought of mixing it up with General Longstreet's Rebels on the Rapidan River, the latest front in the war. "I saw the guards roughly haul straw-littered, dust-coated men out of mattresses, which they had cut open and crawled into to hide. Other men were jerked out of the water closets. Still others were drawn by the feet from beneath bunks," remembered Wilkeson. "One man, who had burrowed into the contents of a water-tight swill-box, which stood in the hall and into which we threw our waste food and coffee slops, was fished out, covered with coffee grounds and bits of bread and shreds of meat, and kicked down stairs and out of the building." And then, without further ceremony, they were paid.

Their blood money stuffed in knapsacks, the prisoners were marched into Albany proper under double guard. "Bounty jumpers!" an onlooker cried. Children pelted them with mud balls. Others hooted and laughed. Before they got to State Street, three jumpers dropped their gear and fled down an alley, only to be shot in their tracks by seasoned guards. "The dead patriots lay by the roadside as we marched by," Wilkeson mused as they passed down Broadway. The jumpers had been killed with no more ado than plugging rabbits in a cornfield. These were the first men he had seen killed in—or, for that matter, out of—the line of duty.

War wasn't turning out the way the callow farm boy had imagined. "Previous to my enlistment," he admitted, "I had imagined that the population of Albany would line the sidewalks to see the defenders of the nation march proudly by, bound for the front, and that we would be cheered, and would unbend sufficiently to accept floral offerings from beautiful maidens." But this was a rogues' spectacle he found himself marching in, and "the people who saw us did not cheer."

At the docks on the Hudson River, the volunteers were herded onto a heavily guarded steamboat. Just to show how much honor there was among thieves, no one dared take off his knapsack. The bounty jumpers were getting desperate. They hadn't figured to get such a thoughtful escort all the way to Virginia. But the prospect of breaking ranks, like the poor sods in Albany, wasn't much of an incentive. Many saw the impending passage as a rite of the condemned. "Bottles, flasks, canteens, full of whiskey, circulated freely among us, and many men got drunk," Wilkeson recalled. "There was an orgie on the North River steamer that night, but comparatively a decent one."

It was a "decent" one because far worse lay ahead. The ship made its first port of call in New York City. On the way to being transferred there to another steamer, four more jumpers were cut down by rifle fire in the act of deserting. The brigands seemed painfully slow to learn that they had more of a chance facing Johnny Reb with a bayonet from a ditch or behind a breastwork than showing their backsides to sharpshooting comrades on the Battery. The desperation to desert must have confirmed to many of the others how awful life really was at the front.

They boarded an ocean steamer, and Wilkeson soon found himself in the bowels of a ship where "promptly the hold was transformed into a floating hell." About 600 men were packed into the hold, and, by Wilkeson's account, "I, who know, say they were as arrant a gang of cowards, thieves, murderers, and blacklegs as were ever gathered inside the walls of Newgate or Sing Sing." They started buying whiskey with their enlistment money at five dollars a canteen. It didn't take long for fights to break out all over. "Drunken men staggered to and fro" in the hold, and the young Wilkeson fought three fights, he reported matter-of-factly, getting licked twice. It was maul or be mauled. He dubbed the ship "The Floating Heaven of American Patriots." And they weren't even close to a battlefield yet.

The ship of fools plodded onward. The guards locked them in the hold and forbade any more bottles of drink from going down the hatch, so to speak. Then it was that two garrulous, well-dressed Yankee gamblers descended beneath decks and opened up shop. They brought with them the chuck-luck cloths and dice boxes, their sole objective to lighten the jumpers' bulging pockets. In a few hours, the massacre was over. Wilkeson, who never received a bounty himself, figured they took the ruffians for the most part of a quarter-million dollars and probably shared their take with Federal officials. The gamblers had to hire soldiers to protect them while they slept with their booty on deck that night. The enraged losers, meanwhile, sought to rob those who had anything left, "and if they protested, their cries were silenced with boot heels stamped into their faces." No one doubted that war was hell, but just getting to hell from New York City was proving be a difficult order.

The bounty jumpers unloaded in Alexandria, Virginia. Their appearance was so vile, reported Wilkeson, that even the street dogs feared to approach them. The men were packed on train cars and sent to Brandy Station, north of the Rapidan River—and five more jumpers bolted from the cars en route and were shot. They arrived at the camp of the 11th New York Battery. The drilling began almost immediately, and Wilkeson was introduced to a maneuver informally known as the "artillery humbug," a routine that didn't include anything so useful as target practice or how to operate in dense woods. "They taught us how to change front to the right, to the rear, and on the several pieces that formed the battery," recounted Wilkeson, "which knowledge was of as much practical use to us as if we had been assiduously drilled to walk on stilts or to play on the banjo." The Albany jumpers had thus far undergone the reverse of the Rebel journey: imprisonment was the first step of their trial by fire, not the last.

Wilkeson's unit struck camp at Brandy Station on a beautiful morning in early May 1864, tramping to the sounds of martial airs played by the regimental band. They marched toward Ely's Ford and began to see signs of stragglers. A regiment of Germans, "ignorant of the power of a southern sun," started dropping some of their burden—knapsacks and boots and blankets and musical instruments—after crossing the Rapidan. That's where Wilkeson heard the advice of his gunner, a fellow named Jellet, that he would hear echoed over and over during the months to come: "'Get food, honestly if you can, but get it.'" The men scavenged what they could find from the well-filled haversacks littering their path—one man's burden was another's booty. As Wilkeson and many others figured it, "To rob a soldier was to rob a man who might be killed next day, and would not need property."

The night before the battle of the Wilderness began, Wilkeson and mates camped on the old Chancellorsville battleground. The bullet-scarred trees and shallow graves made a macabre scene lit up by the Union campfires. "The men who had fallen in that fierce fight had apparently been buried where they fell, and buried hastily," Wilkeson remembered. "Many polished skulls lay on the ground. Leg bones, arm bones, and ribs could be found without trouble. . . . The dead were all around us. Their eyeless skulls seemed to stare steadily at us." Wilkeson and men sat on the makeshift graves, smoking their pipes and listening to the reports of pickets firing in the distance. One infantry-man poked at a shallow grave with his bayonet and rolled a skull in front of them. "'That is what you are all coming to," he said in a low voice, "'and some of you will start toward it to-morrow.'"

The next morning was "delightful," recalled Wilkeson, a bugle calling him to battery where he wolfed down some pork and hardtack. *Get food*, Jellet had said, *honestly if you can*. But the prospects for glory darkened. Since the battle had opened in dense forest, the artillery was use-less; the 11th New York, including Wilkeson and his three-inch gun, was being sent to the rear. Throughout the morning, Wilkeson watched helplessly as the bloodied wounded of the Fifth Corps staggered through the reserve camp. Hav-ing survived one hellish initiation already, Wilkeson wasn't about to miss the one that mat-tered. "By noon I was quite wild with curiosity, and, confident that the artillery would remain in park, I decided to go to the battle-line and see what was going on." It was wiser not to ask permission at all, he knew, since he'd be forced to disobey orders if the request were denied.

Wilkeson boldly made his way up the road, a runaway "running away" to the sound of the guns. He saw a corpse—his first in battle. It had been shot through the chest and "his pockets were turned inside out," a sure sign scavengers were about. A Union sentinel in the woods warned him not to go another step forward, since only soldiers with visible wounds would be allowed back. The warning didn't even give him pause. Wilkeson plodded on until he came within forty yards of the front line, the hum of bullets spitting into trees around him. Suddenly he remembered he didn't even have a gun.

A Yankee corpse lay nearby. Wilkeson didn't think twice about lifting a cartridge belt and rifle from the stiff, still warm to the touch. He found himself in the ranks of the Fifth Corps, in the Union center, but had to admit that "it was not anywhere near as bloody as I had expected a battle to be." Gathering clouds of powder smoke made it seem "as a grand, inspiring spectacle . . . highly unsatisfactory." The Rebs had been feigning an attack, he figured, and the bigger prize lay elsewhere. After dark, young Frank meandered through the woods again, seeking news of the battle from other encamped units and spending the night wrapped in the blankets of another dead man. Wilkeson tried to return to his unit the next morning by going back through the lines, but a guard, mistaking him for a deserter, threatened him with arrest. He was probably the first soldier the sentinel had ever seen who'd gone AWOL *to the front*.

That afternoon, May 6, Wilkeson stood with the Fifth Corps against the advancing troops of A. P. Hill. The young man learned quickly. He picked Reb corpses in the field for food and tobacco. Then came Longstreet's charge, led by "a swish of bullets and a fierce, exultant yell, as of thousands of infuriated tigers." The Fifth Corps balked. "There was great confusion in our line. The men wavered badly. They fired wildly. They hesitated. I feared the line would break." But the Ninth Corps arrived and rallied them. They counterattacked furiously: "We fired and fired and fired, and fell back fighting stubbornly," Wilkeson remembered. "We tore cartridges until our teeth ached," a reference to the infantry ritual of tearing open a cartridge with one's teeth, pouring the powder into a gun barrel, ramming down a ball, and preparing a percussion cap for firing. He saw wounded men from both sides helping each other to shelter, even sharing canteens. Though prone to inflating numbers, Wilkeson said he saw thousands of men on the field who "'had turned up their toes.'" The Union had beaten back Longstreet.

The New York farm boy had seen enough of infantry duty. He threw down his arms and marched with a unit to the rear, blending in with the others so as not to be mistaken for a straggler. His absence had been duly noted. The day of his return to the 11th New York, he endured the rather minor punishment of having to carry a stick of cordwood for being absent without leave. "The stick that one picked up so cheerfully, and stepped off with so briskly, and walked up and down before a sentinel with so gayly in the early morning, had an unaccountable property of growing heavier and heavier as the sun rose higher and higher." What weighed only 12 pounds at sunrise, reflected Wilkeson, felt like it had gained "one hundred and eighty-eight pounds in weight during the time I had carried it."

He was lucky, even if he didn't know it. The more serious punishments meted out to Union men equaled anything Wilkeson would see at Elmira. Severe offenders were tied to the spare wheel of an artillery caisson, spread-eagled on the spokes for five or six hours; sometimes the wheel was rotated a quarter-turn to place the miscreant horizontal to the ground. (It was enough to make most men faint.) Soldiers were tied up by their thumbs under a tree, their dangling feet barely touching the ground. Drunken or disorderly men were "bucked and gagged," their knees pulled up to their chins and their hands at their shins, with a stick inserted under their knees and over their arms, their mouths muzzled with a gag. Even Madame Tussaud would have found the demonstrations most enlightening.

On May 9, Wilkeson's battery arrived near Spotsylvania Court House, where the Rebel infantry had dug in behind a dense maze of earthworks. The next day, the fighting began. On May 12, the Second Corps, including the 11th New York, overran a Confederate division, taking a large crowd of prisoners from the other side of the worm fences. "Our troops caught the battle-exhausted Confederates asleep in their blankets," noted the young artillery private, and two of those among them may have been Marcus Toney and John Rufus King, who would also soon come to know the confines of Barracks No. 3 in Elmira.

Wilkeson took snatches of sleep when he could find them, but there was little time for rest. On May 28, the army crossed the Pamunkey River. As he crossed the bridge, Wilkeson happened to see, standing beneath a tree, the commander in chief of the Union armies. "Grant looked tired. He was sallow. He held a dead cigar firmly between his teeth. His face was as expressionless as a pine board." (He may have looked to Wilkeson the way he appears in so many posed prints by Mathew Brady.) There was grumbling in the ranks that if General George McClellan could be faulted for not going into battle, then Grant suffered from the opposite malaise, one that inspired him to throw his troops like human sacrifices against impenetrable Reb redoubts. "None cheered him, none saluted him," Wilkeson noted of the cold reception. Many of the men seemed only too aware they were marching, in the newly minted words of Julia Ward Howe, to yet another place "where the grapes of wrath were stored."

The Second Corps went into action on June 3. At dawn, Confederate pickets opened fire at Cold Harbor, Virginia, and the light artillery began its bombardment. A hush went around Union lines after the men were informed they were about to attack. "Our cannon became silent," Wilkeson remembered. "The smoke drifted off of the field. I noticed that the sun was not yet up." Then the blue-clad troops "sprang to their feet and dashed at the Confederate earthworks at a run."

During the next 12 hours, the runaway from New York (by all considerations now a man) saw futile charge after charge. The carnage was horrific. The day would see 7,000 Union casualties, though fewer than Wilkeson estimated. By late afternoon, the Second Corps was again given the order to advance. "Not a man stirred from his place," Wilkeson grimly noted. "The army to a man refused to obey the order, presumably from General Grant, to renew the assault. I heard the order given, and I saw it disobeyed." Discipline was breaking down in this, the fourth and bloodiest year of the war. The Cold Harbor engagement was, like so many others, another indecisive struggle where thousands had fallen in a reckless attempt to bring the South to its knees.

A short truce gave Wilkeson his first taste of fraternizing with the enemy, trading Rebs some sugar and coffee for tobacco. A few hours later, he met up with a pair of Johnnie deserters who had gotten lost behind Union lines. "I imagined myself prowling between the front and the rear of the Confederate army," Wilkeson recalled, "with an empty haversack dangling at my side, and nothing to hope for but a Confederate prison, and my heart went out to these men." For the first time, he seemed to see Jellet's dictum—*Get food, honestly if you can*—in a different light. He shared his hardtack with them and pointed the way to the Union rear.

The New York private had more patience with Confederate deserters than Yankee ones. The brave volunteers who had signed up at war's beginning had melted away at Shiloh and Gettysburg, Fredericksburg, Bull Run, and Antietam. Some few had survived, but the ranks were increasingly filled, as no one knew better than Wilkeson, with "mercenaries"—many of them insolent, ill-disciplined, and craven bounty jumpers. Some of these turned out to be what volunteers derisively called "coffee boilers." (The enemy called them "wagon dogs.") They sat, just beyond reach of Rebel artillery, boiling coffee and jawing as Confederate bullets whistled down the road. "It was as though a huge pic-nic were going on in the woods," Wilkeson wrote disgustedly of one such congregation at Petersburg, which he later delighted to see shelled by a rogue Confederate battery. "To call a soldier of the Army of the Potomac a 'coffee boiler' was an insult to be promptly resented."

Wilkeson viewed the bounty jumpers with the scorn of a confirmed nativist. "They were the scum of the slums of the great European and American cities," he offered. "They were conscienceless, cowardly scoundrels, and the clean-minded American and Irish and German volunteers would not associate with them." Bad as they were, he believed, the jumpers weren't the worst species the war engendered. Wilkeson thought of them as nothing more than "white slaves" gathered by northern brokers and sold by the lot to townships anxious to fill enlistment quotas. "A Mississippi slave-dealer was a refined and honorable gentleman in comparison with a Northern bounty-broker," he reckoned. Some of the bounty jumpers surrendered to the enemy rather than risk death, Wilkeson believed— an opinion shared by General Grant—preferring their chances in a Confederate prison to charging a Rebel earthwork at Cold Harbor. And as awful as the alternatives were, they were probably right.

Barely at the front for six weeks, Wilkeson had seen all manner of death and anguish. He saw a soldier with a self-inflicted foot wound who watched in horror as his own leg was sawed off below the knee by surgeons unamused with his prank. He saw a drummer boy leading a wizened old sergeant by the hand, the latter blinded by fire on the picket line—the two of them father and son. He saw a cavalryman's corpse by matchlight being eaten by black beetles near Cold Harbor. A friend in another unit was gambling in camp when a picket's bullet struck an artillery wheel and ricocheted into his side, killing him instantly; "His death ended the game," Wilkeson noted icily. A man could be killed by a small wound gone septic or a touch of the dysentery or a tree falling from a "wash kettle" heaved by a mortar: "The unseen danger is the alarming one to the enlisted men." He had seen men who slept so soundly they seemed to be in the realm of the dead as they dreamed. And Wilkeson knew the terrible moment of truth, the instant when the wounded man peeled away his clothes in horror to see whether the hit he had taken was a mortal one, or blessed permission for an extended trip home.

It was at Cold Harbor that Private Wilkeson was finally given his fighting reprieve. If not, he might have moved with Grant the rest of the war, a fate he could have actually relished had he known an end to the fighting was in sight. Apparently, his cool under fire had been noted. To his surprise, he learned from an adjutant general that he was to be commissioned by the secretary of war as a second lieutenant in the Fourth U.S. Artillery. Wilkeson received a discharge at Cold Harbor and, after some minor skirmishing around Petersburg, arrived in Washington on June 25.

Rumors of Jubal Early's advance spread through Washington in early July. Wilkeson reported to the War Department for assignment on July 10 and was posted to the undermanned garrison at Fort Totten, Maryland. The new lieutenant braced for the imminent assault of Early, who was circling back on the capital from the northeast. Though forever convinced that Early could have taken Washington had he tried, Wilkeson never had to ponder the full consequences of a Rebel attack. The Sixth Corps, newly debarked in Washington, marched to the rescue, and Early's would-be raid on the capital was parried.

Two uneventful months passed, which must have been a strange contrast for young Wilkeson. In September, a part of the Fourth Artillery received its marching orders: the presence of one section of Battery A was required immediately in upstate New York. Wilkeson, though a member of Battery H by his account, was included in the detail, no doubt because of his experience. The truth was that the men were bored, more so than anything he could have conceived during his time at the front. "We marched to the railroad station, and loaded the guns, caissons, and horses on the cars, and left Washington in less than two hours after receiving the order." The detachment of the Fourth was being sent to Elmira, a prison where the Rebs were rumored to be in a state of incipient rebellion.

What Lieutenant Wilkeson found at Elmira in the autumn of 1864 wasn't fit for the back side of a Currier and Ives print. In one sense, he knew very well what to expect. Wilkeson had seen the photographs of Andersonville veterans widely published in the northern press, "grouped and photographed," he wrote, "very unfairly I think," intending to make them look as distraught as possible. But although some returned prisoners were in miserable shape, the 16-year-old conceded, the great majority of thousands of other Yankees that he had seen after exchange were "in good condition." For him, the cruelty of the camps was no surprise: "A military prison, it matters not what people keep it, is not a place where life is enjoyed." His own confinement in Albany had taught him as much.

Being a guard at Elmira—or any prison— was, though far from the front, not without its inconveniences or even tragedies. In effect, guards were something like glorified prisoners, better provisioned than captured Johnnies but still vulnerable to the elements. Camp guards were given full army rations, probably receiving about the same amount of food as prisoners who had jobs. At Elmira they boarded in prisoner-like barracks, though some of them, like the Rebs, camped in flimsy "A" tents. There is no doubt they were better prepared to face the winter, given that blankets and clothing were issued them before they were to Confederates.

But the death rate among guards could also be severe (nearly 200 at Rock Island alone died of disease and exposure). Even the main Union barracks on the other side of Elmira had a stockade fence to discourage desertion.

It was a commonplace that camp guards often weren't the cream of the crop of northern manhood. Union prison personnel typically consisted of those unfit for service at the front, the "invalid corps" as they were known at Elmira and elsewhere: the very young, the very old, the very troubled. Most were known as "100-day (or 90-day) men," so-called for the short tenure of their enlistment. Many prisoners who wrote about Elmira told of being well treated by guards, while complaining no less of a thug or two in blue. Black soldiers, of course, were the most resented of all, perched with a gun on a catwalk above the men who had come to represent the slaveholding South, but they were not particularly common at Elmira. John King claimed to have seen only one in Barracks No. 3, and "he behaved like a gentleman."

Many guards were quartered inside the camp. Others, like Wilkeson's Fourth Artillery, camped on the exterior, creating a ring of protection in case a serious revolt erupted inside. There were several hundred guards on duty at any given time in and around Barracks No. 3, and thousands more were available from the military depot. Although Wilkeson was contemptuous of the 100-day men, deriding their lack of battle experience—an opinion many Rebs shared of their own militias—they did not have an easy task. Patrolling the grounds on foot at night meant that they must meet the challenge of the parapet and properly identify themselves as sentries—or be shot at, mistaken for Rebs. Given positions of power over men who represented an enemy that had killed a brother, a son, a father, or a friend must have been a strong temptation to abuse whatever graybacks came within their reach.

Reports of brutality at Elmira were common enough; many a prisoner like Benson had a fearful incident to relate. A member of the Alabama Third Infantry recalled a lieutenant who regularly beat and stoned the prisoners on his watch, such that most cowered in their barracks when he approached. Keiley told of officers "whose whole intercourse with the prisoners was the essence of brutality," one with a nasty habit of pistol-whipping. And yet John King best remembered "Long Tom," a sergeant who lived in Elmira and provided the barracks with extra coal during the winter—in fact, many guards were warmly recalled by inmates years later. Several of the cruel punishments meted out to prisoners were, as everyone at Elmira knew only too well, as much the signature of the age as the impress of any brutal ideology.

Wilkeson was being arch when he vouched that "I met no Union soldier who had been confined in a Confederate military prison, who thought it to be a pleasant retreat." But the commissioned lieutenant went a step further when he questioned his government's defense of Elmira: "The prisoners, it was alleged, were allowed the same rations, excepting coffee and sugar, that their guards received," he recalled dubiously. "They did not get it." Confederate prisoners "never got more than two thirds rations," he guessed, an estimate that would perhaps have been too low for paid prisoners like Keiley, but was too optimistic for the rank and file. A man who had already seen an exorbitant amount of suffering, Wilkeson was not one to sentimentalize about the demise of Johnnies in Barracks No. 3, men who, in his unvarnished way of putting it, were dying "as sheep with the rot."

The lieutenant now saw a different face of the enemy than he had at the Wilderness. The prisoners were homesick. They were stricken with fever and bowel disorders. They were lethargic and depressed. The transfixing boredom of prison life wasn't lost on a 16-year-old who, despite a rapid succession of campaigns, also knew what it was to helplessly wait as other men decided your fate. As the prisoners huddled before the barracks, "They stood motionless and gazed into one another's haggard faces with despairing eyes. There was no need to talk, as all topics of conversation had long since been exhausted." It was the same malaise that Anthony Keiley reported at Point Lookout when writing of the vicious effects of boredom. The Yankee lieutenant saw overt signs of this desperation from the start, a problem he fully expected to have to confront.

Wilkeson wasn't alone in sympathizing with the prisoners. For some of the Union officers, like Henry Colt and Bennett Munger, a sense of chivalry guided their treatment of men who, as noncombatants, were protected under rules of war. (Although Colt, some prisoners alleged, was ruthless when dealing with those who weren't among his favorites.) And among enlisted Union guards who had seen action, the camaraderie of a shared war could be a profound bond. Still, Wilkeson had more in common with the Rebels in stir than he did with the inexperienced 100-day men who guarded them. As a result, he believed he was more savvy to what they could accomplish when they became desperate.

The sheer "ignorance" of the Rebs troubled him. Many were illiterate, or functionally so, a fact that had inspired some prisoners to start a school in Barracks No. 3. (Private Wilbur Grambling of the Fifth Florida Infantry reported receiving French lessons in December.) "The discipline in the Confederate armies must have been exceedingly severe to have enabled their officers to control these reckless, savage-tempered men," Wilkeson intoned, betraying a prejudice for the civilizing effects of literacy that wasn't entirely defensible. The high literacy rates of the Union rank and file hadn't held down the savagery of the casualty lists at Antietam and the Wilderness, where men were ordered into the maelstrom by officers who were universally of the lettered class.

More than anything, Wilkeson was moved by the Rebs' devotion to work. Outside camp, hundreds were detailed "digging ditches and trenches which were never used," perhaps a pleasing fact to prisoners since in doing so they were hardly abetting the enemy. "They worked faithfully and honestly, and earned their scanty pay," he remarked, anxious to purchase tobacco with it, a currency more negotiable than Confederate paper in Elmira. The work details grew more grim as the temperatures plummeted. "It was pitiful to see the poverty-stricken Confederates breaking the hard, frost-bound earth, while armed sentinels passed to and fro about them, and a battery of artillery moved swiftly over the frozen plain in menacing drill."

Wilkeson, it turned out, got a stomach-full of Rebel defiance the night after he reported for duty. An incident occurred that seems to have been rare in the camps, where the threat of punishment or death kept most agitators at bay. There was, the lieutenant noted politely, "a lack of discipline in the prison." His first encounter with captive Rebs came before he'd even had a chance to develop any sympathy for them. "That night they gathered in mobs, and the Confederate charging-yell rang out clearly," he remembered. "They threw stones at the sentinels. They refused to go into their barracks." A more fractious lot of unarmed men he'd hardly laid eyes on, and the artillery rolled their guns into position and opened the ammunition chests to show they were serious. The edgy Rebs might have reminded Wilkeson of the bounty jumpers he holed up with in Albany—and the thought of mass insubordination unnerved him.

Young Wilkeson attributed the ill-tempered mob to the obvious: the captives had no respect for their guards, who were undisciplined boys or aging and phlegmatic geezers up for short enlistment. The next morning, he went with Lieutenant Howard Cushing to confront the troublemakers in broad daylight. The prisoners were still restive. "One crowd of men followed us to the river bank and jeered us as we inspected the stockade there." It was then that Cushing, his superior, turned on his heels and let fly with a tongue-lashing merited by the likes of unruly grammar schoolers.

"'I am just up from the front, where I have been killing such infernal wretches as you are,'" Cushing began in his fury. "'I have met you in twenty battles. I never lost a gun to you. You never drove a battery I served with from its position. You are a crowd of insolent, cowardly scoundrels, and if I had command of this prison I would discipline you, or kill you, and I should much prefer to kill you. . . . If you will give me occasion I will be glad to dam that river,'" he pointed to the Chemung behind them, "'"with

your worthless carcasses, and silent your insolent tongues forever.'" The peroration had its
intended effect. Such caustic eloquence would
have impressed even the likes of Anthony Keiley. Though the men skulked back to their barracks, noted Wilkeson, he figured their anger
would only fester.

Despite Cushing's bluster, Wilkeson could
hardly begrudge the Rebs their hatred of
Helmira. He had seen the wagons drive out of
camp daily to the town cemetery, the pine
coffins stacked high on the bed, and a sense of
reflected doom gathering over the camp. Even
worse, the approaching winter gave signs of being a bitter one. Having been a "prisoner" himself—and with Yankee warders—the lieutenant
knew how many of the captives could never expect to see home again. Despite wholeheartedly
approving Cushing's harangue, Wilkeson harbored a secret sympathy for the men whose
confinement he was entrusted to keep.

His compassion found a sudden outlet on
the night of October 6. "One night seven or
eight Confederates escaped from the prison by
crawling through a tunnel that they had dug,"
recorded the lieutenant. Wilkeson's disenchant-
ment with bounty jumpers, coffee boilers, and
100-day men in his own ranks led him to transfer his sympathy to the very brutes who had re-
cently threatened him. He then descended into
the realm of the perverse: "I was exceedingly
glad that these men had escaped." Little did

Berry Benson and his confederates imagine that anyone keeping watch over them in a Yankee uniform that night might have approved of their desperate plot.

The Mole Is Out

The moment the tunnelers struck the cool, sweet autumn air in the early morning hours of October 7, Sergeant Berry Benson took a breather, going back to his barrack to get the shoes he'd been saving for the trek south. He said good-bye to William Baxter, not part of the tunnel team, being careful how he did it. A sad occasion it was for Benson. Since Baxter knew nothing about the escape, he was unaware that this was probably the last time the two friends would speak.

Benson furtively gathered a small pile of possessions on his bunk: two pocketknives, a kit to cook in, matches, some cord for a horse bridle, a rough map of the country, and a pocket compass a friend had bought him in camp for thirty cents. He bundled them tightly together and returned to the tunnel tent in the fading darkness. Though the others had decided to go out in pairs, Benson was committed to leaving on his own.

Back in the tent, Benson almost collapsed from fatigue. His head still pounding from the digging he'd done below, he decided to rest for a spell. He started to drift . . . sleep would be so nice . . . only for a moment or two. . . . Then he was jolted awake. There was a shout below: "'They are still in the tunnel!'"

He sat up, disoriented. Had he gone under? How long had he been asleep? Almost as if on cue, the sentry on the parapet called out the hour: "Four o'clock and all's well!" The call started at the front gate and did the complete circuit on the parapet, guard calling out to guard, spinning and repeating like the delicate figures on an elaborate Swiss clock. There were only a couple of hours until daylight.

For the moment, the cloud cover they had was ideal. Everyone knew that this could be their last chance. In the tunnel tent, Benson learned that six men had already made the run, but the others were waiting—for him. They weren't tunnelers. They wanted him to lead the way. Benson called for them to follow behind, and he slid slowly down the chute. He was still feeling drowsy and unfocused from his doze.

Every thrust he had made at the dirt wall in the past five weeks now came back to him with a vengeance. His pulse bludgeoned his brain like blows on an anvil. He moved down the dark barrel of shadows, this time the quickest crawl of all because there was no digging—the only thing left to do at the end was run. "Straightaway I was at the exit of the tunnel, above me the sentry's platform." It was an astonishing thought for Benson or anyone else: the highest-

and lowest-placed men at Elmira prison were now on the same side of the fence.

The mole made a sweep of the camp. "I raised my head and looked out. Across the street stood three guards with rifles, by a fire. I crawled on my belly, under the platform close to the fence, toward the town. Then I got on my hands and knees and went faster, the sentry tramping over my head. When I got a tree between me and the three guards I rose to my feet and walked rapidly down, under the platform, to the corner of the prison." He rested for an instant. Now came a maneuver harder than the funambulist's hop on the trapeze—he must cross the street in full view of the sentries.

"At a quick pace, but not with haste, I came out, crossing the street, not turning my head. I nerved myself for the cry of 'Halt!' and a shot, and to feel a bullet lay me low. But there came no shot—no challenge—I reached the farther side of the street and walked quickly down the pavement." He jumped a fence, only to find himself in a backyard protected by a dog that made a run for him. Benson clambered over the fence like a common thief and found himself in an alley off the street. He stopped and took his bearings. Looking up, he drew a bead on the nearby mountain where Traweek, Maull, Jackson, and the others had agreed to meet. For now, at least, his objective was clear. He started off at a run.

Benson thought about it later as he rested in the darkness outside Elmira, the camp behind him "silent and grim as a burying ground." The tunnel had been a pretty piece of work, a tougher pull than walking out of Point Lookout into the Chesapeake and floating on a wave to freedom. That had been a test of his courage, not his will. But what this escape lacked in nerve, it made up for in vigilance. Now he would have to cross all of Pennsylvania and the Maryland border country before he could feel safe. He was surrounded by land. He had no food. He was lucky to even have a coat because the signs of an early Yankee winter were already showing. Behind him in the early dawn, he could see the lights of the prison. He made for a nearby stretch of woods.

Soon after dawn he was there, the faraway spot they had settled on while staring at the mountains from the yard of Barracks No. 3. Benson called out their names. But "Wash Traweek" and the others came back to him as empty echoes. Surely they hadn't been discovered or he would have heard the alarum. Perhaps they had been delayed by passing patrols. Maybe this wasn't even the place. His head was still throbbing. Benson knew they had to divide up anyway—a group of men on the road, none dressed as soldiers, would have been immediately suspicious. Each man would have to find his own passage home, and Benson had prepared for it better than anyone.

In Elmira the next morning, the escape was reported. Rumors of the break flew through barracks. Marcus Toney got wind of the false floor and the raisin box used for shuttling dirt, but the feat got garbled in translation: *fifteen* men had gotten out, he heard, all of them headed to Canada. John King learned that *five* men had absconded and two were caught; Wilbur Grambling of Florida heard that *twenty-five* had actually made the break. The prison was rife with rumors, which were high entertainment given the lack of competing spectacles.

On October 8, the *Advertiser* reported seven men had escaped and "there was a suspicion of their whereabouts." They were being optimistic. Two days later, it correctly recounted that ten men had eloped. The newspaper made the unusual inference that the tunnel had been built crooked as a deliberate diversion. It had, in all, taken days to sort out just how many men had gone, since the Confederate ward sergeants withheld the names of missing prisoners to confuse the Yankees. The tunnel was quickly destroyed, the commandant figuring out that the dirt had been dumped in the sinks. For days afterward, the prisoners were subjected, as both a punishment and a warning, to long and thorough searches in the increasingly cold temperatures.

Benson turned west instead of south, intending to cross the Chemung further upstream just in case the river was guarded closer to camp. He picked apples and wild grapes the first day, living off the land in what seemed to him a "beautiful picture" of orchards and farms. (In the previous five months, he'd had three pieces of fruit, all given him by a friend.) First he resolved to sleep by day and travel cross-country in darkness. By using his matches, he would be able to read the compass. The first night he spent crossing a mountain, having to "get on my hands and knees and crawl zigzag, holding by the bushes," but it seemed a sure way of getting hurt. He resolved to go by roads instead, still at night, even if he knew that patrols would be scouring the countryside for them. He didn't dare make a fire the first night.

He knew the woods. As a boy he loved them more than school, and he spent much of his time learning the names of the trees and plants and herbs that dwelled there. Even then he had scavenged, scouring trash piles for treasures, pilfering a neighbor's fig trees. Berry had become lost in the woods once—abandoned, he thought, by his Negro nurse—but when he was found, the boy showed no sign of emotion. He wasn't afraid to forage on his own. Once he had even run away from home, crossed the river on a borrowed boat, and only been enticed back by his mother with the promise of a new cap. He thought about that time as if it had taken place in another life. Now he was navigating the hardwood forests of a boreal land nearly 1,000 miles to the north—and might have given a good deal for such a cap.

On the second day, he came to a schoolhouse somewhere between Elmira and Corning, then crawled in through a window. "I hoped to find the half of a dinner some pretty girl had left," he wrote lightly. "But I found only slates and books, the greedy things. And a blackboard." Benson looked around him for an opportunity and, as seemed his habit, had an inspiration. He picked up a piece of chalk and composed a message in his mind:

Mr. A. M. Benson,
Augusta, Georgia.
DEAR FATHER: I escaped to-day from
Elmira Prison. I am on my way back to Lee's
army.
Corporal B. K. Benson,
1st South Carolina Volunteers

Elmira papers, New York papers, Richmond
papers, Augusta papers, please copy.

The papers would print it, he felt sure. But he faltered. There was no sense giving the enemy any knowledge of his whereabouts. For all he knew, the message might be discovered within an hour. So he put down the chalk. It was a sage decision, but one with more consequences than he figured. Besides humbling the Yankees, the chalkboard announcement would have brought more joy to one home than he ever could have imagined. Little did Benson suspect that his own family had given him up for dead months before, hearing reports that he had been killed trying to escape Point Lookout. The chalkboard dispatch would have seemed like a voice from the dead to his parents in Augusta. In fact, as it turned out, his decision not to write them any letters from Elmira at all only seemed to confirm his supposed "death" at the point.

Benson spent the night in a tobacco barn, and the next morning he followed the Chemung away from Elmira. But the river was no course to follow: headed due northwest at this rate, he would be in Canada in another two weeks, farther from home than ever. He turned south, away from the river. By his reckoning, on October 8, a Saturday, it began to snow. His coat offered little protection, so he slept in whatever shelter he could find: inside a barn, beneath a church. He followed a railway bed that, despite its early promise, started to lead north. The roads seemed determined to do the same. Something awful wanted to lead him back to Elmira.

Benson hadn't made good time: by dawn of the fourth day, he was only 20 miles southwest of the prison. He'd had little water, relying on apples alone for solid and liquid nourishment. (Near Corning, he'd spent an hour vainly trying to corner a rooster.) One night he fell asleep by a set of railroad tracks, woke up later, and set off on his way until being overtaken by a bewildering sense of déjà vu. Finally he realized that he was walking *north*, returning the way he'd come the day before because he'd forgotten which side of the tracks he fell asleep on.

When at last he righted himself, he found he was in coal country, where the village men dressed in black and wore candles in their hats. At the small town of Fall Brook, Pennsylvania, he knocked at a door and was given bread and tea— "the first tea I had tasted in three years." The man of the house was named Adams; Benson called himself Jefferson. It was a modest meeting of two "ex-presidents," he mused later, noting that in his hunger "I destroyed everything but the crockery." He trudged off to Canton, a town he remembered coming through on the train ride to Elmira, nine miles down the road.

In no time, Berry Benson became an accomplished sneak thief. To put it another way, he became an efficient forager for a one-man army in the field. First it was a pair of trousers and stockings on a back-door banister—when he later took them off, his legs were black with coal dust. Before he got to Canton, "I walked all night, stopping but twice, once to borrow a chicken." Five miles south of town near a railroad shanty, a barrel of potatoes seized his eye. "When a man has lived at a hotel in Elmira from July to October he realizes that roasted potatoes go well with broiled chicken."

The cold of winter was drawing close, especially for a fugitive who moved, like a frightened mole, in the hours after dusk. So he snitched an overcoat from an open window and then "dusted." He had accumulated the wardrobe of a wealthy tramp (which he was forced to wear all at once) and could note with a grim sort of pride, "I now summed up that I had eleven pockets." He only lacked for something to fill them up with. A ways past Canton, he vigorously shook a chestnut tree until its vintage fell with the force of a military tattoo, yielding nine pockets full of chestnuts. "Somewhere near Ralston, pains in my stomach reminded me of the obligation I was under to repay the owner for the chicken I borrowed the night before. So I borrowed another, a good fat hen, to repay him should I meet him," he jibed. "I had no desire to return to him one that was any less fat. I would do no man injustice."

Benson's instincts took him further south, following the rocky valleys and railroad cuts that wedged a gap through the Appalachians. He still traveled by night, longing to see the beautiful country he passed through in daylight, if only that were possible. On the 11th, he saw the moon set twice, scrawling notes to himself on scraps of paper. The next day marked almost a week since the escape. He thought of the "poor boys" back in Elmira. Meanwhile, word of the prisoners had dried up in the *Advertiser*, the paper having soured on a story in which a pack of Rebs vanished in a region full of Copperheads— that is, the more deadly human variety.

Now that Elmira was a distance to his rear, Benson had a brilliant stroke. The best thing might be to march into a Yankee camp and play a supreme bluff. "Why not enlist," he imagined, "get a thousand dollars bounty, go down as a recruit to Richmond, and then, the first night on picket, walk over?" It was wonderfully simple. Maybe he'd have to talk flat and clipped like a Yankee to fake it, but the strain shouldn't do his mouth serious harm. There was only one detail that scared him. It was one thing to pull on another man's trousers but another to mouth his most hallowed words. Reciting the oath of loyalty to the Union—a ritual required of recruits—was a bitter lie for a man who took pride in being honest. Besides, Benson remembered his miserable failure at impersonating a Yankee at Spotsylvania five months before; an image of a hanging tree stood mute in his memory, the branches now black and bare. He promptly discarded the idea and set a course for Williamsport.

Benson followed the Susquehanna River south, his commissary fast dwindling. In Williamsport he spotted scraps of hardtack on the ground before the train depot. "Some were as big as a dollar," the hungry soldier recalled. "Once I came mighty near finding a whole one." His shoes were so tattered that one of them had worn clear through, making it impossible for him to step between railroad ties on rough stones.

On the night of the 13th, he stole a rowboat moored at the river's edge. He'd never pulled an oar before in his life, and it showed. Benson beached the boat twice because his right hand was pulling harder than his left—a watery reminder of the same mistake they had made digging the Elmira tunnel. When finally he got the knack of pulling, he rowed down the Susquehanna, eating chestnuts in a lazy reverie and recalling "there was not a man that enjoyed that night as I did, in all Pennsylvania"—until the sound of an approaching falls forced him to pull for shore. The honeymoon (and the moon was full) had been short. He berthed at a nearby lumberyard where he found another coat. He now had a grand total of 15 pockets, as he toted them up. In one of the newest ones was a license to distill liquor; the sober veteran tore it to bits and "scattered them to the four winds."

He trudged by moonlight down the rugged backbone of Pennsylvania. In Northumberland, he knocked on a door with a light inside and, pleading he had lost his horse, was given a serving of bread and butter. There was no way his shoes would hold up 'til Virginia. Either he had to steal another pair, he realized, or borrow a horse. But Benson could never quite bring himself to take a horse. In fact, he could steal anything *but* a horse—except the time in May he had taken the mount behind Yankee lines at Spotsylvania. Many was the occasion he called himself a coward after Elmira for his failure to jump a grazing mare. Instead he plodded on, and when he met strangers on the road he would tell them he was looking for his mount, "Blaze," who had run off and left him a poor straggler. For a man who had dug a hole halfway to Shanghai, it was a rather weak fiction by which to travel in the coal-driven world of Billy Yank.

There was one other way to save leather. Benson knew the quickest route south wasn't by following the valleys and rivers, but by taking the course the Yankees had already surveyed for him: the iron rails. He'd been afraid to ask the way to the railroad for fear of seeming an utter stranger, but on October 14 he happened upon a set of tracks and hopped a lumber freight to Sunbury. It was such an easy jaunt that, further down the line, he resolved to board a passenger train for Harrisburg. He had no money for a ticket—even the chickens he'd carried under his coat were long since devoured. Benson's appearance, by this time, had improved some. The only Reb article of clothing left him was a black cavalry hat, found at the Wilderness, which he stuffed in his coat and replaced with a plasterer's hat coated with mortar. He felt something like an unpeeled vegetable, wearing layers of clothing that, were he ever forced to remove them one by one, would eventually reveal his essence as a South Carolina sharpshooter and chicken thief.

The Harrisburg train stopped at Sunbury. "All was bustle. Everybody was getting off, and everybody was getting on. I stood, hesitating. I was eager to ride; I was afraid." Benson boarded at dusk. He figured to avoid the conductor by hiding out on the platform between cars. As the conductor approached the platform, Benson went down the steps and wrapped himself around the car exterior, clutching the hand-holds on the side. The ticket-taker passed by. But when he came back through a second time, unexpectedly, he caught Benson sitting on the step in the gathering darkness. "I know he sees me. Then, suddenly, my shadow on the step shortens. I know he is holding his lamp over me, looking at me. I sit still. I am wondering what he will say."

Benson hunched over. He was brave enough to have dug out of prison and traveled incognito 200 miles, but too afraid now to turn his back even a few inches. "He remains silent a hundred years, and then—he says nothing. He goes away."

The "lickety-split, lickety-split" sound of the rails passing beneath seemed to drag on for a continent. The Elmira escapee sat there for two more hours, no doubt marveling at how the good luck he found at Spotsylvania was, though a little worse for the wear, still clinging to him as he rode the rails southbound somewhere between home and Helmira.

By now, he was nearer Maryland than New York. Benson changed at Harrisburg for a train headed south. Again he performed his trapeze act on the car exterior—and again a conductor caught him, this time in the act of clinging to the side. Benson pleaded he was on his way to

York to visit his sick sister. The conductor took pity on him and told him to get off at the next stop. At York, Benson disembarked and continued the trek southward on foot. On October 15 he crossed the Mason–Dixon line into Maryland. He had been "marching merrily, whistling Dixie," striding the final miles through Pennsylvania. The small town of Gettysburg, late of epic battle fame, lay 30 miles to the west.

Though Benson was jubilant to have crossed the slave line, he knew the borderlands were treacherous. While imprisoned at the Old Capitol in July, he'd read a story of an escaped Reb who revealed his identity to a stranger in Maryland—and was carted off to prison for the indiscretion. Benson continued due south to Baltimore, the next stop in his pilgrim's progress, where an Elmira friend had given him the name of a southern sympathizer.

A train loaded with beef on the hoof crawled by, a troop of Yankee guards riding on the car tops. Against his better judgment, Benson decided to hitch a ride. He now reasoned that the most audacious mode of travel was the least suspicious. When one soldier engaged him in conversation and tried to talk him into enlisting, a conductor—once again—saved his skin, this time ordering him off the train and saving him the awful prospect of having to take the oath of allegiance to Lincoln. On the morning of the 17th, he entered Baltimore, a Federal-occupied city in a slave state, on foot.

Strolling policemen made Benson nervous. So he put to use some of the swagger he had seen in Traweek at Elmira. He walked the streets like he had been born there, though with a rapidly pounding heart. When at last he found the address he had been given, a Negro maid told him that the woman Benson sought, said to be domiciled on North Eutaw Street, was not there, nor had anyone even heard of her. Shortly after, Benson saw a handsome young couple through a basement window and he broke down, asking them for something to eat. They kindly gave him a serving of bread and mutton with no questions. A gang of boys on the street offered him an apple, one of them saying he looked like a Reb. Benson laughed and strolled off. Though longing to tell some-one his story, he thought better of it. Baltimore was not safe.

Endowed with the instincts of a migratory fowl, Benson made his way ever south. He would have to make a wide arc to the west to avoid the federal capital and was determined to aim for Leesburg, Virginia, on the far side of the Potomac, where a friend lived. Benson con-tinued his freebooting ways, skimming the cream off earthen crocks of milk and eating de-licious winesaps until the juice "burnt my mouth like pepper." He was now almost two weeks from Elmira. For the first time in months, he began to feel like a free man. It was different, he realized, when the sentiment of liberty had to be earned. He had ridden on many slave patrols before the war. Though his recognition of the shared experience was dim, he began to understand what the fleeing bondsman felt.

Deeper South

The tunnel break of October 6 was the largest-ever Reb escape from Elmira. But it was soon to be dwarfed by a more public—and far more pitiful—exodus from Barracks No. 3. In late September, word had begun circulating of a prisoner exchange, the most heartening hearsay the Rebs had yet entertained during their long months of captivity in the Chemung Valley.

Anthony Keiley greeted the reports, like so much else, with skepticism. After all, the Union had been refusing an exchange of prisoners since 1863, when the controversy erupted over captured black soldiers. And the Yankees, so "Beast" Butler had told Keiley in June, had no intentions of recanting their position. If anyone were to be exchanged, Keiley figured, it would be a cynical attempt by Lincoln to undercut George McClellan, the Democratic candidate for president whose party platform promised a general exchange of prisoners in anticipation of the November general election.

The fall of 1864 was not a good time in Elmira. Foster's Pond had deteriorated into a stagnant backwash of effluvia. The excellent well water nearby was in danger of being contaminated by seepage from the pond latrine. Scurvy was on the rise. The majority of prisoners—and their guards—lived in rows of tents inside the stockade, exposed to the icy autumn of New York. Commissary-General Hoffman had, in August, embargoed parcels to "healthy" prisoners and cut back on the general ration. Even someone less than a cynic might have seen in that order a thinly disguised Malthusian prescription. In September alone, prisoner deaths more than tripled to 385. The ruts were getting deeper for the thousands of men in the Elmira bullpen.

The town of Elmira went about its daily affairs. The Know-Nothings sent thugs to rant against the Irish. Military agents arrived with their soapbox to sign up soldier substitutes and meet the draft quota. A minstrel show at Ely Hall brought down the house with its "exuberance of negro fancy." A touring menagerie, the tragedy of *Macbeth*, the Siamese twins, the world's greatest ventriloquist, and sundry lectures—on "Marriage No Lottery" and temperance, among other topics—came and went. Knotholes in the prison fence offered a look at the grounds otherwise off-limits to the public, except for the observatory. "People from the country are hardly willing to go home after their shopping is done," reported the *Advertiser*, "without a peep at the varmints."

The gossip of deliverance was soon borne out. The prisoner exchange seemed all but final for those men incapacitated for fighting. "The knowing ones are rubbing up their old complaints, getting their asthmas, rheumatisms, lame legs, etc. in working order for the examination about to take place," Keiley wrote. For it was the meek, not the muscular, who were about to walk away from Elmira. The surgeons made the rounds of the hospital on October 1, making a list of prisoners whose wounds would render them unfit for duty for at least 60 days. Keiley knew full well he wasn't likely to make the grade of the walking wounded, not even with the ball he took at Malvern Hill. "Full rations of beef, a quiet conscience, and a good digestion, have left me in an awkward exuberance of health which precludes all hope of discharge on the ground of unfitness," he noted sadly. It was entirely possible, he mused, that he had eaten himself out of an early parole.

The cagey lawyer from Petersburg could only watch as the men presented themselves for inspection. Each one who stepped forward was hoping to be judged unfit for "age, or sickness, or wounds . . . while the rest were sent back sorrowing." The result of the muster was both a commentary on the desperate state of recruits in the South and the horrible conditions of Elmira. At the end of the doctor's tally, a week later, fully one in eight prisoners, over 1,200 men, were deemed eligible for exchange. Many of Keiley's fellow Petersburg militiamen, too old for regular service, were among them. Never had a shabbier group of specimens been appointed such an envied elect.

"Four or five officers took the paroles on the long porch which ran along the front of the hospitals, and having nothing better to do, I spent an hour or two watching the scene," Keiley related, observing, as always, from a privileged perch. "As soon as the announcement was made in the various hospitals that the parole lists were ready, those who had been notified that they had been entered for exchange began to crawl from their cots, and turn their faces towards the door. On they came, a ghastly tide, with skeleton bodies and lustreless eyes, and brains bereft of but one thought, and hearts purged of all feelings but one—the thought of freedom, the love of home.

"On they came on their crutches, on their cots, borne in the arms of their friends, creeping, some of them, on hands and knees, pale, gaunt, emaciated, some with the seal of death stamped on their wasted cheeks and shrivelled limbs, yet fearing less death than the added agony of death in the hands of enemies." It looked like a nightmare out of Dante—or a premonition of scenes to ensue in the prisoner camps of the next century. And how Keiley longed to be among them.

The parolees looked a scruffier lot than the Federal prisoners that Keiley, always anxious to affront the North, had seen released from southern camps before his capture. But their fate, even with the promise of release, hung slender. Between October 3, the day they were mustered out as parolees, and October 11, when the group finally departed Elmira, several of the chosen prisoners died. Keiley desperately cast about for a way to find a seat on the train, the "hegira" as he called it—what may have been, for all anyone knew, their last chance to get out of Elmira alive.

"Many a brawny fellow with the thews of Alcides would gladly exchange his exuberant health and perfect strength, for the most helpless frame and the puniest limbs in the hospital," he recounted glibly, "and numberless expedients to elude the vigilance, or corrupt the integrity of the examiners were practised, and with very encouraging success." One prisoner bribed a surgeon with five dollars (federal) for the favor of imagining a gunshot wound that pierced his left arm—earning him parole. The cleverer ones, Keiley heard, faked epileptic fits. "Thus the poor ones had to rely on their wits, while the better-off ones bribed."

Keiley preferred his wits. He wasn't a dirt-digger like Benson—though he gloated over the "eleven enterprising beavers" and their escape. Nor were petty falsehoods his forte. He would earn his parole by private arrangement, he seems to have resolved, or not at all. The first week in October, he put out word that he was more than ready to give up his sumptuous lodgings for an extended ride on the Erie. Better than money, it turned out, he had friends in high places. And better than friends, Keiley could argue that he was a private citizen of Petersburg, not a member of the regular Confederate army. Unfortunately, only the headstones for the Rebel graves in the Elmira cemetery seemed to distinguish between the two because the Yankees were not always inclined to care.

On October 9, news came. "A knock at my door ten minutes after nine; my friend D. calls me out with the gravity of a lord-chancellor, and *sotto voce*, announces, 'Major Colt has just put your name down on the list.'" If Keiley had paid out any money for the privilege, he wasn't telling. Most of his Petersburg friends from the militia would accompany him, citizens considered too old to fight. Keiley made haste to ready his departure. He went about distributing what he couldn't carry with him to the unlucky souls who remained—an act of Christian charity mixed with profound relief.

It was October 11, only days after Berry Benson and his "beavers" had fled. The parolees, still some 1,200 strong, were divided into three squads and marched through the barracks yard toward the Erie train station. Keiley had a final meeting with Major Colt, his benefactor, near the gate. "His eyes filled as he bade me goodbye at parting, and I fear my own were not altogether dry, as for the last time I wrung the hand of the true man, and humane, courteous official, Major Colt." The commandant gave him the name of a Union lieutenant colonel held prisoner in the South, hoping that Keiley, a gentleman of his word, would return the favor. The hatred of North and South, if only for a moment, became a casualty of the war. The two men parted with a kind word and a handshake.

The parolees marched through the gate to the city center, where three trains of sixty boxcars awaited them at the brick depot. "Those unable to sit up were carefully taken in military wagons from the Barracks to the cars on cots," wrote the *Advertiser*. "The cars they occupied were covered with fresh clean hay." Men like John King, Marcus Toney, J. B. Stamp, James Huffman, and Joe Womack no doubt watched them disappear through the stockade with a mixture of emotions. Some of their comrades were free. But those who stayed behind were learning that they were almost as likely to perish of chronic diarrhea in Elmira as they had been of a minié ball or bayonet at Bloody Angle, a fate unthinkable at war's beginning.

Keiley's conveyance to captivity in July—the Erie Railroad—became his means of deliverance in October. Headed southeast, the train stopped at frequent intervals, chugging at a snail's pace for over 200 miles. Spending the first night in a space three feet by six inches, as he remembered, he stuffed himself with "fabulous quantities of crackers." The bored Keiley matched wits in transit with a lieutenant from Maine who claimed that all Rebels deserved to be hanged—until the lawyer sharply reminded him that George Washington had been a rebel fit for the gibbet, too. It took 40 hours to get to Baltimore. "Whenever the train stopped, the guards robbed the nearest orchards." When they reached the "city of monuments" on the thirteenth, at least five of the prisoners were already dead, "the first toll of the dread Reaper on our journey home."

Keiley watched from his open boxcar as civilians crowded on the train platforms to find if relatives were lying therein, only to be wagged away by Yankee guards. Having been frustrated for months by the mail censors at Elmira, he had an inspired idea of how to write a friend who lived in the city. "Tearing a leaf from my note-book, I jotted down a few lines, and rolling the letter in as small a compass as possible, I watched my opportunity when the guards were not looking in my direction, to hold it up with a gesture that attracted one of the ladies," he recounted.

The scene could have been lifted out of a musketeer novel of Dumas. "As soon as a fair opportunity offered, I shot the 'paper pellet' towards her, and was much gratified to observe the diplomatic nonchalance with which she put her foot on the missive, quietly continuing her conversation with a female friend meanwhile. A moment or two afterwards she *accidentally* let fall her handkerchief, and stooping to recover it, picked up my note with it, and conveyed both to her pocket—all this without a look towards me." A few moments later, she offered him a sly glance of assurance that the message would be delivered—or Baltimore wasn't a hotbed of secesh sympathizers. Somehow Keiley retained his good spirits even when crammed like a bovine passenger in the boxcar.

In Baltimore, they unloaded for transfer. Keiley jumped on an ambulance driven by a drunken Yankee who offered an impromptu tour of the city. (Little did he guess that four days later, Berry Benson, one of the Elmira tunnelers, would walk the same streets even more anxious and hungry than he was.) Portside, the parolees trooped onto a steamer headed south down the Chesapeake Bay. Their destination, dreaded and familiar: Point Lookout. There they would check out of their Yankee hostelry as they had checked in several months before.

The condition of the paroled prisoners was disputed. Keiley made them seem no better than lepers from Capernaum, but the *Advertiser*, a solid pro-Lincoln paper, placed the exodus from Elmira in a much better light on October 12: "Each of these sick cars was well provided with attendants and pails of water and every care taken to make the invalids comfortable." Two days later, a U.S. army surgeon in Baltimore begged to differ, writing to Hoffman that "the condition of these men was pitiable in the extreme and evinces criminal neglect and inhumanity on the part of the medical officers in making the selection of the men to be transferred." Another surgeon boarded the steamer bound for Point Lookout and reported 40 men who "should not have been sent on such a journey."

It would have surprised Keiley to learn that his old nemesis, the "murderous" camp doctor E. F. Sanger, heartily agreed. Sanger complained soon thereafter that the prisoners had been sent off with neither provisions nor nurses, nor with blankets proper to such a difficult remove. Nor was his a newfound compassion. The chief surgeon had long been lodging complaints with the Union brass regarding the treatment of Elmira's Rebs. From early August, he had been fomenting against the lack of fresh vegetables, the epidemic proportions of scurvy, insufficient hospital wards, improper feeding practices, and particularly the sickly putrescence of Foster's Pond, a place that "left a festering mass of corruption, impregnating the entire atmosphere of the camp with its pestilential odors, night and day." Keiley, at least in this much, was wrong about the clubfooted doctor, who, whatever his personal arrogance, had begged Washington for the most basic of sanitary comforts.

In mid-October, the steamer dropped anchor at Point Lookout. At dawn commenced the thankless task of unloading the sick. "A gangway plank was stretched from the side of the ship to two flour-barrels standing on the dock, and down this 'shute' the poor helpless, maimed creatures were slid like coal into a vault."

Healthier prisoners like Keiley were assigned to the "'officer's pen,'"—his old haunt in camp—and told to make themselves "as comfortable as possible."

The only consolation of finding himself a recidivist at Point Lookout was the likelihood that Keiley's exile would soon end. Before he had even settled into his old routine, however, he was unceremoniously "flanked." His pack, filled with clothing and the handiwork of some of his Elmira comrades, was filched one night. He suspected a camp official of the crime, though his own fellows chided him for having left anything in Yankeedom unattended in the first place. The satchel, after being thoroughly pilfered, was returned to him, and Keiley claimed to have later recognized some of its contents on the back of a Yankee orderly.

The Elmira contingent hunkered down on the Chesapeake Bay, where the exchange officials waited for 5,000 convalescent Rebs to gather. The men were confined to tents and beds of straw. The daily routine, such as it was, was even less bearable in cold weather. The Rebs were put on half rations—sick men, according to prevailing military logic, didn't merit any more. Keiley volunteered for "administering hospital slops and allopathic boluses" in the convalescent ward. Never had any man been so anxious to volunteer for the trying labors of hospital duty. He had found yet another way by which to "endure the tedium of my cage."

On October 28, the men were mustered for inspection. It was the last time they would be counted up like a herd of shriveled Holsteins. Everyone eligible for exchange was expected to have an ailment—the more pronounced, the better. The census of afflictions began. Keiley knew that Major Colt's blessing was no guarantee of freedom here. Even with a limp, he was walking better than most of the others, not a promising sign to the examining judges. And it would have staggered even the self-composed Keiley to be turned away just at the point of being redeemed. He thought hard as the doctors approached. Then his brazen self-confidence came to the rescue: "When called on by the doctor," he bragged later, "I drawled out a disease with a name as long as a Nantucket 'sea sarpint'—and was passed."

The prisoners were stripped of blankets on October 30 and began boarding three vessels in the morning. One of them was the *Northern Light*, a steamer that before the war had plied the California route around Cape Horn. Two decks on the *Northern Light* had been fitted with around 1,000 hammocks altogether, and by nightfall the prisoners were still loading. Since many of them suffered from night blindness, a common ailment in the camps, Keiley volunteered to help them up the rope ladder, the thought of losing a man overboard unbearable this close to home. But as bad as Point Lookout had been, the next leg of the trip wasn't one

Keiley relished. "Although Friar Peyton told Henry VIII that the road to heaven was as short by water as by land," he recalled, "the same is not as true of the road to Dixie."

The *Northern Light* steamed off with a full hold. The next day they reached Hampton Roads, Virginia, where David Dixon Porter commanded a flotilla of Union gunboats in the harbor. The steamer dropped anchor for a week, a delay Keiley found far from salutary. "Boat-loads of soldiers are constantly passing down the river," he noted November 6, the men evidently furloughed to vote in the presidential election on the eighth. But there was another, more unsettling movement under way. "Every morning we saw coffins going over the side in numbers which suggested uncomfortable reflections on the uncertain tenure of life on a prison-ship." They were still a long way from home.

Steaming near land to avoid a squall, they followed the coastline south. On November 9 they reached Hilton Head and moored adjacent to Fort Pulaski. Nearby was the celebrated Mitchell-town, an experimental burg dedicated to educating freed slaves, an idea that struck Keiley as absurd. It was a futile task, he argued, to instruct a race whose "passing generations have not left a trace on the page of history." Such a project only worked to salve the Union conscience, he believed, and give employment to a few nosey Connecticut schoolmarms. Five months in Yankee lockup had not softened him on the Negro question.

There was even less to keep them busy below decks than there had been in the officer's pen at Point Lookout. For once, however, Keiley seemed grateful to be bored. The hours of waiting would soon be paid with due recompense. "Many of us lounged on deck till morning, too much exhilarated by the safe termination of our captivity, and the near approach of home, to waste our hours in the prosaic stupidity of sleep."

A steamer called the *New York* arrived at Hilton Head the next day. The Rebs were boarded and hustled 10 miles up the Savannah River to the agreed-upon "truce-ground." A deputation of Savannah citizens was waiting, and the exchange was completed. The city fathers escorted the soldiers onto a makeshift flatboat that steamed up the river to "the most beautiful Atlantic city of the South," as Keiley called Savannah. They were met downtown at noon by a band playing Dixie. And thanks to a "general massacre of all bipeds furnished with feathers," a citywide feast ensued that made the scraps of Elmira salt pork seem like an ancient memory, at least for an afternoon. They were prisoners no longer, permitted even the extravagant liberty of walking the streets without escort.

Keiley wasted no time preparing to return to Petersburg the next evening. "Sixty days," as he put it, "are an aeon in these times." Following an impatient train ride, he arrived in darkness.

His beautiful Petersburg stood like a ghost beneath "an imperial autumn moon." The crack of rifle fire echoed through the empty streets. "I passed the churches, and found that their yards had been converted into burial grounds—the public cemetery being within reach of the enemy's guns. . . . In many private-grounds I noticed embankments with which bomb-proofs were covered, for the safety of the citizens during the frequent bombardments. Many of the lower stories of buildings were protected by barricades of cotton-bales." The city whose church bells had stirred his passion to fight in late spring was now eerily quiet.

Petersburg had been under siege since the day of his capture. Now Keiley could see the depressing story that the *News Express* might have told—if it had been delivered in Elmira at all. "In leaving prison, I found I had not come to peace," he wrote gravely, "but to the presence and the centre of war." Anthony Keiley walked in the shadows of familiar buildings that had already made most of the improvised conversion to rubble. Petersburg itself was a captive of the war. And though Keiley didn't suspect it, his days in the Yankee "bastilles" were still not over.

Keiley had been fortunate. So too, in a different way, had been Benson. Yet the escape of the "Elmira ten" made Yankee prisons seem more like makeshift holding pens than onerous "bastilles." In fact, they were far from porous.

Stone fortresses like Warren and McHenry were as hard to flee as the Chateau d'If. A camp like Johnson's Island, three miles from shore in Lake Erie, presented an escapee with serious navigational problems. Rock Island, a small clump of land in the Mississippi River, offered running Rebels the prospect of swimming the Father of Waters, the southern channel 400 feet wide. Of course, none of this might have been too much for the likes of Berry Benson. But even Benson, following his stroll into the Chesapeake from Point Lookout, had been re-captured.

Camps like Elmira and Morton, surrounded by wooden stockades instead of masonry walls or large bodies of water, would seem to have been promising grounds for a breakout. Given that local language and customs weren't a barrier to flight—a problem for POWs in most wars—the actual number of escapes was small, however. Although large-scale breakouts happened several times in the southern camps, they were virtually unknown in the North, even allowing for the conservative escape numbers usually reported. Rock Island, Illinois, saw 41 successful escapes out of an aggregate population of 12,000. In the last year of the war, Alton, Illinois, had about 30; Johnson's Island, 9; and Point Lookout, filled to bursting, 17. For that matter, only 17 successfully absconded from Elmira (which had over 12,000 total inmates), most of them in the Benson break. It was one of the lowest rates for a major prison in the North, a fact no doubt abetted by its remove from the South and the severely weakened condition of its captives.

If few in number, Elmira escapees wanted nothing in the way of shrewdness. A Georgia sergeant nicknamed "Buttons"—named for the brass buttons that covered his chest like a plate of armor—was said to have had prisoners lay him in a coffin and lightly cover it one day in November. The coffin was loaded on the burial wagon by prisoners. When the wagon halted outside camp on the way to the cemetery, Buttons rose up from the pine case like a corpse come to life—then scrambled away when the teamster was too shocked to protest. (Benson, who also knew a "Buttons"—if indeed it was the same man—doubted this story.) For months afterward, the Elmira guards were said to be meticulous about inspecting all bodies as they came into the dead-house south of Foster's Pond, making sure the coffins were nailed firmly shut. The first to escape Elmira were two Johnnies who went over the fence on a ladder in July 1864; the last was in April of the following year, when an enterprising Reb hid in the camp "swill" wagon containing the cookhouse garbage and made a not-so-glorious ride to freedom.

One prisoner who escaped Elmira was a mere child, Bennie Orcutt. A South Carolina lad employed as an errand boy by the camp clerks, Orcutt was the recipient of a piece of good fortune in December. It turned out that he bore a more-than-striking resemblance to Jimmie Dumars, the son of a Yankee officer in Barracks No. 3. Orcutt appears to have kept his eye on Jimmie as he came and went at the camp, doing little more than calling out his last name to the guard when passing out the gate. One day, when Jimmie didn't come, Orcutt saw his chance. He pinched a clerk's coat, waited until dusk, and then shuffled to the front wicket and mumbled "Dumars"—and the gate opened. Nothing more was heard from Orcutt later, save a letter to the clerk in which he apologized for having swiped the coat.

But it was Sergeant Joe Womack who conceived the most bald-faced escape. Womack had been an early partner of Benson's in the "gofer" (tunneling) business, watching with him as their best effort was caved in by Yankee guards in August. The sergeant of his ward, Womack, a man who could write well and was blessed with good manners, had struck up a friendship with several Yankee officers, one of whom was accustomed to lend him books. It so happened that in one of the tomes Womack found, stuck between the pages, was the Barracks No. 3 equivalent of a genie in a bottle: a blank pass authorizing the bearer to enter and exit the prison.

When he showed the pass to Benson, whose tunnel was still unfinished, Berry urged him to get the camp forger, a man named Miller, to fake Colt's signature on it and be off. Miller, an engraver by trade, had been forging the major's signature on sutler's orders for months. The administration had tried to stop the mysterious forgeries by numbering orders, then printing them in red ink, then finally using an embossed print. And every time Miller met their challenge with an improved fake. But this case seemed too easy. Womack suspected the pass had been planted there deliberately to see whom it might tempt. At the last minute, he lost his nerve and returned the book—pass included—to the officer. Failure to get through the gate, after all, would mean solitary confinement and maybe the sweatbox.

On October 7, Womack woke up with the rest of the camp to find that Benson and his subterranean tribe had made their own tunnel on the sly. He was hurt at being excluded and didn't understand their silence about the scheme until much later. But he wasn't deterred. In mid-October, Womack borrowed the officer's book again—relieved to find the pass still in it—and went to work on a solo job. He practiced forging Colt's signature himself on orders to the sutler, and marveled as each one he took for redemption to the store was cashed without a hitch.

In the gray hours of October 26, Womack was ready to bolt. In the fading daylight, he donned some citizen's clothing a friend had sent him, lifted an officer's coat from Union quarters, and donned a precious pair of blue pants.

Posing as "Reynolds" of the 110th New York Volunteers, he presented his forged pass at the gate. After some hesitation, he was passed through by a suspicious sentry.

No sooner had Womack cleared the checkpoint than he froze. He realized, to his horror, he had left his pass with the guard. No sane soldier would have done so. Turning on his heels, he proceeded back to the sentry post and politely asked for the pass, a corrective he later believed ensured his credibility. The forgery was returned to him, and he strode toward the city, picking up speed the further he got from camp. With the help of some Copperheads in nearby Waverly, he caught a train south and quickly headed for Richmond.

Richmond, it turned out, was exactly the direction his old accomplice Berry Benson was headed.

Secretary of War Edwin Stanton directed policy for Confederate prisoners with
an iron hand. (National Archives and Records Administration, B-3932)

Confederate soldiers (foreground) under guard at Union camp in Virginia. (Library of Congress, Prints and Photographs Division, LC B8184-10079)

Confederate dead at Spotsylvania, May 1864, the grim alternative to capture.
(Library of Congress, Prints and Photographs Division, LC-USZ62-104044)

Rebels taken at Spotsylvania on May 12, 1864, the day John King and Marcus Toney were captured. (Library of Congress, Prints and Photographs Division, LC B8184-4796)

Rebel prisoners and colors being marched to the Union rear at Chancellorsville, Edwin Forbes, artist. (Library of Congress, Prints and Photographs Division, LC-USZ62-12810)

Rebel officers taken at Petersburg, relaxing on a steamer in the James River, Edwin Forbes, artist. (Library of Congress, Prints and Photographs Division, LC-USZ62-14642)

The Old Capitol Prison, Washington, D.C., stood on the future site of the U.S. Supreme Court. (Library of Congress, Prints and Photographs Division, LC B8171-1019)

Prisoners caught in the act of escaping were returned to do "barrel duty" at Point Lookout, Maryland. (The Morrow Collection of the W. H. Over State Museum, Vermilion, S.D.)

Anonymous group of Confederate prisoners. (National Archives and Records Administration, B-6262)

Elmira Prison Camp.

The prison barracks of Elmira, some not completed until the winter of 1864. (Library of Congress, Prints and Photographs Division, LC-USZ62-15596)

Confederate Prison Camp. Elmira. N.Y. 1864-5.

Roll call for Elmira prisoners. (Chemung County Historical Society)

Anthony Keiley, model prisoner and politician. (Valentine Richmond History Center)

Berry Benson in 1877. (By permission of Frances Benson Thompson, the Benson Papers, #2636, Southern Historical Collection, Library of the University of North Carolina at Chapel Hill, Volume 10, page 260A)

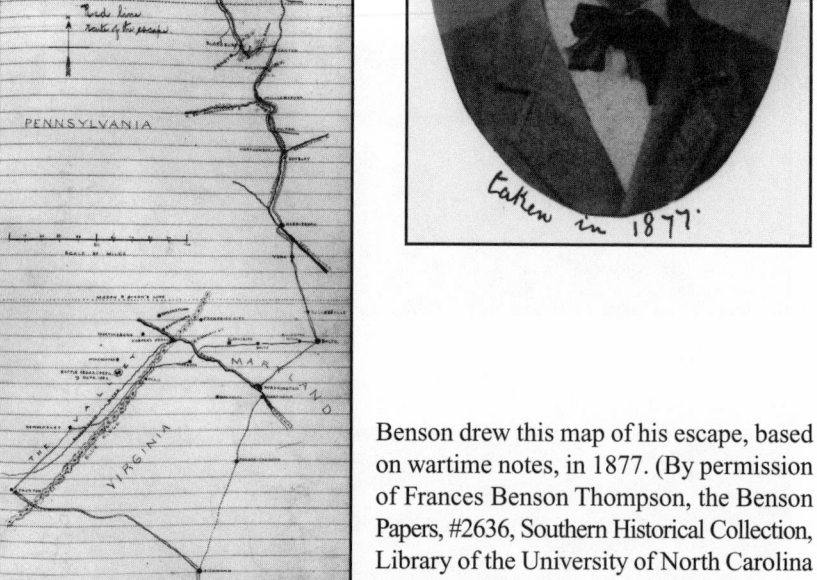

Benson drew this map of his escape, based on wartime notes, in 1877. (By permission of Frances Benson Thompson, the Benson Papers, #2636, Southern Historical Collection, Library of the University of North Carolina at Chapel Hill, Volume 10, page 289)

This rail pass was given Benson when he reached interior Confederate lines in late 1864. (By permission of Frances Benson Thompson, the Benson Papers, Southern Historical Collection, Library of the University of North Carolina at Chapel Hill, Volume 10, page 318)

Marcus Toney was known as "Private Toney" long after the war ended. (Library of Congress, General Collection)

Toney, at center in light duster, stands with fellow prisoners in front of the Elmira train depot before returning home. (Library of Congress, General Collection)

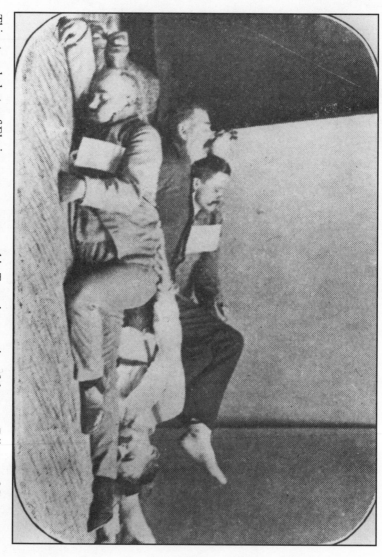

This staged photo of Elmira corpses appeared in Toney's memoirs of the war. (Library of Congress, General Collection)

John King, circa 1916.
(Library of Congress,
General Collection)

King (right) lived through presidential administrations from John Tyler to
Franklin Roosevelt. On the left is brother Cyrus, whom he pulled to safety at
Gettysburg. (Courtesy of Martha Stump Benson)

The Erie train station in Elmira. (Photograph by author)

Foster's Pond, today. (Photograph by author)

The view from Barracks No. 3 looking across the river. (Photograph by author)

Woodlawn National Cemetery, burial place for the Confederate dead. (Photograph by author)

CHAPTER 4

City of Indigents

A S the crow flies, Sergeant Berry Benson was no more than halfway to Charleston. But by the time he was ready to cross the Potomac at Edward's Ferry on the evening of October 19, his meager belongings tied in a bundle, at least he knew he almost had both feet in Dixie. He was far from complacent on the subject: northern Virginia was Yankee-held territory, and there was no telling what colors the next troop of cavalry down the road would be wearing. (He'd also heard tell of "Jessie's Scouts"—Federals who rode the region dressed in Rebel gray.) Besides, Benson hadn't forgotten his last visit to General Washington and Lee's home state: being thrown in the Alexandria guardhouse was his sole reward for swimming the Potomac while gingerly balancing a pack of matches on his head.

On the night of the 18th, he heard the wonderful noise he had been seeking—the splashing shoals of the Potomac. A Federal cavalryman rode picket on the other side, and Benson hid in the bushes. A stray horse was grazing nearby and he tried, without success, to get it into the river. The next day, Benson claimed, he could hear gunfire from the battle of Cedar Creek, a good 50 miles distant. He tied his clothes up inside his biggest coat and lashed them to a plank he found at river's edge. In case he lost the bundle in the crossing, he decided to wear his shirt and pants. Pressing down on the empty side of the plank to keep the bundle dry, he stepped into the river and soon found himself treading deep water. Though forced to swim, it was still an easier crossing than the one he had done near Alexandria.

No sooner had he made the ford at Edward's Ferry than he realized something was wrong. His compass had fallen out of a pocket as he made the passage. A lesser man might have taken it for a bad omen. Benson, instead, saw in it an auspicious sign: he no longer needed any guidance, to his way of thinking, since his journey was so close to an end. It was a learned trait in many a veteran to tame the worst turn of fate into a sign of hidden favor. And so Benson surrendered himself, blissful and dripping and famished, to the mystery of fortune, happy to be alive again inside the original borders of the Rebellion.

He approached a house by the shore on the Virginia side. Barely able to contain himself, he knocked loudly on the door. A voice from inside peppered him with more questions than St. Peter. Only after the sergeant had revealed his command, his regiment, and the full itinerary of his tour of Yankeedom did the door open. Coincidence had struck again: the owner had had a son in the Old Capitol prison with Benson and was overjoyed to have news of his boy—still bedding down in Washington, he said, with free board from the Federals. At first, the old man had thought Benson was a spy.

The sergeant found a welcoming bed and meal, but stayed only two nights. The following day he set his course south by southwest, angling for the mountains to be out of reach of Union troops in the upper Shenandoah Valley. He stopped two days in Leesburg with a friend, Judge Gray, who gave him a gray coat that could pass for uniform or mufti. On October 23, continuing his back-road odyssey and drawing closer to Confederate lines, he stopped at another house in his path. Night was falling. The owner kindly offered him dinner but said there wasn't a bed to be spared. Benson politely proposed to sleep in the barn. The man, a little too cagily, said the barn was "full."

They eyed each other suspiciously. When the owner finally invited Benson into his parlor, the sharpshooter decided he was too far gone on his journey not to accept the risk. What he found inside was the most pleasant surprise of the journey: sitting before the fire were a half-dozen disheveled military men dressed in various shades of butternut and gray. Not only were they Rebs, he learned later, but they were also part of John Mosby's command, a guerrilla unit notorious through the upper South for its slash-and-burn offensives. Benson had stumbled into a nest of cavalry on the eve of a big raid.

For the parlor-sitters, Benson was an "intruder." He told them the name of his unit. When they realized he didn't know the First South Carolina was stationed in Richmond, he smelled like a deserter. And when he told them he'd escaped from Elmira, they were even more skeptical. "Men don't escape from prison every day," one of them drawled. Then Benson ran through the litany of his northern jails like a string of holiday hotels. It wasn't until he recited the names of some of Mosby's own men at the Old Capitol—Waterhouse, Crowley, and Underwood—that the tension broke. It was as though he'd showed them a daguerreotype of his own cell. They begged for a full account of his exploits, and before he left the next morning they'd taken up a collection of Confederate paper, greenbacks, and a little silver for the foot-sore raconteur from North Augusta. This group was a far cry from the "buttermilk cavalry" that foot soldiers usually disparaged as weak and skittish. Benson later claimed that Mosby himself had been one of his interrogators.

Benson stumbled on until the evening of October 27, when at last he penetrated Confederate lines in the Shenandoah. It had been three weeks since he left Elmira. A skulking stranger on the moonlit back roads of Pennsylvania, he fast became something of a camp celebrity once he arrived on the other side of the front. The Rebs in camp were amazed to hear where this gangly maverick had walked from. To his new-found Confederate mates, Benson gabbed on about his imprisonment and escapes, what was surprising since he regarded himself "a very in-different talker." General Bradley Johnson, local commanding officer, marveled at his exploits and had Benson sleep in his own tent after offering him his saddle for a pillow. Benson dreamt that night of a sweetheart with blue eyes.

He wasn't home yet. Continuing to New Market the next day, "South C'lina" reached the command of General Jubal Early, late instigator of the raid on Washington. Some of the men had the effrontery to jeer Benson, thinking him a straggler from a unit that had fled to the mountains in a recent skirmish. Finding the 12th Georgia Battalion present, the fugitive prisoner sought out an old school friend, Robert "Hood" Hitt. When Hood saw him coming up the path, Benson recalled later, he looked like he'd just seen a ghost. And he had.

"'How are you, Hood?'" he asked, holding out his hand.

Hood stood with his mouth agape.

"'Why, Hood, don't you know me? I'm Berry Benson.'"

"'Well, well, well,'" he sighed. He took Benson's hand and barely shook it.

"'Why, what's the matter, Hood?'"

His boyhood friend looked about as frightened as the wagon driver had, according to the story, when "Buttons" had hopped out of his casket on the way to the Elmira cemetery.

"'Why, man you are dead!'" cried Hood. "'You are dead! You have been dead for months! Your brother and your folks at home know you are dead!'"

The story Hood proceeded to recount was enough to make Benson pale—and then shout for the sheer joy of it. It so happened, Hood told him, that a fellow prisoner and acquaintance at Point Lookout, Michael Duffy, had seen a prisoner's body on the beach the same evening that Benson had flanked out in May. Since he never saw Benson after that, he assumed the body was his. Once exchanged from prison, Duffy duly informed Benson's family that their son had been killed trying to escape from Maryland's western shore. Berry Greenwood was as dead to them as Alexander the Great.

With new urgency, Benson requested a pass to travel by stagecoach to Staunton, where he rode on top with the driver before hopping a train to continue his trek to Richmond. (This time, the fare was paid.) In the Confederate capital, he sent the first telegram of his life: "'Dear Father: I am not dead, but alive and well. Just escaped from prison.'" (The last time he was in such an office, he had been a boy vainly begging his father to buy him a telegraph.) The words would be a wonderful tonic, but that was enough said. As far as Benson was concerned, there was a war on.

Out of combat for five months, he could hardly wait to get back to his unit, now encamped in a war-weary Petersburg withstanding the siege. Just about everyone in the First South Carolina knew Berry Benson's story: present at Fort Sumter; served with distinction at Manassas, Antietam, and Chancellorsville; captured at Spotsylvania on special mission; and killed by Federals trying to escape at Point Lookout. It was indeed a tragic end for one who'd enlisted as a "Minute Man" before his 18th birthday. So as he strode up the path along the Petersburg entrenchments, conversations broke off midsentence. Haggard faces gave way to astonished looks. A few men muttered his name. Sergeant Benson walked through the Confederate camp like Lazarus armed.

His brother Blackwood, from a distance, saw the apparition approaching. He was dumbfounded. His beloved older brother had been taken from him months ago. He had to know if the phantom was real. He ran up and pulled Berry's head down by the hair and began beating him on the back with his fists. Blackwood never said a word except to look up and ask his brother when he'd been exchanged. "Escaped," said Berry proudly, and his brother fell to pummeling him again, as though to prove to himself that the specter was made of flesh and blood.

"That night, when he thought I was asleep," Berry Benson recalled, "I felt my brother's arms steal around me."

The Petersburg trenches were no place for a reunion. As Benson soon learned, his family had, for most of the past five months, believed him dead. And yet somehow they had gotten news, only a few days before his telegram, that he hadn't been killed at Point Lookout after all. He didn't have very long to ponder the mystery of the matter. The next day, the Benson boys were sent off together on a scout. Almost six months of fear, tedium, despair, and anxiety collapsed in a span of hours. It was as though the sergeant from North Augusta had never left the front at all.

Boots and Saddles

Not everyone who left Barracks No. 3 on the lam that fall was a devotee of Longstreet and Lee. It was "intensely dark," Lieutenant Frank Wilkeson recalled of the autumn night he would beat his own hasty retreat from the precincts of Elmira. A ruckus had broken out in the stockade, and a rifle was fired. "I stood in the door of my tent listening to the uproar in the Confederate pen," he wrote, camped outside the barracks with the Fourth Artillery. "I judged that the prisoners were divided into two groups; one standing by the river bank, the other near the gate. Both groups were yelling at the top of their voices." The gathering tempest that Lieutenant Cushing had smothered earlier appeared to be erupting all over again. The guards on the ramparts warned the Rebs to desist. Wilkeson, officer of the guard, had the bugler blow "Boots and Saddles."

The troops came running from their tents. Another rifle fired. Somewhat brashly, Wilkeson had one of his cannons trained on the prison, then ordered a sergeant to fire a blank round on the camp, thus signaling a contingent of troops in downtown Elmira of the riot. He remembered how Cushing had dismissed an earlier mob with a few icy words—if only he were so eloquent. The boy-lieutenant resorted to a show of force instead.

"I saw the flash of his gun," recalled Wilkeson, "heard a shot scream close above my head, and then heard the crash of timber as the shot tore through a barrack, and this was followed by cries of alarm." The warning had its desired effect. "Instantly the uproar ceased. The great prison was as silent as death." Wilkeson felt as though he had won his first skirmish as an officer.

To an impartial observer, he had acted more like a farm boy than a hardened veteran of Cold Harbor. Firing ordnance at unarmed prisoners not overtly engaged in escape was against every regulation in the book—and, if it ever became public, could imperil Union captives in the South. Given the plenitude of Federal guards and their firepower, prisoners were rarely willing to test their mettle. Not only that, but captivity had weakened their ability to rise up and resist. None less than Berry Benson, when he later heard of the incident, wrote Wilkeson off as a fool who had panicked in the presence of what had probably been an unusually emotional prayer meeting.

Lieutenant Cushing rode up after the explosion, his face creased with worry: "'You will be court-martialed, sure,'" he advised Wilkeson grimly. Another officer arrived with a severe reprimand for firing on the prisoners. Wilkeson had pulled the trigger too soon. Worse, he had endangered his own men within the prison walls. Cushing told the second lieutenant to plan a quick escape from Elmira and report back to Battery H—wherever *they* might be.

Wilkeson believed he had done his duty. He couldn't, by his own admission, have been more than 16 at the time, what would have made Benson seem a mature specimen and Anthony Keiley, twice his age, the equivalent of a town elder. It was, if anything, a youthful indiscretion: he had ordered a piece of ordnance fired on a crowd of unarmed but rowdy Rebs. A boy who had experienced the violence of Yankee bounty jumpers firsthand wasn't likely to look on as a helpless Quaker when the passions of a mob wearing gray approached the boiling point.

He had fired swiftly—and a blank round at that. What was held to be a virtue in the field, as he was now to learn, could be considered a blunder in prison. But perhaps he had a point to prove. For in all the greenery of his years, Frank Wilkeson had grown to detest the officer corps he now was a part of, describing them as "shoulder-strapped office-holders" unfit to command men in battle. For three long years, Yankee volunteers had fallen under ignorant orders from the men whose pledge it was to lead them to victory. Wilkeson detested the typical West Point man as a schoolboy soldier who knew everything about the history of war and nothing about its cost. It was as though, once he earned his own commission, he was pledged not to put his own men in jeopardy—even if it meant recklessly endangering others.

Cushing was worried that the 100-day men might arrest Wilkeson for the gaffe—a fitting irony for Elmira. For Washington was willing to suspend humanitarian concerns in managing the camp—cutting rations, overcrowding the men, skimping on medical care, and refusing for months to drain the execrable swamp named Foster's Pond. But let a boy officer lob a single projectile on the camp to quell an uprising in progress, and the wrath of the military gods would be swift. Wilkeson knew he was in a pickle.

The next morning he said goodbye to Elmira in a hurry. Overnight he had gained a telegram, at Cushing's behest, ordering him to report back to Battery H of the Fourth Artillery, which was apparently in Tennessee. In the weeks to come, Wilkeson learned the details of what had transpired the night before. A stone, not a shell, had been fired on the camp. And if it was any comfort to Wilkeson, the suspicion he left under soon dissipated: "I afterwards learned that a few Confederates were wounded by splinters when the stone struck the barrack, and that they never again made night hideous by their yells and howls." When Benson later heard about the incident, he labeled Wilkeson a "crazy fool."

As it was, Lieutenant Wilkeson became one of the first *Yankees* to escape Barracks No. 3, recognizing full well that "the military prison at Elmira was a place to be avoided by men of good taste." But a prison, he was soon to learn, wasn't the only place where the war had herded human beings into a pitiful and pathetic mass. Wilkeson looked for his unit in Nashville, and, failing to find them there, turned to Stevenson, Alabama, still in search of the Fourth. There he found a grisly place that must have seemed half-familiar: a refugee camp for civilians displaced in the guerrilla campaigns along the mountain borders of the South.

Stevenson, he found, was a twisted mirror of Elmira. "I saw hundreds of tall, gaunt, frouzy-headed, snuff-dipping, pipe-smoking, unclean women," the lieutenant marveled later. "Some were clad in homespun stuffs, others in calico, others in bagging. Many of them were unshod. There were hundreds and hundreds of vermin-infested and supremely dirty children in the camp. Some families lived in tents, some in flimsy barracks. All lived in discomfort. All drew rations from the government. All were utterly poor. It seemed that they were too poor to ever again get a start in life." They were even too abject to riot.

The war, he learned, had wrought the same ruin on noncombatants as it had on the miserable gray jackets captured at the Wilderness. Just when Frank Wilkeson thought he had seen the worst that the fratricide could offer, he found a group of creatures even more stricken. The vengeance harbored by some of the Stevenson refugees made the usual mountain feud seem trivial. These, he sensed, were the real prisoners of the war—those who, once released, found nothing but an empty and bitter "freedom" in the ashes of a hard-won peace. Disillusioned even more, he set off again in search of the Fourth Artillery, a trip as lonely, in its own way, as the odyssey of escape forged by Berry Benson.

A Winter's Tale

Lieutenant Wilkeson was rid of Elmira forever. For that matter, so were Keiley and Benson. But thousands of other Rebels continued to live and toil in a plank-walled metropolis locked away from the dim light of winter. By the fall of 1864, the barracks/city would boast almost as many inhabitants as Elmira proper, a bustling burg fully half the size of Philadelphia during the Revolution—until its numbers started to dwindle.

Barracks No. 3 was a city unto itself, a settlement with amenities urban dwellers of the day took for granted. There were broad streets that lined the barracks. There was a marketplace (and a thriving black market). The camp had negotiable currencies and a system of exchange. Myriad social classes, dens of iniquity, a functioning barbershop, and (haphazard) mail delivery all grew up faster than a field of oats. The camp had touts and craftsmen, buyers who bought low and sellers who sold high, policemen and spies, true believers, sneak thieves, and bullies. Worship services and secret societies abounded. Confirmed brutes and brilliant scholars were counted among the ranks, devotees of Beelzebub and Baudelaire.

The camp wasn't so much a real city as it was a town of shadows—teeming, filthy, gray, infected, cramped, and decomposing. The demographics of Barracks No. 3 were sterile, as though a part of the human race had been sequestered for a sordid experiment in seasonal mortality. Aside from the spouses of Union officers, among its residents were no women. There were no births, no marriages, no children, and no families to speak of. Elmira prison was *half* a city, stripped of luxuries (except fricasseed rodent), of high culture (save for a desultory library), of the free circulation of trade and commerce (save for the rutted road to the cemetery), of a living bridge to a world beyond the front gate. It was a city where no one had asked to live in the first place. And a city in which thousands of men would not have the good fortune, when the war finally did end, to leave the environs by virtue of the New York and Erie Railroad.

John Rufus King, for one, would enter and leave Elmira with little fuss. Like so many others, he had entered the limbo of Point Lookout and matriculated in the summer of 1864. Shipped to western New York, he would reside in Barracks No. 3 for almost a year, making Keiley and Benson seem like passing tourists. Being neither an escape artist nor a well-oiled politician, he was doomed to never again see the Confederacy—at least not until the surrender had made it a political relic. King never seemed to have even considered fleeing Elmira. He accepted his fate as one that was his to bear, doing so with the relative cheer of a faithful Confederate. He soldiered on in prison as he had in the field.

King had been captured at Spotsylvania in May 1864. It was only through the intercession of a young boy that he was saved after the battle during a frenzied fit of choler. Days after the battle, walking the decks of a steamer headed for Maryland's western shore as a new prisoner, he beheld something of a miracle in his path. Lying beneath a heap of blankets at his feet was none other than John Keener, the Rebel companion the Yankees had "killed" after his capture at the Bloody Angle only a few days before.

Keener turned out to be as fleshy an apparition as the "ghost" of Berry Benson was. The wounded but garrulous captive regaled King with a tale as old as time—or at least as old as the history of powder and ball—and repeated by many another veteran through the war. "His girl's picture in his side pocket had miraculously saved him," King marveled later. "It was in a case and the bullet that might have penetrated his heart, glanced on the picture and ploughed through the flesh on his breast." The story reminded King "what noble creatures the young girls are," a benign moral given the sweet stamp of mountain chivalry. King himself was as religious as he was romantic. He carried a Bible through the war that his father had given him, his own personal kind of talisman against stray shot and ball.

On May 20, King marched through the prison gate at Point Lookout, where he and a small mess of mates were given the vacant officers' "bull pen." The pen was, in a Yankee kind of way, neatly symmetrical: there were ten rows of tents, each allotted 18 men, and streets about 20 feet wide dividing the rows. King was a member of the prisoners' Tenth Division, which was fortunately situated adjacent the hospital, a place many residents were destined to visit.

Talk of freedom made the rounds. Prisoners were permitted to swim in the bay during daylight, a recreation that pleased King except for being stung by "sea nettles." But the camp gates closed for security at dusk. (As Benson would find to his good fortune, sometimes they closed a little late.) King, however, was more aware of the voluntary exodus from camp than he was by any planned subterfuge. The Yankees, he noted sourly, were recruiting captives to take what they called "the oath of loyalty." If a Johnnie swore fealty to Washington and could provide evidence—proof of desertion or impressment— release from camp was usually forthcoming with the promise they would not take up arms again. Though hundreds of prisoners at Point Lookout would take the proffered carrot, King would only demur that "I am happy to say that your humble servant was not included." Within three days of King's arrival, Berry Benson had come and gone in the gathering dusk.

The grub at Point Lookout, King recalled, was dreadful. Prisoners took two meals—at 8 A.M. and 3 P.M.—each consisting of three ounces of bread, two or three ounces of beef or pork, and vegetable soup. King took the camp contractors for speculators, buying damaged goods and selling them to the government for a profit; even the pickled beef, he thought, was tainted. A mock charge by his company only months before on a field of ripe corn was soon, as he sat daydreaming in his tent, a memory edged in gilt.

On July 4 King and a friend crept into the commissary building and enjoyed a holiday "I will never forget." With a Reb trusty looking on, they set to gorging themselves on food that had been sent by parcel to other prisoners. What made their pilfering less than loathsome was that the intended recipients weren't going to miss the delicacies any time soon. A surplus of provisions—apples, cakes, and soda pop—had gathered in storage in the wake of a high mortality rate—many of the addressees were dead. The veteran of the Upshur Grays referred to the escapade as "flanking," or stealing rations from fellow prisoners, a practice widely detested (though not uncommon) in the prisons. For most men, of course, there was no dishonor in "flanking" the dead. John King ate his fill that day, with a Yankee guard joining the feast.

King dwelled in the purgatory of Point Lookout for two months. On July 27 he embarked on the typical POW tour—Hampton Roads, New York City, and points northwest. Four days of travel by boat and train ensued. His contingent of "thousands" arrived at Elmira on July 30, only three weeks after Keiley debarked. He was placed in a group of men who were assigned a tent—not a barracks—in Ward 39, perhaps not an objectionable fate in the doldrums of a New York summer. The change of venue seemed auspicious. Elmira looked cleaner than Point Lookout, he believed, and the drinking water was far superior. Besides, "There were hills on the east," King remembered, "which kept our minds on the beauty and majesty of nature." He was officially installed as prisoner no. 4403 on the Chemung.

A fine summer brought pestilence in its wake. Foster's Pond, fast becoming the latrine and garbage dump on the prison's south side, was to be the source of more than one epidemic. The rats that frequented the camp were known to drown in the nearby wells. King figured a beaver dam had long ago diverted the course of the Chemung to make the bend in front of the camp. The pond was "not healthful," he realized from the start, but the farther vista of hills was kinder than had been the bleak waves of the Chesapeake, an opinion shared by Keiley. King was all of 22 years old at the start of his sojourn in the North, a Gettysburg veteran who had not yet seen the worst the war could do.

Like hundreds of thousands of other men in 1864, John King was a working authority on military digs. Much of the previous fall he'd spent in a dog tent with two Rebs, snuggling for body heat as temperatures plummeted outside. He had camped near the family burial ground of President James Madison near Montpelier, Virginia, what must have been an inspired bivouac for a young patriot. He built a rickety shanty near Orange Court House, where General Lee wintered before the spring campaign of 1864, and even appeared before a military court and did time in the guardhouse when charged for burning fence rails to keep warm at night. He knew all kinds of habitations. But King had done most of his campaigning in northern Virginia, where winter usually arrived later and departed sooner than it did in its more bitter New York guise.

King's new home, Ward 39, was a hopeful bit of army idiom if there ever was one. The name had more substance in it than a piece of army tent canvas would suggest. The problem was that Elmira was taking in more prisoners than it could adequately shelter. In June, an army inspector had informed Hoffman that 3,000 men could be comfortably quartered at Barracks No. 3. By September, the number of residents had reached 9,000, but the request for additional barracks had been mysteriously tabled. Only in October, by which time the area had been touched with its first snowfall, did Colonel Hoffman relent, issuing the order to build barracks sufficient to house 10,000 prisoners. It was a simple but costly piece of procrastination. By Christmas, 900 men were still living in tents.

The men of Ward 39 had to wait months before moving into their spanking new home on the Chemung. One hundred feet long by about 25 feet wide, the new barrack wasn't finished until almost Christmas, the weather having turned bitter even by the standards of a hill-country Reb. A good man with a hammer, King wasn't overly impressed with the handiwork: the barracks lacked a ceiling; there was no plaster; the bunk bottoms, three tiers to a wall, were hewn from rough plank; and the wooden stoves were inadequate (although these were later replaced with cast-iron coal burners). The Yankees denied the lodgers any bedding for fear it would engender lice, the soldier's constant companion and the frequent cause of "camp itch," the most common of the war's minor ailments. "It mattered little to us for we were already well supplied [with lice]," King quipped. Ward 39 was to be home for about 200 men. Even so, for those who had lived in "gopher holes" the previous winter, Elmira was going to be a step up.

The Yankee larder was distinctly worse than the lodgings. Twice every day, the men were ordered by a "war sergeant"—often a fellow prisoner—to fall out and trot to a large cookhouse where they stood before long tables. The daily special didn't vary much: King recalled they breakfasted in the morning on bread and meat and supped in the evening on soup and bread. To hold the soup ("Four beans to a gallon of water," remembered prisoner Marcus Toney), the men fashioned canteens, buckets, cans, pitchers, and coffee pots. The gruel was dished out to them on the spot, and they had to depart cradling piping hot containers in their hands. "Those who could not carry it with them," recalled King, "did without soup."

It took three hours of efficient ladling to feed a garrison of what was, at its height, almost 10,000 men. The prisoners were fed as though in a factory, a military version of *Oliver Twist*, except the boy orphans had become a gruesome species of men ("old rags and strings and long unkept hair. . . . Our legs were spindling and weak") and the headmaster carried a loaded Colt revolver. (Benson remembered the men being forced to eat beneath two large Union flags that hung on the wall.) The only Yanks who treated them with any sympathy, King believed, were the veterans who had been to the front and knew what it was like to face a day's fighting without a bellyful of food. Rations were skimmed and stolen by men on both sides, a daily struggle for life and death within a stone's throw of civilized Elmira College and city hall. "I was assured by the guard that the same rations were issued to the prisoners as to the U.S. troops stationed there," remembered prisoner Erastus Palmer of Cobb's Legion. "[But] there seemed to me to be some bad leak in it before it got to us."

King recalled the Elmira banquets in humbling detail. The bread ration he measured with his forefinger—five-and-a-half inches long by one-and-a-half inches thick. The meat served was mule, by his reckoning, for the ribs were too round to come from any self-respecting cow. The broth was of slender substance, for "often we could see through the soup to the bottom of the pan." When someone in the ward misbehaved, his companions went on reduced "detailed rations" while the offender served his punishment. "While they were being punished," King complained, "we nearly starved." No doubt they missed the informal Reb meal in the field of wrapping a slab of dough on a ramrod and roasting it over a fire—or the gray jacket's hash of beef, bacon, and biscuit affectionately known as "cush." And yet there were Rebs at Elmira who could remember having gone days in the field with nothing more than dry cornmeal in their rucksack, the prospect of barely adequate government rations that only dwindled over the course of the war.

The burden of such privation grew heavy. "Many men, once strong, would cry for something to eat," King recalled later. "I know from experience." When a package of food arrived from his sister Elizabeth—cakes, dried apples, biscuits, and butter—he was too sick to partake. He gave most of the treasure to his bunk mate Jaco Hale, a brawny member of the Stonewall Brigade who was glad to relieve him of the surplus—and so became his steadfast protector ever after.

POW diets were meager on either side of the Mason–Dixon. Federal policy required that prisoners receive the same amount of food as their captors—an idea commonly ridiculed as "paper rations." The official army meat ration posted by the *Advertiser* in July 1864 was 14 ounces of pork or bacon and 14 ounces of beef per *day*—a helping of wildly optimistic proportion where the prisoners were concerned. Like much in the camps, theory was kinder than fact. The ration of beef at Elmira was reduced by the commandant under the claim that it was "unfit for issue." Prisoner rations were cut and resold to build an emergency "prison fund" for hospital patients or camp "luxuries" like barrack stoves, and, in the case of Elmira, additional barracks—what seemed a sensible accounting tactic to the authorities.

Everyone, living and dead, contributed to the fund. The sutler gave 10 percent of his take. Money and valuables from expired captives were diverted to the pot. Daily rations were skimmed for the proverbial rainy day. Wages paid to prisoners for public works, like laying the sluice pipe to Foster's Pond (a dime per diem), derived from the same source. Thus, the camp was permitted to garner a fictional "surplus" by cutting rations and turning "inside out" the pockets of the deceased. The prison fund was an accounting sleight of hand, a way to shore up inadequate camp infrastructure at the expense of inmates while dignifying the process under the sober imprimatur of "accounts receivable." At war's end, unspent monies in the fund totaled nearly $60,000 and were returned to the federal government. The combined funds from all northern camps at the end of the war totaled nearly $2 million.

Most men arrived hungry—and stayed so. At Elmira, they scoured the grounds for culinary delicacies. "The prisoners ate every rat they could find and it is well for the rat I didn't find any," King himself admitted, who never forgot that "they smelt very good while frying." J. B. Stamp remembered seeing an apple core trampled in the mud before being rescued by a prisoner and devoured, while Keiley recalled seeing prisoners beg for refuse from the kitchen bonecart. Still others wrote of prisoners who rifled the night-stool refuse from the hospital, sometimes coated in excrement, and washing it off before imbibing.

Rations could always be supplemented through the sutler, but price gouging was common. Although King complained of prison inflation, he was fortunate to have anything to spend at all. His family, in West Virginia, was in territory occupied by the Federals, so they could send him money through the U.S. mails, an alternative that didn't always exist for other men.

As atrocity stories about POWs in the South escalated in 1864 (newspapers fanned the hysteria), Washington retaliated by cutting rations 20 percent. After August, prisoners in the North received two meals a day, totaling a few ounces of meat (or fat), soup, a loaf of bread, infrequent portions of beans and potatoes, and a very little coffee—much the regimen King remembered. "I myself often watched for the bones, after the meat had been eaten off," he wrote. "I got up many times in my bunk with a bone and after gnawing the soft ends, sucked at the bone for hours at a time."

Some Rebs later attested to being well fed at Elmira, a fact not hard to explain. Prisoners who worked in camp typically were given *double* rations and per diem pay. Anthony Keiley, for example, was amply fed for performing clerical duties. Ward sergeants, cooks, and laborers were similarly rewarded. But in a city of almost 10,000 men, such jobs barely amounted to 400 at any given time. For yeoman soldiers like John Rufus King, either not fortunate enough to find work nor flexible enough to accept it, the result was serious malnutrition. J. C. Rutherford of the 52nd Virginia Infantry spoke for many when he observed, "The food as a general thing was very good, but not enough of it. There was just enough to make us hungry."

As winter approached, the executive command of Barracks No. 3 changed hands. Major Colt, the camp commandant who had been in charge since the first prisoners arrived in July, was relieved of duties in early December and succeeded by Lieutenant Colonel Stephen Moore. Colonel Benjamin Tracy of the 127th U.S. Colored Troops had replaced Seth Eastman as depot commander of Elmira in September. Tracy's dilatory response in pressing for additional prisoner barracks and a cleanup of the pond made him complicit with Washington in the festering sore that was Barracks No. 3. Neither Moore nor Tracy (who would become secretary of the navy in the Benjamin Harrison administration), whatever their intentions, was able to appease the death rate of the coming winter.

The cold, beginning in October, had turned glacial by December. Of course, northern winters were anathema to men from the Deep South, many of whom had never experienced a run of subfreezing weather. Elmira, as King wrote, was "an excellent place for [prisoners] to find their graves in the winter," an opinion that the mortality tables bore out. True, some gray jackets were already used to going weeks on end without a change of clothes. But King couldn't figure out why the well-provisioned North didn't provide for them better. "The pants I had when arriving at Elmira were in such a bad condition that for a long time I wore nothing but my underwear," he wrote, having to patch up his pants as winter approached. When his shoes wore out, he wrapped his feet in rags, and not until February, by then stricken with a case of frostbite, was he issued a new pair of boots. (A shipment of Confederate cotton that winter was intended to supply northern prisoners with clothing, but the first delivery didn't arrive at Elmira until late February.) He compared his bandy legs to those of a turkey gobbler's.

Severe strictures were placed on clothing sent to "healthy" prisoners from the outside, another concession to the "Remember Andersonville" crowd. Any clothing in blue was forbidden. The government did issue some overcoats: the tail on one side hung almost a foot longer than the other, a giveaway if the owner should ever try to escape. King was one of the lucky ones so adorned. "Should we have been out in the world in such costume, one might have mistaken us for scarecrows eloping from the neighboring cornfield." But the ungainly uniforms helped get them through the winter. King's shared bunk had two blankets—a luxury always in danger of being stolen by an unscrupulous neighbor.

Before long, camp conditions rendered King a ghost of himself. Confined to a field hospital once with constipation before his capture, he wasn't prepared for the inferno at Elmira. He had already caught a bad cold on the way to New York, an event he claimed had lowered his high-pitched voice a register or two. He did a month in prison hospital with "stubborn diarrhea," a condition he imputed to eating tainted crackers. It was a common ailment on both sides—prisons and military camps—particularly early in the war. (Rebel mortality for dysentery and diarrhea was 10 percent in the field.) He estimated that "thousands" of Rebs were so stricken at Elmira, and the unlucky ones "died rapidly, despondent, homesick, hungry, and wretched." The official weekly inspection reports of the camp barely mention the affliction, perhaps an acknowledgment that it was as common as grass. In some ways, Elmira wasn't so much an abomination as an extreme exaggeration of wartime conditions. After all, the average soldier in Rebel ranks was doomed to be wounded or sick a half-dozen times during the war.

King suffered as well from vitamin-deficiency blindness, commonly called "gravel." Unable to see at night, he needed a guide to direct him home if darkness fell when he was away from Ward 39. Before long he could add scurvy to his list of ailments, too, his mouth and gums "so spongy and sore that portions could be removed with the fingers. Others were afflicted in their limbs, the flesh became spotted and the pains were almost unbearable."

Caused by vitamin C deficiency, scurvy, a by-product of malnutrition, produced myriad symptoms. The body weakened and tired. The gums rotted, and the breath turned foul. In some men, saliva dried up and their hair fell out. The joints swelled and ached. Wounds wouldn't properly heal. Patches of skin turned reddish-brown, caused by hemorrhaging through the capillaries. Unlike pneumonia victims, the afflicted didn't cough; unlike malaria, there were no sweats. Those stricken with the disease didn't typically feel sick, except that they were being worn down from within and suffered from general lassitude, making the bearer more susceptible to other disease. So few doctors had actually seen scurvy before the war that it was difficult to diagnose. Union authorities prescribed "desiccated," or dried, potatoes as an antiscorbutic in camps and prisons, but the drying process only robbed the spuds of nutrients.

Forty men in the ward were also afflicted with smallpox. King, who was vaccinated as a boy, avoided the epidemic that raged through the winter, fortunately immune to the most feared of the camp diseases. Vaccinations, given in camp, were often infected with bacteria and resulted in huge open sores on the arms of those treated. Through ailments seen and unseen, winter's harvest spread. In December alone, 269 prisoners perished. The coffins were being piled as high on the cemetery shuttle as the food on the commissary wagons that rolled through the front gate.

Marcus B. Toney of the 44th Virginia reached Elmira on or about August 2. He was registered as prisoner no. 4621. Like Keiley, he would work for his captors and grow slightly well fed for his trouble. Quartered first in a tent that had to be struck for inspection daily, he was appointed sergeant of Ward 36; his duty was to call roll, report on the sick, and distribute rations. He was particularly good at the latter, managing to squeeze extra food in his requisitions until, by his own account, he weighed a robust 180 pounds. But Toney resisted leaving Elmira on anything but his own terms, considering his Confederate oath, as King did, a sacred pledge. His fate, in fact, was strangely tied to King's: both men had been captured on May 12 at the Bloody Angle, both entered Point Lookout on or about May 18, and both arrived at Elmira during the same week.

For a prisoner who had apprenticed at Point Lookout, Elmira could not have been a complete shock. Toney had spent five weeks in the Maryland camp without a change of clothing, washing his only garments in the Chesapeake Bay and sun-drying them on the sand while he stood up to his chin in saltwater to avoid sunburn. He did eventually find a way to improve his lot. Having saved two days' worth of food rations, he sold them to a fellow prisoner for five cents and bought a stamp and two sheets of paper. Writing with urgency to a friend in Baltimore (the dispatch stamped "Prisoner's letter, examined and approved"), he received a parcel stuffed with clothing and a 10-pound gift of smoking tobacco, a treasured commodity in camp.

The man who had left good pieces of land behind him in Tennessee and Virginia wasn't very enamored of Maryland's western shore. Camp life ranged from dull to dangerous. Toney told of two prisoners being shot one day, their offense being a rush to glean the latest gossip from a returning work detail. The two Rebs, it turned out, had inadvertently pushed over the "deadline," a no-man's-land several feet short of the stockade, and were wounded by a sharp-shooting sentry. With orders to extinguish all lights by 9 P.M. and trigger-happy guards liable to shoot at the smallest noise, "Point Lookout, with its army of ten thousand men," Toney described of the night hours, "was nearly as quiet as a cemetery."

Even had the captives been freed by some miracle, many couldn't have gotten far after dusk. Like King at Elmira, scores of the prisoners suffered from night blindness, a condition attributed by the camp doctor, wrote Toney, to the "sun's heat and reflection from the water, the sand, and the white tents." No doubt the prison diet of salt pork, soup, hardtack, and occasional binges of fresh meat, a regimen notably deficient in vitamin A, was even more responsible. Scurvy was a common malady there, too, as prominent as it would have been a century before among British mariners drawing the borders of empire—or even among vegetable-starved Confederate troops in the field.

Bad as Point Lookout was, Toney didn't evince any strong desire to leave it for another camp. Like many, he may have preferred the known nightmare to the unknown. But the arrival of new prisoners from Lee's army soon meant that some camp veterans would be transferred. With about 1,000 other prisoners, Toney boarded an overloaded transport on July 30, which slowly steamed northward. In Jersey City, the Rebs were tightly packed into railroad cars where "the car windows were small, and there was no chance to get out," Toney recalled. "While en route we were not allowed to speak to any one at the various stations at which we stopped."

On August 2, they debarked at Elmira. Toney's first impressions, as he emerged from the boxcar into the streets of the humming city, were favorable. The Chemung River was "a beautiful, clear, limpid mountain stream," he gushed, and the men were "comfortably quartered in tents." The stockade, he noticed, was more imposing and better anchored than Point Lookout's—and he knew why. In Maryland, the Chesapeake Bay had been a formidable barrier to escape. At Elmira, more careful precautions would be required, as Benson and his gang of gophers would prove.

The barrack for Toney's Ward 36 was built in the early fall, well before King's. Ranged in rows, the bunks lined the length of the building. Two men were assigned each bunk and issued two blankets apiece, Toney remembered. When the weather turned cold, four men typically slept to a bunk: "Two of them slept with their heads toward the east, and two with heads toward the west, and of course had to be on their sides, and when ready to change positions one would call out, 'All turn to the right'; and the next call would be 'All turn to the left'; The turns had to be made as stated, or there would be collisions." Like much in the camps, it was only a regimented reflection of war's routine. It was common practice in cold weather for soldiers in the field to sleep in a tight row, front to back, and collectively turn in unison, a movement known by veterans as "spooning." With doors and windows closed in winter, the barracks were as dark as caves.

The typical barrack had two stoves. John King's ward had a deadline "nailed to the floor

three feet in circumference" around each of
them, presumably to keep a few toughs from
hogging all the warmth. When a guard saw anyone cross over that line, wrote King, he "would
become enraged and would run cursing, striking
right and left through the crowd, little caring
who received the blow or what he did." "With
an open building," added Toney of his own barracks, "the heat was not very intense." Following
in the steps of the resourceful Keiley, Toney
"bought" another stove for Ward 36 and had it
installed in his personal room, which measured
about 8 by 10 feet and was at the front of the
barrack, a reward for doing business with the
commandant.

Suffering from spinal pain and chills in late
January, Toney suddenly seemed to go on mental leave. He was, a friend later told him, "delirious for two days, and climbing up and down the
bunk." He couldn't believe it when he was diag-
nosed with smallpox, defiantly showing the Yankee sawbones a vaccination scar. On January 25,
however, he was admitted to the smallpox hospital, a series of A-tents across the frozen pond on
the camp's nether side.

Toney moved into a tent with two other men,
going to great pains to choose the least-afflicted
bunk mates he could find. His two comrades
turned out to have no appetite at all, giving
Toney the benefit of their rations. But the cold
tea and bread were hardly enough for even one
man. It had come to this for the good Methodist

of Edgefield, a man raised with affection by his black nanny, the owner of slaves and a fair stretch of land in Dixie—dying on a small cot, forgotten in a field of ice none of his people would ever see, much less imagine, from their faraway farm in the beautiful poplar forests near Nashville. When he awoke in the morning, Toney could see none of his colored folks standing outside in the snow to fetch him home.

The temperature sunk below zero. "The second night one of our bedfellows died," Toney wrote, "and all the vermin came to us, and we had plenty of company. The vermin will leave a body as soon as it gets cold." The eight blankets the three had been sharing could now be split among two, but it was cold comfort with only a piece of canvas for an exterior wall. The lack of substantial shelter hardly seemed a major problem to the authorities, since "bad air" was considered a cause of disease, and ventilation in the hospitals was encouraged. Typically the smallpox corpses were hauled in front of the tents and left there until the burial detail arrived, but usually not before the bodies had frozen in an array of grotesque poses, like the sculptures of a winter carnival gone bad.

Toney was no "hospital rat." He wanted out of his miserable tent before he was allowed to find his own chilly grave. Four days later, he was released from the smallpox "hospital," the official euphemism accorded the tent city across the water. Apparently he showed signs of recovery, though he hadn't seen a doctor the whole time. After the Yankees burned his gray togs and replaced them with a blue suit, a sergeant briskly cut the tails of the coat so he couldn't pass for a Union man. Since the fever had affected his eyesight, he purchased a pair of green-tinted spectacles from the sutler. When he walked back into barracks on January 29, the men of Ward 36 didn't even recognize him. Most figured his trip across the pond was the Elmira equivalent of crossing the bar. Marcus Toney had come back from the smallpox dressed like a Yankee.

Life in Prison

During the fall and winter, Toney got to know the camp from end to end during his spare hours—which was almost all the time. He could expound on the economics of Barracks No. 3 like the author of a learned treatise: "As there was very little currency in prison, tobacco, rats, pickles, pork, and light bread were mediums of exchange. Five chews of tobacco would buy a rat, a rat would buy five chews of tobacco." The currency wasn't only negotiable, it appears, but recyclable. "I have seen men go hungry a day and save their rations and trade them for tobacco," he remembered. "I have seen a prisoner discharge a quid of tobacco from his mouth and another one pick it up, dry, and smoke it." Five chews of tobacco, valued in the camp at about a dollar a pound, also bought a shave.

James Marion Howard, a God-fearing Christian of the 12th Alabama, was a good example of the entrepreneurial spirit Toney knew. Howard cut a deal with a carpenter from Elmira who would buy a plug of tobacco for ten cents in town and sell it to him on the sly for twelve and a half. Howard would then retail the plugs on his own, underselling the hated sutler, who was asking fifteen cents. Some days he cleared as much as a half dollar, with which he could buy extra rations from one of the mess waiters—an infraction of the rules that once cost him several days on bread and water in the guardhouse. Howard later volunteered for the graveyard detail, during which time he typically sold rings and watch chains to curious civilians, and earned five cents a day and three meals for his labors. He had $64 in his pocket when he was discharged at war's end.

Dissatisfied with the sutler's prices, men frequently traded rations for tobacco or money and swapped them again. (Crackers or tobacco bought a cup of hot coffee near the pond.) Prisoners weren't permitted to receive money from the outside, presumably to reduce the chances for bribery. Money posted them from the world beyond was confiscated and credited to their account by prison clerks like Keiley, negotiable in the form of sutler purchases. Thus there turned out to be a hefty business in forged receipts redeemable by the sutler, as Joe Womack discovered while experimenting in the handwriting trade.

The camp bustled with underground activity. A black market grew up around prisoner-made crafts, prized exports of Barracks No. 3. Rings made of gutta-percha, from Yankee soldiers' buttons, were a bustling cottage industry if one didn't take the phrase too literally. Using a cut cracker box with a needle for a drill, they fashioned a flywheel that would move the drill up and down. The guards smuggled in small pieces of silver for ring-fittings, and the prisoners hammered them out and joined them to the gutta-percha in the shape of two hearts or two hands joined. (King remembered toothpicks made of bone, a parasol of white pine, and even "a rude engine"; Benson recalled a fiddle of white pine for sale near the guardhouse.) The guards smuggled the finished rings into town and sold them easily, probably under guise of a charity. They apparently split the proceeds with the craftsmen, a working trust that Toney says was rarely broken—a point that Keiley disputed. Captain John Kidder of the 121st New York Volunteers claimed to have made $200 in the ring trade his first three weeks in camp and later averred that his moonlighting helped him double his military income.

For those who preferred to work in another medium, there were necklaces or watch fobs made of horsehair. Prisoners worked with pine splinters for their needles, the ambitious ones sewing the hair almost like a crocheting maid on a front-porch swing. But the market for raw materials was unsteady. At first the men stealthily cut bunches of hair from any equine mane or tail within reach, especially on the supply wagons, until "finally the horses were about to lose their hair appendages," wrote Toney, "and a guard was sent with each wagon."

There was free movement inside Barracks No. 3 until dusk—provided one stayed several feet short of the stockade wall. The men had preaching every Sunday and regular prayer meetings, some of which got rather boisterous, as Wilkeson may have discovered. Otherwise, they were left to their own devices, which for some men were more war-worthy than others.

The rest of the world was beyond reach. Keiley could only remember a few familial visits permitted prisoners during his months at Elmira. Entrance to the camp was so strictly controlled that reporters from the *Advertiser* didn't have access until after the surrender. Any civilian entering Barracks No. 3 had to swear his loyalty to the Union, what would have made impossible a visit from most friends and relatives of the captives. The most direct contact the Rebs had with the outside world were the paying spectators who watched them from the observatories—and those who, not wanting to pay the price of an elevated view, watched the Johnnies from the knotholes and cracks in the plank stockade. Benson, for one, wasn't averse to seeing women in the towers, noting it was the only chance the men had to see the fairer sex.

As Keiley had learned, the mind, if not diverted, could turn on itself with a vengeance in confinement. "Melancholia" (depression) was common, especially the variant known to strike the young soldier in the field—"nostalgia," or homesickness. No one, as contemporary medical thinking had it, was immune from nostalgia in the camps, neither young men with excitable sexual imaginations nor married men forced to depart from their families. Coming to grips with prolonged confinement, the body began to falter. The heartbeat slowed. Appetite waned. Within days, conversation wandered. Anxiety, accompanied by insomnia, set in. Many were those who, no longer able to get out of bed in the morning, finally came to the point when they no longer got up at all, by which time they were only a step removed from the cemetery at Woodlawn.

There was a class of men in the camps, known by some Rebs as "drones," who did little but sit and lay about, refusing to join the craft industry, the prayer meetings, and almost everything but meals. Many a man who had probably not been out of his home county before the war now had to endure the privation of not seeing his home and family for months, even years. As a group, they had watched as friends and comrades had disappeared, lost a leg or arm to the surgeon's saw, or bled to death in the trenches. And many were those without families who brooded that sweethearts long absent would marry civilians before the war had even ended. Their prospects looked dim, and the winter gloom that descended over the barracks enveloped the drones like an endless and suffocating mist.

They were not completely alone. Letters poured in and out of Barracks No. 3 by the thousands every day. Prisoners were permitted "to write and receive letters not exceeding one page of common letter paper, provided the matter is strictly of a private nature," the regulations read. Like their fellows in the field, many frugally responded in the same envelope they received from home. But news of the war, much less of the prison, was contraband and thus censored. Many an envelope arrived home with only a few lines and a signature, a bitter disappointment for anxious loved ones. ("The people at home never knew how we suffered in prison," wrote King of the censor.) At Camp Morton, Indianapolis, the growing volume of sweetheart mail encouraged authorities to restrict letters to family only. Prison correspondents at Camp Douglas took to flying kites above Chicago in a novel attempt at air mail in the Victorian Age, an enterprising way to escape the censor's knife.

In some ways, Elmira was a poorly appointed pen. *The Vidette*, a prisoner newspaper at Camp Douglas in Chicago, advertised novelties ranging from tobacco pipes and medicinal remedies to in-camp variety shows. A photo studio there permitted inmates to send their portraits to worried relatives at home. The Prisoners' Masonic Association was quartered in its own barrack and given a Yankee Mason for a guard. There were hospital flush toilets, a sewer system connected to Lake Michigan, a circulating library, a garrison police force, and a fire department (five engines) as large as Chicago's. Prisoners fashioned violins, guitars, and banjos from discarded scraps, and in 1863 black inmates staged a minstrel show (admission: twenty-five cents) but had to change locale due to a crushing run on seats. Though alcohol was forbidden, other vices flourished. One prisoner was said to have made $10,000 (federal) dealing faro to comrades who had somehow amassed a disposable income.

But prisons were prisons. Whatever diversions they may have enjoyed in some places, the men were confined to barracks at nightfall, and lights and talking were forbidden by 8 or 9 P.M. At Douglas, a lit candle (a common tunneling tool) would draw a sentry's gunfire at night. Three or more prisoners congregating on the streets might be subject to disciplinary action. Men going to the latrines at Douglas in the dark could neither veer from their path nor wear any clothing—or they had to face the consequences. One inmate was killed by a guard for urinating in the street.

Woe be it to anyone who committed a major offense like insubordination or, far worse, attempted escape. Offenders might be hung by their thumbs, an experience so excruciating many would faint or vomit within minutes. Others were made to clamber aboard the "mule," a piece of sharpened wood on legs that wrongdoers "rode" for hours at a time, sometimes with weights tied to their ankles. They were whipped with belt buckles, forced to sit bare-bottomed in the snow, and gagged with a baton of wood that could split a mouth at the corners. The chosen few were given solitary confinement on bread and water—the fate that Wash Traweek endured and that Joe Womack would have faced had his forgery been discovered—cramped in small holes or sweatboxes and clamped to a ball and chain. Gone were the days when being a prisoner of war in Lee's winter camp in northern Virginia meant being taken in a mock snowball battle by fellow Rebs and given a friendly shove.

There were other, more public humiliations. Misdemeanor offenders might be dressed in the "barrel shirt," a whiskey or flour barrel punched out at one end with a hole drilled in the other side for the head. The barrel was posted with a sign announcing the transgression ("I Am a Thief"), and the guilty began his painful promenade along the barrack streets. Nor was it always a badge of honor among the prisoners to be so acknowledged. Toney noted that "a prisoner carrying a barrel shirt, 'I stole my messmate's rations' was hissed all around the camp." A scarlet letter would hardly have been more damning.

Yet certain "crimes" were eminently respectable. Some prisoners preferred to steal from the Yankees than be given their rations outright. (Benson was proud of having filched a stack of wood from an unsuspecting guard.) The officer in the camp bakery complained to authorities one day that his prize lapdog, worth over $100 (federal), had disappeared. Elmira prison, of course, wasn't a good place to bring a dog in the first place. The home of 10,000 hungry men, the barracks must have inspired consuming visions of "protein on the paw." The Union authorities, however, couldn't tolerate such insolence. The dognappers were discovered, though empty-handed, and "as the prisoners had nothing to pay with," Toney remembered, "they were treated to the barrel-shirt." The culprits were hardly jeered. "The ones who carried the placard 'Dog Eater,' had the sympathies of the entire camp," Toney explained, "because many of them would have enjoyed a piece of the fresh meat. When twitted about it, they said: 'It was not a common cur, but a Spitz, and tasted like mutton.'"

Toney remembered being thrown in the guardhouse for tossing a pail of water in the street—fortunately, he appealed to Major Colt, who bailed him out. And even modest John King became an adept of the barrel walk. Defying regulations one day, he crossed a restricted work area and was arrested. His punishment: to saunter back and forth across the compound in a "barrel shirt." He took a turn or two of the grounds, after which, on the advice of a Yankee guard, he applied for a temporary job sawing wood, and "the old measly pork barrel and I parted company forever." Still in jail after a week, King was finally released by the commandant for lack of charges. It wasn't often, in fact, that he agreed to use his trade skills in camp. The Yankees once approached him with an offer of a carpenter's job: "Our wages would have been 5 and 10 cents per day according to our capabilities; [but] this didn't tempt me." His warders, King suspected, only wanted him to hammer together coffins.

Yankee justice could be vicious, but its principles were hardly novel to the men in gray. The ball and chain, barrel shirt, buck and gag, mule, solitary confinement, and hard labor, not to mention shaving a head, branding an ear or a palm, and hanging by the thumbs, were common court-martial sentences for disciplinary infractions in the South. Even the threat of death by minié ball for crossing the deadline at camps like Point Lookout wasn't a difficult concept for Rebs to grasp: desertion from their own ranks was commonly punished with execution. (At any given time, some tens of thousands of Rebs were on unauthorized leave from their units.) As Frank Wilkeson had found at the ripe old age of 16, his people meted out as harsh a brand of justice to their own kind as to any roughneck enemies they captured. The prison experience was only a more lethal version of the brutal conditions that reigned in the field.

John King was painfully aware that less honorable options remained. Rebel informers—called "razor backs"—earned extra rations for betraying escape attempts or other infractions. Others went so far as to take the oath of loyalty, derisively called "the dog" or "swallowing the eagle" by most Johnnies. In fact, King never forgot the startling sight he found upon his arrival in Elmira. The first Rebs he laid eyes on inside the stockade were 300 soldiers who had taken the oath at Point Lookout—only to be confined to Barracks No. 3 as their just reward. King was proud he hadn't been tricked by the offer of reprieve—and was openly disdainful of those who had. (No doubt he felt guilty at being coerced by General Rosecrans into taking the Union oath early in the war.) He remembered with pride the time he had seen General Lee talking to his regiment at Mine Run, Virginia, in late 1863, a splendid vision of the man who so bravely rallied them, a leader he would not desert even while in prison.

Oath-takers were billeted in separate barracks while their "applications" were processed and given jobs like hospital orderly for their trouble. When requests were approved, they were paroled with the provision that they stay within northern lines. Many were those who, upon taking the oath, agreed to become "galvanized Yankees," enlisting in the army to fight

Indians on the frontier and freeing Union troops for the final, and crucial, assaults on the Army of Northern Virginia. Nearly 6,000 Rebels in the North took this desperate course. But many others remained firm in their allegiance. G. W. D. Porter of the 44th Tennessee Infantry recalled being told he would be used as a hostage in battle if he didn't take the oath—and offered, by way of scorning the threat, to volunteer for the duty.

Contempt for oath-takers was near universal, even among guards. "These fellows looked like they had stolen something and been caught with it," remembered prisoner John Copley regarding the "galvanized" Yanks at Camp Douglas. "The ground had a special attraction for their eyes." Added Toney contemptuously, "We had more respect for the men who stood guard over us." The Rebs didn't ask for help in exacting a little vigilante justice, either. Some oath-takers were beaten up and thrown out of barracks when their true colors were discovered. More of them likely took the oath from hunger pangs than for any love of being what Copley called a "Tory," though the hatred they engendered was no less.

Not every hungry Johnny in a slouch hat was beholden to old Jeff Davis. One Elmira captive, a South Carolina printer, wrote the *Advertiser* to plead his case for parole. He related how he had been unwillingly drafted in the South before he "voluntarily surrendered" on the field, going so

far as to get one of his company-mates at Elmira
to attest to his desertion in writing—a favor the
comrade granted him with the caveat that
"should he ever be returned to the South, he
would certainly be shot." The desertion rate at
Douglas, where galvanized troops were actively
recruited, was 13 percent. At Elmira, over 150
rebels "swallowed the eagle" before Lee's surrender. John King and Marcus Toney never
ceased to be disgusted by the very thought.

The fact was that Barracks No. 3 couldn't run
without Confederate grease. And cooperation
with the enemy took many forms. Some men
earned nominal wages to dig ditches. Others, like
Toney, did administrative work, gaining precious
extra rations and privileges. (It wasn't a coincidence that a man like Keiley put on weight in
prison.) The Confederate "cook-house rats" who
oversaw the mess were still another group in the
shady area between ward and warder, who shifted
for themselves at every turn. J. L. Williams of the
Ninth Alabama Infantry claimed, with an accomplice who worked in the mess, to have flanked
10,000 prisoner rations during his eight months
at Elmira, a number that, even if grossly inflated,
puts the case against the niggardly Union in a
somewhat different light.

The lure of collaboration must have been
great. Although death began as a trickle at
Elmira—"only" 11 men perished in July—it had
become a freshet by midwinter, with February's
toll reaching 426. (The *Advertiser* stopped re-

counting the monthly figures as they began to mount.) One prisoner in ten would never leave the northern camps alive. The odds of surviving, in fact, were no better than they were in the field.

For those who didn't survive the war, the most sensitive ritual of Barracks No. 3 was reserved. It was as if, lacking other activities of normal civic life, the prisoners and their guards observed last rites with a meticulous attention. "When a prisoner died, his name, company, and regiment were written on a slip of paper and pinned on the lapel of his coat," recounted Toney. "If he did not have a coat, it was pinned on his vest: and if the vest was gone, then it was pinned on the shirt."

"The body was removed to a house called the dead house, a building some thirty feet by forty feet." The building had been erected at the western edge of Foster's Pond, as far removed from the barracks as possible. It was a place to be avoided, if only because of the stench it exuded, especially in warmer weather. Guards, in particular, were known to abhor the place. "In this building were a large lot of boxes made out of poplar, not coffin-shaped, but straight boxes that resembled gun boxes, and into the box the body was deposited." The caskets, of course, were knocked together by the inmates. The only Reb who went into the dead-house prone and came out again breathing was, if the common rumor was to be believed, the audacious Sergeant Buttons.

The Yankees handled the dead as deliberately as the shuffling line of Rebs at mess. "On the lid of the box was nailed a headboard," Toney continued. "The inscription was removed from the body, and copied in large letters . . . then placed in a dry mineral water bottle, corked perfectly tight, and placed under the armpit. Each grave was numbered, and an alphabetically arranged book kept in which the names were entered, and opposite the names were the numbers of the graves." The grave diggers even had to chink a hole in the coffins with a pick so as to sink them in the marshy burial ground. As Toney figured, after hearing quite enough of the elaborate ceremony, "The care of the dead was better than that bestowed on the living."

The winter of 1864–1865 was among the worst in memory—in January, the Chemung had ice over a foot thick. Indeed, some prisoners attested later that, under the circumstances, they could not have expected better treatment. Keiley's own supervisor at Elmira, Stephen Hopkins, professed that many Rebels were "better housed, better clothed, better fed, than they had ever been before in their lives." But Hopkins left in the early fall, before the snow and ice came.

For the men who did make it through the cold months, the only thing worse than an Elmira winter was the prospect of a hasty spring. And that was soon upon them with a fury.

CHAPTER 5

Death in the Ranks

THE winter of 1864–1865 would not be forgotten any time soon. The snow, which had started falling before Benson left on the night of October 6, didn't let up for five months. In December, the government issued emergency clothing for 2,000 men—though the garrison comprised four times that many prisoners. By February, the snow on the ground was packed to a depth of several feet. Men were ordered out for roll call, some freezing their feet while tramping their legs to keep warm in the icy morning temperatures. Those afflicted with dysentery would mess their pants while waiting for the frosty ordeal to end.

Slowly the cold receded, but not so the dangers of life in Barracks No. 3. A series of heavy rains in March brought tidings of a terrible spring. On March 16, the Chemung overflowed its banks, inundating the adjacent camp. "The water came into our prison higher and higher, and in a short time the small pox hospital [where Toney had been] across the creek had to be abandoned," John King remembered. "The water increased and in a few hours it reached nearly every house in the prison. The lower bunks were submerged and the second row was threatened. We were surrounded by a wilderness of water."

The south stockade wall washed away, and even the railroad near the river was mangled. Pickets were posted on the terraces above the pond to watch for anyone in trouble—or trying to escape. About 3,000 feet of prison fence was destroyed. For once, the rest of the world was open to Barracks No. 3. Perhaps an enterprising soul like Berry Benson would have tried to swim to freedom, but it was hard to be enterprising when you were cold and sick and counting the hours until the next call to mess. In the entire course of the adventure, only one prisoner seems to have even tried to abscond, an aide to Colonel Moore who was grabbed before he could get far on the aptly named north border of the camp, Water Street.

For days the men "roosted" in the upper bunks in their barracks, having only the brackish water of the Chemung to drink. King and his mates watched with grim amusement as the Yanks rowed into the barracks to deliver them food. The sick had to be transferred from the hospitals, on low ground, and it was all they could do to keep from falling in the water. King saw one prisoner leave the hospital who fell into the drink while boarding a boat and was shortly

222

pulled out—alive, for the time being. Down-stream, people were warned to be careful about what they fished out of the river, given that the smallpox hospital had been washed away in the freshet. Rumors drifted out that Confederate coffins had floated away in the Chemung, a grisly tale that the *Advertiser* did its best to quash.

Within a few days, the waters started to subside. The camp had been splotched with a thick residue of mud. "As soon as we could with safety we waded out to the highest pump in the prison, which was near the deadhouse, to get some water," King wrote. The dead-house, on higher ground, had remained above the soaking for the most part. "On my way to the pump I noticed several old blankets near my feet. Looking closer I discovered a number of dead men concealed under them. The high water had prevented the people from taking them to the graveyard."

Though Noah had foresight, he had nothing on the Yankees in the alacrity of their response to the flood. "The walls were rebuilt and in a week or so our old prison was in its natural condition," King noted, with a twinge of regret. It was only a few days after the flood that he would be forced to perform the barrel walk for a minor dereliction. But the spring was to have more, and greater, tragedies in store for many of Elmira's residents, old and new.

On April 9, the inevitable happened: General Lee went to parley with General Grant at

Appomattox Court House. The news of the meeting couldn't have been shocking, given the steady train of Rebel defeats the camp commandant was only too willing to announce through regular bulletins. The Lincoln-loving town celebrated. "There was great rejoicing and ringing bells at Elmira when the news came that Lee had surrendered," wrote King. "After that we received better treatment from the Yankees and were not guarded so closely."

Marcus Toney shared the bittersweet sentiments of his comrades taken at the Bloody Angle. "This is a dark day for us," he wrote in his diary on April 10, "and the officers celebrated by getting drunk." Toney had been born some ten miles from the McLean house at Appomattox Court House where the surrender was signed. The next day the *Advertiser* reported that "the rebel prisoners are rejoicing with the rest over the prospect of peace," a partisan platitude still lined with a modicum of truth. Since Lincoln's reelection, the Confederacy had been doomed. The end of the war was the only sure way most men would be able to exit through the gates of Barracks No. 3 while still breathing. It wouldn't be long before men like Toney and King would be able to go south with their honor.

Five days after the surrender came the second jolt—the assassination of President Lincoln. Feelings among prisoners ranged from shock to depression to fear of the future to morbid guilt—and, not last, to grim satisfaction. Most of them, after all, had supported George McClellan in the election of 1864. And men who had witnessed wanton carnage on the battlefield might be assumed to be somewhat inured to isolated acts of criminal violence. But this was the first assassination of a sitting American president. It was believed that an Elmira prisoner who had taken the loyalty oath just before John Wilkes Booth struck was the last man to have the name of Abraham Lincoln affixed to his pardon. Colonel Benjamin Tracy, Elmira depot commander, was said by the *Advertiser* to have had the document "framed as a sacred souvenir," signed as it was the day before the president's death. The president's body passed through Elmira a week later on its trek to Illinois.

Hatred of Lincoln, deep-seated through the South, was well nourished in Barracks No. 3. One day a Reb in the yard had the foolishness to yell out that "'old Abe ought to have been killed long ago!'" It was, at that moment, as though someone had leveled a curse on the entire camp. In the tension that ensued, any of the prisoners might have seemed, to a grieving, gun-toting guard on the wall, the kith and kin of John Wilkes Booth or Mary Surratt. Many prisoners, although no friends of Lincoln, had to despise the man for his recklessness. The courage of those who had survived the camp, men like King and Toney, might have all been in vain for such an ill-timed remark. "I believe the artillery would have been turned on us, but for the guards who were stationed throughout the camp," Toney recalled. The guards rushed the offender to headquarters, where he was ordered to be hung by his thumbs. "No one sympathized with the fellow tied up," Toney explained, "because he jeopardized so many lives."

Although a die-hard disciple of the Cause, Toney took Lincoln's loss hard, or at least he later claimed to. With Old Abe in office, he conceded years later, "I do not believe we would have had the five years of carpetbag rule and other troubles incident to the reconstruction policy adopted by the government." Sentiment among the gray jackets at Elmira was subdued. King acknowledged that most prisoners had supported McClellan, but "it was sad to hear the bells tolling in the city when the news came." Even so, he remarked, the Yankees tried to turn the tragedy to their advantage. They circulated a paper among the prisoners saying that those who would sign their names to a statement showing regret for the president's death would be the first to be paroled. But "we did not care to express our sorrow in that way."

The warmer weather brought equal doses of hope and melancholy. "As the spring passed the number in our wards decreased," lamented King. "At roll call there was no answer to nearly a third of the names." Many of these were fatalities wrought by disease and exposure—camp deaths peaked in March at 491, though they dropped to nearly half that (267) in April. But there was another reason for the missing hands: in February, the prisoner exchange had recommenced. Elmira inmates willing to take parole were being shuttled home until, by April, barely 5,000 prisoners remained in camp. There was a growing sentiment, as the armies of the South crumpled, to take the Federal oath of loyalty. In a camp where so few men had escaped, it had become clear that the only way out of Elmira was in the wake of a personal, if not a general, surrender.

Once Lee capitulated, the dam was broken. In May, over 1,000 men were paroled after taking the oath. The week beginning June 13, by which time all Confederate armies in the field had surrendered, nearly 2,000 more followed. The process of repatriation was slow, braked by the logistics of transportation in an age when the iron horse was the fleetest means of conveyance. And hundreds of men at Elmira were simply too sick to travel in the spring. Men like King and Toney had bided their time, faithful until the end, soon to understand that home was just a short journey away.

Visitors

What was left to see as Barracks No. 3 emptied out? The prison had been closed to public visitation during the war. And any outsider admitted in an official capacity seems to have agreed to examine the barracks with one eye closed.

Commissary-General Hoffman, visiting in July 1864, was reported by the *Advertiser* to be "highly pleased with the accommodations and arrangements which have been devised for [the prisoners'] comfort." The *New York Post*, permitted a peek at the camp in August, offered that "the treatment of the rebels is exceedingly humane and liberal," noting that the wealthier among them "dress with taste, and even elegance."

Such sunny assessments were perhaps defensible at the start. But the passage of time did little to shake the official optimism on Elmira. Dorothea Dix, celebrated humanitarian and social reformer (Keiley hated her because she was said to employ only ugly nurses), came for a visit during the late fall, when conditions at the camp were about their worst. Thousands of men were still billeted without barracks, and Foster's Pond, the acre-large cesspool, was only beginning to have circulating water. Just a few weeks before her visit, Surgeon E. F. Sanger had reported, while discussing the dire state of camp medicine, that "at this rate the entire command will be admitted to hospital in less than a year and 36 per cent die."

Dix's visit was a smashing success. She reported on November 25 that the Rebels were "receiving all necessary care, and provision fully adequate to all necessities." She seems to have believed that there were "but few cases" of serious illness and that the mortality rate was "low."

(Two hundred and seven prisoners died in November, a number far exceeding the figure for any other northern prison but Camp Douglas.) Added the *Advertiser* of her sojourn, "Her only wish seemed to be that our prisoners in the South should be as well provided for as those at Elmira now are."

There seems to have been a conspiracy about Elmira in which an official catechism spread from the weekly army inspectors and newspaper correspondents to humanitarian reformers and Washington brass. The weekly reports reveal less about camp conditions than they do about the prerogatives of military bureaucracy. On November 13, Captain William Jordan reported so many "good" ratings for camp conditions that one might have been reading an advertisement for an upscale sanatorium. On December 11, another inspector gushed that "the prisoners are now well clothed, having all that is requisite for their comfort, except a few pairs of pants." The *Danville* (Va.) *Advertiser* reported in March that "they who visit them are universal in expressing their opinion that they are too well kept."

Some of the reports were troubling. Captain Bennett Munger, one of Washington Traweek's teachers before the war and a favorite Union officer of many prisoners, commented that prisoner clothing was deficient on August 21. A month later he advised that prisoners inhabiting tents were suffering and that "numbers have died both in quarters and hospital for want of proper food."

Colonel Tracy added with alarm, on October 20, that "the mortality in this camp is so great as to justify, it seems to me, the most rigid investigation as to its cause." (A subsequent investigation recommended the establishment of washing facilities.) On February 12, a frank inspector commented on the "very bad" health of many prisoners, ascribing it, as the administrators of Elmira often did, to circumstances beyond their control: a recent group of sick prisoners from Fort Fisher said to have infected the camp.

And so, when the *Advertiser* staff was permitted to enter through the front gates of Barracks No. 3 on April 24, two weeks after Lee surrendered, they offered a shocking assessment of what was probably the most notorious prisoner of war camp in the North: "The first things that greeted our eyes on passing the gate, were elegant drives, beautiful lawns, handsome walks, tasteful gardens, and all the paraphernalia of cultivation and refinement," the paper cooed. Little did they imagine that much of the work had been hastily done after the cessation of hostilities. When the *Advertiser* declared it "the most beautiful spot in Elmira, or within a hundred miles of Elmira," it was clear that the smear instinct of gutter journalism in the North had found a most reputable alternative.

The last Rebs were stuck in stir, either waiting permission to go home or refusing outright the terms of freedom. Those who had chosen to take the oath before Richmond fell were given priority leave. Departing prisoners were even allowed to shop in downtown Elmira on their way to the railroad depot—a group leaving May 19 was described as "hale and hearty" by the *Advertiser* and said to be thankful for their treatment. A handful of departing prisoners would often stay on in town, restless souls who had no roots in the South and weren't anxious to revisit what was now a defeated and trampled land. Meanwhile, the newspaper groaned, the Rebel dead were buried with more respect at Woodlawn than were the men in blue.

If a buyer couldn't be found, the government announced, the barracks were due to be razed. One day the *Advertiser* lamented that considerable improvements by the prisoners had made the barracks "a small Eden"; the next day, it solemnly declared, "the business of the Prison Camp is at an end." Convalescing prisoners had the duty of cleaning the barracks previous to destruction. On July 17, a "farewell hop" was held by departing officers, a gay affair by all accounts where "tempting viands and luxuries of the season tested the appetite." The next day, Battery A of the Fourth U.S. Artillery, Frank Wilkeson's old unit, pulled out of town.

In August, the *Advertiser* noted that the pesthouse contents were soon to be burned. The dead-house itself was bought by a local entrepreneur, relocated, and used for storage. Officers' houses and some barracks were moved away and turned into private residences; others became barns and garages. The rest of the camp buildings lingered on, however, and were not entirely dismantled until early 1866. By this time, Anthony Keiley had gone back to publishing angry editorials and Berry Benson was accumulating materials for his lifelong memoir. In the years to come, a neighborhood would grow up on the old campsite, filling in the ground where the barracks had stood between Water Street and the river, not about to be a testament to anything but the present.

A Reckoning

"Helmira" became the burial place for nearly 3,000 prisoners. The approximately 2,950 dead comprised 24 percent of the inmates (over 12,000 total), a mortality rate approaching Andersonville's. Camps like Elmira, Alton, and Delaware (and others like Andersonville and Salisbury in the South) were not, as some men may have first expected, a haven from death, but a place where they were perhaps more likely to find their Maker than any other. And that the Confederate graves at Woodlawn were under the supervision of a black man probably didn't endear the prisoners any more to their final resting place.

John Jones was born a slave in 1817 in Leesburg, Virginia, the same town where Berry Benson found refuge on his journey southward in 1864. In 1844, fearing the consequences of what would happen to him when his aging owner died, Jones ran away from Leesburg, armed with a pistol and knife. With several other slaves, he fled on foot in darkness and crossed Maryland and Pennsylvania before reaching Elmira. A 27-year-old Negro without a stitch of education, Jones decided to get some book learning in the North. Save one winter's worth of instruction from a sympathetic ladies' academy, he was denied entrance to local schools.

Through hard work, Jones made himself a solid citizen of Elmira and was appointed sexton of the First Baptist Church in 1847. Within a few years, he had found another, though unofficial, position in town, this one as an agent of the Underground Railroad. For the nine years that Jones was a conductor on the line, over 800 escaped slaves were said to have passed through Elmira, a key station on the route connecting Philadelphia with St. Catharine's, Ontario. It was Jones who convinced the Northern Central Railroad to stow away escapees, the 4 A.M. train out of Elmira being most popular. While helping one group of fugitives from Leesburg, Jones learned in passing that his former master—and his own mother—had died during his long absence.

In 1859 Jones was appointed sexton of newly established Woodlawn Cemetery, north of downtown Elmira. When the Rebel camp opened in 1864 and Colonel Hoffman ordered that the army lease a plot for the Confederate dead, the government offered a grave digger

$40 per month in wages. Jones, as sexton, came to supervise the burials. The government eventually paid him $2.50 apiece—over $7,000 in total, enough to help him buy a house in town and become one of Elmira's most respected citizens after the war. The bottom rail, as many black soldiers had cried out at passing Rebel prisoners throughout the North, was now on top. Even in death, Elmira's revenge on the South had found its mark. A former slave watched as the remains of slavery's defenders were lowered into the earth.

CHAPTER 6

When Johnny Came Marching Home

APPOMATTOX wasn't quite the end of the matter. After Joe Johnston's surrender in North Carolina, the Rebels under Kirby Smith in Louisiana didn't acquiesce until May 26, and Galveston ran up the white flag a week later. It was the second week of June when someone whispered to John King that he was on the list for exchange. A friend, Parnell, told him to be ready to go the next day. With ten cents to his name, King marched to the barracks tailor and asked for dispensation from the usual twenty-five-cent fare for turning a blanket into a pair of trousers. Seeing that King was homeward bound, the tailor agreed. ("I believe Wanamaker would have made a better fit," his customer later judged.) That afternoon a friend gave him a free shave, since young King had determined to look better than at any time since the day he enlisted at Warm Springs two years before.

The next morning, June 14, several hundred prisoners were called out to assemble in the cookhouse. The objective was to have them swallow something more vile than a mouthful of rancid meat: the Yankee oath of allegiance. It was an indignity King was willing to suffer this time, there being no point in being mule-stubborn anymore since everyone in the field had come in. "I will never forget the march from the cookhouse to the big gate," he remembered. "All the prisoners who were left behind congregated near the street as we went out. . . . Many of the poor fellows left behind waved us farewells, for but few ever met again."

Given two days' rations, they were marched out of camp to board a train for Baltimore, but the hungry King had devoured all of his food before they walked through the front gate. While waiting for the train in town, he sold an old U.S.–issue blanket for forty cents and supped on bread and cheese with the proceeds, most of it gone before the transport rolled in. The prisoners were given free rail or boat passage as far as it would take them on the journey home. It was the first sign they had of a reconciliation with the Union.

For a time, King almost forgot who'd won the war. They passed trains loaded with Yankee soldiers headed home in the opposite direction, and "they cheered us as they passed," he remembered brightly. Near Baltimore, a Negro girl threw the prisoners some hot clove onions. In Camden Street Station, King was tearfully gnawing on one when he caught the eye of some local women. Just when he thought they were admiring the cut of his new pants, one of them tenderly remarked how "pitiful" he looked. "I concluded I would eat more onions, as it was comforting for some one to look at me kindly." Traveling with another veteran of Ward 39, Hoy Reger, he took a train to Grafton, West Virginia, the furthest a government ticket would take them, and spent the night there with an uncle.

With Reger at his side, King arrived in his old stomping grounds the next day after dark. They were afraid to stop and ask anyone for help, not sure what local sentiment about the war was like. But King seemed unaccountably shy about his own people: "Timid to approach the [family] house, we slept in a pasture field." The next morning, they kept on walking toward Buckhannon, where Reger took his leave of King for home. The young carpenter crossed the river at Hyer's Mill that evening, and went up to the family house and stood on the porch. There was a shout of recognition when his people saw him. John Rufus King had walked the last 36 miles to the happiest reunion in his life. Two years and one month after enlisting, Johnny had finally come marching home.

The bitterness of the war didn't stick with John King for long, even if it had rent his family. His brother Cyrus, captured at Gettysburg, was released in March 1865 to spend the remainder of the war retired on half pay, overseeing a group of slaves on a plantation in Pittsylvania County, Virginia. Their eldest brother, Joshua James, had fought for the Union. Joshua enlisted with the 17th West Virginia in 1864 and received a bounty of $400, which he later used to buy 100 acres near the Ohio River. "He was a good brother and I liked him," King wrote later, "and I would not have fired at him in the war, if he had appeared arrayed against me in battle."

Unlike Joshua, John King got nothing from the war. His soldiering wages were made next to worthless by inflation. He'd had to surrender two months' pay in Confederate bills just to buy a pocketknife. (The month after he was captured, pay for privates rose from $11 to $18 a month.) It was only by dealing tobacco—which he took pride in never using—that he was able to purchase enough luxuries to get as far as Spotsylvania. And then the Yankees had been good enough to offer him a spell of free room and board on the Chemung.

Within two years of the surrender, King married Mary Ellen Waggy, and they settled down to farm in Lewis County, West Virginia. He spent the last 70 years of his life there. Mary Ellen bore him six children. They raised corn, potatoes, horses, cows, and sheep on their 71-acre farm. At the urging of his wife, John King even became a devout Methodist. The war, after all, had been little but a short eruption in a long and peaceful life. On his way back from Elmira, King had even come partway home over the

Baltimore and Ohio Railroad, and he noticed some of the same red and rusty rails they had torched on a mission early in the war. The sight of the burned rails made him feel almost ashamed, like a vandal.

The days before the war were gone forever. He sat out on the farm on a Sunday afternoon, thinking back to the days in Marion County, West Virginia (formerly Virginia). John King could still remember when windows were pieces of greased paper. When a locked door was nothing but a string tied to a latch from the inside. He recalled when scythes were hand cut, and one sharpened them by first hammering out the edges and whetting them with vinegar. When there were corn huskings where a young man got a kiss if he found a red ear of corn. The time was, before the war came around, when granulated sugar was as unknown as a railroad whistle in Upshur County or as strange as an airtight jar for jellies or a dollar for a day's work.

He was a young man before he ever held a dime or nickel in his hand. He walked barefoot to Sunday school, wearing rolled-up pants and a palm-leaf hat. He used a goose-quill pen and a slate in school while hogs rooted beneath the floorboards. It was a time when the shoemaker made house calls; men wore woolen suits instead of coats, and women gathered up their hair in sunbonnets and carried a dried turkey wing for a fan in summer. Then . . . then he would think of Gettysburg, the memory unbidden, the sight of a dead Yankee, his severed head lying casual as a rock at the side of the road. The memories came and went, some separated by almost a century.

King had no political fevers, though he quietly prided himself on being a lifelong Democrat. He didn't vote in a presidential election until 1872, when he was already 30, being forbidden the vote during the war and denied it again, as a veteran of the South, during Reconstruction. The election of 1872 was his only "lapse," when he cast his ballot for Horace Greeley, the abolitionist that Marcus Toney saw watching the prisoners from the Elmira observatory one day. King's only excuse, he mused later, was that Greeley was running as a Democrat.

Prison had been a torture—it took many years for King's nasty case of frostbite to subside. But there was a comradeship with those men that he treasured. "It brings a sadness to my heart that I can hardly shake off at times," he recalled, in his seventies, of those he had bunked with in Ward 39 and never saw again after boarding the train for Baltimore. Each of the last ten years of his life, he went to nearby Weston to commemorate his fallen comrades and mingle with men who'd worn both the blue and the gray. In 1932, King regaled Union veterans at one reunion with stories of battle and prison life that seemed a world away from what most had heard about the mechanized massacre of the Great War.

He was a patriot to the last. His grandfather Joshua Hedges King was a friend, as a young man, of the aging George Washington. It was John King's boast (for one little given to boasting) that he had held the hand of a man who had gripped the hand of the Father of His Country. It was a reminder that such a link could exist between General Washington, who died in 1799, and John Rufus King, who wouldn't pass away until the Great Depression, the last surviving Confederate veteran in Lewis County. In a handshake was pressed a bond that ran from the cabins of Valley Forge to the Gettysburg fields to the barracks of Elmira to the grim shantytowns of coal country in the Roosevelt years. John King died of a heart condition in 1936, just short of his ninety-fifth birthday. Until the end, he kept the signed parole given to him the day he left Elmira.

Though Marcus Toney was among the last to leave Elmira, it's not that he lacked for opportunities. On April 24, May 24, and again on June 8, he recalled, camp authorities put out a call for prisoners to take the oath of allegiance and put the war behind them. Each time, Toney refused. By summer, the camp had been opened to visitors, and the sale of rings and prisoner-made trinkets was brisk. Toney, a little too vainly, counted himself among a very few holdouts in mid-June who refused to take the pledge (there were still 1,000 by the end of the month). The men asked the commandant what plans he had for the unredeemed souls in his charge: "He said that he would send us to Dry Tortugas to die," reported Toney. As there were stragglers in war, so there were in peace.

The Tortugas, which harbored an island prison in the Gulf of Mexico, seemed a fate worse than Elmira, if such were possible. A missive from a Tennessee friend soon convinced Toney that it was time to go home and find work. His family needed him. Resistance seemed absurd at this point. The holdouts finally subscribed to the ritual of surrender on June 14 (the same day as John King) and "swallowed the eagle" with a collective gulp. They packed what little they had and strode through town, for the first and only time, as free men. Waiting for a train in downtown Elmira, as Keiley and King and thousands of others had done before him, Toney paid a photographer a quarter to take a picture of him and his comrades. He was the only one of the group with a quarter to his name. It would, they figured, be a unique keepsake of their deliverance.

That photograph at Elmira station Toney kept for many decades. "The effect of the prison diet can be seen in the faces of the men," he wrote later. "One has lost his teeth and has his jaw tied up with a rag, another is as pale as a ghost, and several of them are very dark. One poor fellow can be seen on the right with a blanket twisted and thrown around him; he is too weak to stand, and is sitting down." Still another, with a cup dangling from his neck, "is supposed to be on the lookout for buttermilk, coffee, or probably something stronger." They have the grim look of factory workers coming off a shift, of urban toughs posing for a tintype.

Toney's health had come through the war intact. Like Keiley, he had done almost too good a job of surviving: he weighed 180 pounds on release, no doubt thanks to the culinary favors he enjoyed as ward sergeant. Toney took the train to Louisville via Indianapolis, then dropped south to Nashville. His last fifty cents went to a hotel meal before taking the ferry across the Cumberland River to his home ground. There, returned for the first time in years, he unaccountably got lost.

"We found change written upon everything," Toney recalled sadly after seeing the land scarred by the likes of an Old Testament plague. The hardwood forests—poplars, hickory, and walnuts—had disappeared. And so had every salvageable piece of timber therein. "I looked for the old homestead, and there was a piece of house that resembled it; but the weatherboarding had been stripped off for some distance, and not a piece of fence was in sight. The trees my mother planted in 1845, the year before she died, were all gone." On the night he came home, he boarded with friends down the road. Unable to sleep in a real bed after bunking on prison planks for more than a year, he took a quilt and tromped off to the front yard to curl up under an apple tree. "It was nearly a month before I got used to a bed."

There was no sign of the proverbial girl that Toney, as the First Tennessee regimental band played in 1861, "had left behind me." But there was a bigger shock in store. Much to Toney's anger and amazement, he found little mulatto children playing on the front porch of the family home. Where could they have come from? He was told that one of the family slaves had married a white Yankee woman—an act he found intolerable. "Jim and his wife had to vamoose the ranch," he recounted bitterly, a western idiom that didn't hide the very southern nature of its sentiments.

The family farm was in ruin. Toney's days as an aspiring member of the landed gentry were over. He found a position with the Southern Express Company, and later with the New York Central Railroad, but he soured at not being recognized as a man who had stood the field at Chickamauga. As a Confederate veteran, he couldn't vote, and he couldn't buy a piece of government land under the Homestead Act, but all the while he had to pay taxes. The Rebs returned to find that they had much less of a voice in their lives than in 1861. Toney soon took the oath of amnesty, "forgiving" him for his service against the Union—a privilege for which he surrendered $1.25. And it wouldn't be long before a disillusioned yeoman farmer from Edgefield would turn into a confident vigilante.

There seemed to be nothing to talk about but the war. Perhaps for that reason, the first soldier reunions were depressing affairs. Toney's old comrades in the Rock City Guards, Company B, had been buried all over the South. Of the 104 who had marched out to the tunes of a band after Fort Sumter, only 32 had returned by August 1865. Barely half of those would show up that fall to have their picture taken in bow ties and long-tailed coats, a more respectable pose than the scruffy photo Toney had taken at the Elmira depot. Even the formal dress and poses, however, couldn't hide the abject status of returning Johnnies.

Toney joined the Masons and earned his third degree from the society in 1867. But his penchant for secrecy had a darker side. He followed the path of many an ex-soldier when he joined what he called the "auxiliaries of the police," known to posterity as the Ku Klux Klan, whose local chapter frequently met at the Masonic temple. He was defensive about the charge that the Klan was prejudiced: "It was not done especially to intimidate the blacks, but whites as well if guilty of wrongdoing. The blacks who behaved themselves had the best of friends in the Ku Klux Klan." The defiant critic of *Uncle Tom's Cabin* argued that the Klan "only" committed one killing in the area, and that of a persistent northern detective who insisted on snooping around. When the vote was restored to Confederate veterans in Tennessee in 1870, the local chapter was disbanded. Toney naïvely believed the secret society was finished "forever."

Bloody Angle, Devil's Den, the burning Wilderness: even the surrender didn't bring an end to the disasters man could wreak. In late 1868, Toney was returning to Nashville from Cincinnati on the steamer *United States* when, in the middle of a stormy December night, they collided in the darkness with another steamer, the *America*. Thirty barrels of coal oil in the bow of the *United States* suddenly went up in fire. In Toney's words, "Our vessel commenced to burn and sink at the same time."

Toney scrambled through the smoke and confusion, returning to his room to claim his watch and money. He crawled 200 feet along the deck beneath the smothering smoke. "Mothers were calling for husbands and children, husbands shrieking for wife and children. In all my privations in life I have never witnessed such a heart-rending scene, and I was powerless to aid any one." He tried to jump onto the *America* before it pulled away in the confusion, but was prevented by heaps of burning hay.

His battle instincts—at least those that called for full retreat—proved worthy. When the *America* finally pulled clear, Toney leaped from the deck, plummeted a dozen feet into the Ohio River, and began swimming through the icy water for shore. He made landfall as a shivering wreck, clad in nothing but his underwear. He probably would have died of exposure had a flat boatman not carried him on his back and restored him in his own boat to the *America*. One hundred and thirty passengers on the *United States* went down—what would have been a good week's work for the Reaper at Elmira. The strange symbolism of the event may have been lost on him: the *United States* had collided with the *America*, and Toney had survived yet again, having lost nothing more this time than a favorite overcoat.

The war remained a source of pride. Marcus Toney greeted the end of Reconstruction like a bitter Reb: "We had been slaves to our own slaves, and now we were freemen, as the yoke of slavery had been lifted from our necks." His belief in the Cause never wavered. When some Yankee veterans suggested that pensions be paid by the government to their southern comrades-in-arms, Toney, like many others, was revolted by the prospect. "A Southern soldier who deserted his flag and joined the enemy and now receives a pension is getting a premium on perjury," he advised, still as contrarian as the prisoner who sweated through much of the spring of 1865 in an emptying Yankee camp. Not for nothing did his friends call him "Private" Toney.

Toney made at least two pilgrimages to Elmira. In 1901, he visited the graves of "our fallen heroes" at Woodlawn Cemetery and was surprised at how well manicured the site was.

He found only one thing wanting: "With only a narrow path dividing, sleep the boys who wore the blue, and the only difference in the graves were the marble slabs of the blue, where our wooden head boards had all rotted away." In the ensuing years, he assisted in having marble headstones quarried and cut for the boys in gray, which were finally installed in 1907.

Barracks No. 3 had disappeared, made invisible by the buildings of peacetime. Ward 36 had been replaced by the town pumping station, the smallpox hospital had given way to ice sheds, and the cookhouse was now a nursery. Toney visited amiably with Melvin Conklin (now the Elmira postmaster), the Union spy who had discovered many of the camp tunnels and had them destroyed. The visitor was chagrined to learn from Conklin that John Jones, "the old darky," had died a few weeks before. It was as cozy a reception as any ex-slaveholder could have expected in a former depot of the Underground Railroad.

In 1913 Toney came back with an invitation. He wore Confederate gray in presenting a formal address to an audience filled with Union veterans, Masonic adepts, and Sons of the American Revolution, all crammed into seats in the Congregational Park Church. He told a few war stories and spoke rather kindly of the camp. The *Advertiser* commented on the chumminess of the visit: Toney was greeted by a former prisoner who decided, after the war, to settle permanently in town. The old man from Nashville also took up with another old "friend," the custodian of the church who had been in charge, 48 years earlier, of one of the camp observatories on Water Street. Rip Van Winkle seems to have been recognized by just about everyone.

Marcus Toney, husband of Sally Hill Claiborne and father of two daughters, lived longer than most of his fellow veterans. At age 89, he was confined to his Nashville home by an extended illness. On November 1, 1929, three days after the stock market crashed, he died. A longtime employee of the New York Central Railroad, he was never quite able to escape the reach of the Empire State.

The fate of Anthony Keiley was quite another matter. Upon his release from Elmira in late 1864, he had unfinished business to attend to. Keiley was, after all, missing in action from the state legislature. He decamped in Richmond in December to attend the second session of the Virginia statehouse, thus reentering the intellectual scuffles that picked up where the military ones had left off. The following spring, on the heels of General Lee's surrender, he coestablished the *Daily News* of Petersburg, unable to get the proselytizing instinct out of his blood.

His pointed editorials against Secretary of War Edwin Stanton ran afoul of the occupying authorities. In June 1865, he was arrested and incarcerated in Richmond's Castle Thunder, where he passed a mercifully short sentence of three days. By his own account, he was imprisoned "for the crime of calling Clement C. Clay [a Confederate senator from Alabama] a gentleman and refusing that compliment to Major-General David Hunter and his associates on the Military Commission," which was founded to try the conspirators responsible for the assassination of President Lincoln. The *Daily News* was effectively banned from future publication, but Keiley founded another sheet, the *Index*, the day after his release, which felicitously fell on July 4. His travels in Yankee prisons had come to an end.

The diary he kept at Elmira had been more than a gentleman's conceit. Keiley turned it into a book before the war was over, publishing *Prisoner of War* in 1865, but most of the copies burned in a Richmond warehouse during the last days of the conflict. The Elmira *Advertiser* ran extended excerpts from it beginning in July 1865, more a testament to Keiley's luxurious prose than the paper's evenhanded politics. The book was reprinted the next year in New York as *In Vinculis* and proved, like his war wound at Malvern Hill, another valuable credential in the postwar South after the carpetbaggers were finally sent packing. He was no doubt proud that on June 9, 1866, the children of Petersburg put flowers on the graves of fallen Confederate soldiers, thus commemorating the second anniversary of the day the city was saved by Archer's Battalion—the day that Anthony Keiley was ignominiously captured.

In the fall of the year before, 1865, Keiley, 33 years of age, married Rebecca Davis, daughter of a prominent Jewish family in Richmond. They had two sons and a daughter, all of them raised in the Catholic Church, as his mother would have dearly wanted. Keiley continued to sit in the House of Delegates and began consolidating political support, serving on the executive board of the Virginia Historical Society. Five years after returning to a shell-shocked Richmond, the man who said of prison life that it was "certain to make [men] hogs, and very likely to make them devils," was elected the mayor of the former capital of the Confederacy, serving from 1871 until 1876. The memory of the Cause did not wither on his watch: the walls of his mayoral office were adorned with the portraits of Stonewall Jackson and Robert E. Lee.

Public service, as in the classical Roman style, would be Keiley's credo. He fought for relief of the city poor and served as president of the national Irish Catholic Benevolent Union for over a decade. (During the same time, he bitterly resisted the enfranchisement of Negroes.) Following his mayoral tour, Keiley served for ten years as city attorney of Richmond. He never ceased to defend, even rationalize, his headstrong support of the South: in 1879, while addressing a Memorial Day crowd at a Confederate burial ground near Baltimore, he intoned that "not one in twenty of those who lie here, or in any Southern cemetery, owned or ever expected to own a slave," a retreat, if a grudging one, from his strong endorsement of the peculiar institution.

Keiley's ambitions extended far beyond Richmond. Chairman of the Democratic state committee in 1881, his long work for the party came to fruition when the Republicans were ousted from the White House. In 1885, President-Elect Grover Cleveland nominated Keiley as minister plenipotentiary to Italy, an act soon confirmed by the U.S. Senate. But the Italians, it seemed, wanted to have nothing to do with the spirited public servant. Fourteen years earlier, Keiley had made an impassioned speech in Richmond denouncing the invasion of papal territory by the secular state, calling it the act of "socialists and infidels," words that now served to sabotage his political future. Under pressure, Keiley resigned his commission rather than risk a political imbroglio. The ultimate insider, he seemed compelled from time to time to publicly remember his outsider roots as the son of an apostate Irish immigrant.

It was no surprise that Keiley's mouth had gotten him in trouble. Now his marriage was to prove just as much a handicap. In 1885 Cleveland, determined to reward Keiley for services rendered, nominated him as an envoy to Austria–Hungary. Again he was rebuffed, this time for what he avowed were "reasons which in the nineteenth century are an affront to the common sense of mankind." The problem, he and others alleged, was that Keiley had married a Jew. Whether religious bigotry was the reason for his refusal or simply that Austria–Hungary was reluctant to offend its Italian ally is unclear. But Keiley was again turned away on the threshold of diplomatic prominence.

In 1886, Cleveland finally found Keiley a post more fitting to his temperament: a judgeship. He moved to Cairo, Egypt, then to Alexandria, where he served, for the next sixteen years, on the International Court of First Instance and the Court of Appeals, forums for adjudicating the status of foreigners living within the Ottoman Empire. His exotic life had dramatically diverged from the cows and sheep of John King and the old soldier reunions and railroad business of Marcus Toney. Keiley was, as always, a man of leisure and taste, though now far removed from his native land and reportedly with no intentions of returning. In 1902 he retired and moved to London to fill his hours with chess and music, a devotee of the piano and violin.

A few years later, Keiley traveled to Paris to taste the joys of the French capital. On a January day in 1905, he was crossing the Place de la Concorde, not far from where the obelisk stood, a vivid reminder of his Egyptian service. Keiley, the practiced world traveler, would never get to the other side. Traversing the square, he was struck by an automobile and rushed to the nearby Beaujon Charity Hospital. A few hours later, he was pronounced dead. He was 72 years old, and his demise was front-page news in the Richmond papers. "Providence . . . had preserved me unharmed," he wrote forty years earlier of another, more arduous, journey, "amid the perils of Yankee prisons, the raging ocean, and the Piedmont Railroad." But Providence had retired from the field. Only an accident concocted of the modern world, it seems, could have brought his charmed and determined life to a sudden end.

As for Frank Wilkeson, death and danger followed him like an old friend. Upon leaving Elmira, he wandered southwest in search of the Fourth U.S. Artillery, the late phantom unit he had left in Washington for his Elmira tour. The search was an adventure. In the Alabama mountains, he discovered barefooted refugees fleeing from starvation and murder. He watched at the Paint Rock River in Alabama as a raft full of Union volunteers sank under the sheer weight of humanity, a half dozen drowning with barely a notice. He saw escaped slaves, burdened with trunks and boxes they had taken from their cotton plantations, forced from a train and dumped on the tracks, made to gather their belongings—and their masters'—and creep under a pelting rain to seek cover in a nearby woods.

Neither deserter nor straggler, Lieutenant Wilkeson was a victim of evasive maneuvers—but his own unit, not the enemy's, was the culprit. Just where *was* Battery H of the Fourth Artillery? Everyone told him something different. Near Huntsville, Alabama, Wilkeson missed a train and set off in search of the next station, tramping through the Alabama backcountry. One day he was offered lodgings by a planter whose gang of 20 slaves had run away. The man and his sole remaining bondservant, a yellow-complexioned fellow who appeared to be his son, seemed to the young Yankee an untrustworthy pair. That night his host tried to betray him to a Rebel guerrilla, and Wilkeson only escaped with the help of a large-caliber revolver.

Still in search of the Fourth, he took a steamer up the Tennessee River before the war's end, an exercise in helpless and stultifying fear, the soldiers and crew constantly under fire from Rebel bushwhackers along the shore. "Going up the Tennessee River in a steamboat was not as monotonous then as it is now," Wilkeson recalled 20 years later. The approaching demise of the Confederacy, if anything, only fired the vengeance of the ragtag, invisible Rebel rearguard.

It was only at Eastport, Tennessee, that Wilkeson learned the absurd truth of his odyssey. The Fourth's H company had returned to the capital a month before he even left Elmira, a mistake that seemed a crowning example of military inefficiency. "I had travelled on an order from Elmira, New York," he mused, "by car, by steamer, on horseback, and on foot, for thousands of miles, through many States, searching for a battery of artillery which was all the while at Washington, and whose commander daily expected me to appear."

Four weeks before Lee's surrender, he was brevetted a first lieutenant and captain for meritorious service. But the army wasn't a proper place for a young man seeking excitement, not during peacetime. "I had no interest in the regular army, no desire to continue to loaf around barracks, and to drill foreign-born soldiers," Wilkeson wrote. He resigned his commission in 1866.

He was a wanderer forever after. In 1869 Wilkeson married Mary Crouse in Johnstown, Pennsylvania, and fathered three children. In the years to follow he lived a life as wonderful and strange as anything dreamt of the day he ran off to join the 11th New York Battery. Wilkeson started as a civil engineer for the Northern Pacific Railroad, lived among the Blackfeet Indians, did a barometrical survey of the Cascade Mountains region in the Northwest, and followed in his father's footsteps as a journalist, working as a correspondent for both the *New York Times* and *New York Sun*.

By 1870 he had settled his family on a ranch in Gypsum, Kansas, near Salina, his base of operations for the next 40 years. After a career that included running for political office and unsuccessfully attempting to organize a regiment for the Spanish-American War, Wilkeson succumbed to kidney failure in his sixty-fifth year. When he died on April 22, 1913, he had a cross tattooed on his breast and a horse on his right forearm, and by that time he weighed a hefty 230 pounds. He described himself until the end as a "farmer."

Berry Benson was given a much-deserved furlough after his October escape from Elmira. But he didn't stay home for long. He fought in the Savannah campaign in December, staying until the city was evacuated before Sherman's splendid victory parade. In January he reported to Petersburg, where the siege curtain had pulled so tightly around the city that both sides could tell time by the courthouse clock tower, the one whose bells had first brought the militia out to fight on the previous 9th of June.

Hopping from trench to trench, Benson and the sharpshooters of the First South Carolina, including his brother Blackwood, repulsed the Yankee onslaughts for weeks. Berry fired a captured Spencer repeating rifle, loaded with a seven-shot magazine, until it grew so hot he had to put the weapon down to cool it off. By early spring, Petersburg held the distinction of having withstood the longest military siege in American history—and not even the British had been able to take it in

1781. It had been more than nine months since Archer's Battalion had made their stand on the Jerusalem Plank Road, A. W. Keiley coddling a misshapen smoothbore in defense of his adopted homeland.

Petersburg was evacuated on April 2; the next day, the First Michigan Sharpshooters raised the Union flag over the courthouse. Chased from the city earthworks a day or two earlier, Benson and a dozen or more sharpshooters fled west along the Appomattox River, hoping to find a ford and join the main bulk of the Confederate army fleeing Richmond. Traipsing through the woods, the small band of men sang "Jubilo," a Negro tune whose hope belied the impossible position they now faced.

At Sutherland's Station, on April 2, the Benson brothers fought their last engagement. Standing up in a shallow ditch to return a Yankee fusillade, Berry claimed to have seen the unseeable that day: a "black spot in the air," he reported, that whizzed by his left ear, "and if it had hit me I would have seen the bullet that killed me." (If dodging bullets seems unlikely, it was more than possible to evade a whistling mortar shell.) At the surrender a week later, the Benson boys, though officially paroled, slipped off from the ranks and fled to join General Joseph Johnston in North Carolina. They took their rifles with them, preferring not to give them up as the surrender terms required. Berry carried his old Enfield home with him in May, and it hung on his living room wall for years.

Only 22, Berry Greenwood Benson had a life ahead of him at war's end. Perhaps befitting a young man who had faced down death so many times, no vocation seemed beyond him. Benson became something of a dabbler. He taught school. He became a public accountant and authored a classic text on double-entry bookkeeping. The study of mushrooms took his fancy, and he wrote a regular nature column for the *Augusta Chronicle*. He traveled as a tourist to Mexico and Cuba and published philosophical commentaries in major magazines. (Brother Blackwood wrote several novels based on his war experiences.) Berry even became a self-declared expert on cryptography, a field he was introduced to at Petersburg when he sought to decode Yankee flag signals from the trenches. His urgent missives to Secretary of War Elihu Root on improving army ciphers were summarily dismissed around the turn of the century.

Benson was married in 1868 to Jeanie Oliver, daughter of a Confederate officer, who bore him six children. As he grew older, his Elmira adventure became a personal passion. Ten years after the surrender, he took an oath, with tunnel companion John Fox Maull, to remember the Elmira escape with a toast (of water) every October 7. He corresponded, on the same date every year, with Maull, Cecrops Malone, John Putegnat, and others he could still locate who had made the dash across Water Street that

cloudy autumn night. When most of his com-
panions-in-arms died before him, he kept up
the correspondence with their widows, writing
to one in 1912, on the eve of his seventieth
birthday, that his trek across Pennsylvania long
ago didn't seem all that outlandish, since he was
still capable of walking 20 miles on a Sunday.
His escape from Elmira had led to a return
there, if only in spirit, year after year.

What began as a simple anniversary became a
quest to remember his adventure with everything memory could bear. He wrote to northern
authorities to obtain maps of the country he had
crossed, mostly at night. To those who had
helped him during his flight as a fugitive, a passing pathetic stranger, he wrote letters of thanks,
even if it was only to their surviving relatives. He
did what he could for his fellow escapees who
had fallen into poverty, sending them money
when possible. He wrote many a letter and
placed many an advertisement in vain to find the
whereabouts of the Yankee corporal in the New
York 12th Infantry who had taken Benson's
pocketknife when he was captured at Spotsylvania—the weapon he had claimed from his dead
cousin, Zack Benson. He had little use for grand
veterans' organizations with this, his own sacred
fraternity of Confederate chums. Fifty years after the escape, he was still signing letters to a fellow conspirator "your old comrade mole."

Benson was well known locally as a Confederate hero. He posed for a monument to Con-

federate soldiers that was erected in Augusta, and he attended, as an honored veteran, the Civil War reunion/march in Washington in 1917. Benson walked in tattered trousers with his Enfield in arm at the head of the Georgia delegation, afraid of what some of the women might think of his immodest apparel. Marching down Pennsylvania Avenue, he was asked to stop en route so men with movie cameras could capture his image, furiously turning their cranks as he stood erect, the soul of Confederate gravity. (Later, he saw the film in a Washington movie theater.) The veterans rushed forward to shake hands with President Woodrow Wilson, the first Southerner in the White House for over 60 years, but the men in blue gently turned them away. "The police knew better than to start that sort of riot," Benson mused in a letter to Blackwood.

The following day, the spry Elmira alumnus took an automobile/camping tour to Point Lookout prison, some 50 miles distant. He had the pleasure of pointing out to his companions, at almost every turn of the macadam, a little church, a lonely farmhouse, a stream, a break in the woods—all that he recalled from his harried flight. More often than not, much to his companions' surprise, he was right about what lay around the next bend. They found a gutta-percha button, vintage 1850, on the site of the old prison, and Benson, with superior eyesight even in his seventies, could make out in the inscription a misplaced letter and a period posing as an apostrophe. The official historian for both of his escapes, Sergeant Benson was still a stickler for details.

Fate wouldn't have let Berry Benson forget Elmira even if he'd wanted. A member of the Augusta *Chronicle* staff, D. G. Stebbins, informed Benson one day that they had made their first acquaintance during the war. Stebbins, it turned out, had served in the 102nd New York regiment and been a guard at Elmira— and, of course, had been on duty the night of October 6. Nor did Benson's karma end there. In 1922, Benson wrote a series of letters to the G. & C. Merriam Company to complain about mistaken definitions in their *Webster's* dictionary. Eventually, his querulous missives were made known to the president of the firm, one H. Curtis Rowley. Rowley, recognizing the name of his correspondent, informed Benson that he had been a guard at Elmira, too, a private in the New York 54th, who was patrolling the camp interior on the night of the escape.

The reunions, the correspondence, the passage of time—all healed whatever old wounds remained from the war. Benson even sought out Melvin Conklin, the former Elmira camp spy whose mere name, not many years before, had made the South Carolina veteran fairly bristle. Late in life, Benson remarked that on either side of his short Enfield at home hung portraits of Robert E. Lee and Abraham Lincoln, "and I am ashamed of neither." He was a patriot of the Union evermore.

His memory fading, Benson became a connoisseur of exotic causes. Following the Great War, he sponsored a young French war orphan with yearly stipends—actively encouraging others to do the same—and so became her generous "grandpapa in America." He wrote irascible letters to the newspapers complaining about the "unintelligible rot" of their horoscopes. But in a letter to Sir Arthur Conan Doyle, he professed, nonetheless, a belief in reincarnation and karma, declaring himself a confirmed "theosophist."

If anyone could reflect on the majestic machinery of the universe, it was Berry Benson, a man who had survived imminent execution as a spy, imprisonment at Point Lookout and Elmira, a wound at Chancellorsville, the siege of Petersburg, and more than 50 years as a bluff and outspoken veteran of the Cause. When he died on New Year's Day, 1923, six weeks shy of his eightieth birthday, he was remembered by friends and family for the peacefulness of his final escape.

EPILOGUE

TODAY, Elmira, New York, a town of over 30,000 people, is more likely to remember its popular postwar summer resident, Mark Twain, than it is the Confederate camp on the Chemung. The city is much more sedate than the wild river town it was 150 years ago. Some of the buildings that the prisoners would have seen in their first or last tramp through the streets are still standing: Elmira College, the Chemung County Historical Society (formerly a bank), the county courthouse, and the Erie train station. Nearby shopping malls have stolen customers from the once-vibrant downtown, and it's hard to say whether the old business district is half-expired or halfway back on the road to recovery.

Nothing remains of the camp. The buildings were torn down long ago. There is a flagpole, reputed to have been in the barracks, that was uprooted from a private yard and moved next to a prison memorial on Water Street that was dedicated in 1995. Otherwise, the residential neighborhood that grew up in its place is lined with maples and honey locusts and picket fences, its frame and stucco houses endowed with generous front porches for street watching. Two plaques on Water Street mark the boundaries of the camp. One can walk down the street trying to imagine Berry Benson emerging from the earth below on a gloomy October night—but it is hard in the sunlight, with the leisurely traffic, in the full colors of a splendid fall.

Between the Water Street house lots and the river lies Foster's Pond, now a small remnant of its former size. Within living memory it was a popular place for ice-skating, a sport that some of the prisoners even availed themselves of. The pond seems idyllic, shaded with towering hardwoods, the water sunk below the earthen terrace built up as a wall after the flood of 1972. The place is apparently on the beaten path of younger residents. Near the pond I find a school textbook on the jogging path—*A History of the American Republic to 1877*—the binding wrapped with black electrical tape, already on its fourth owner, looking more lost than abandoned. Across the river to the south are the hills touched with orange that King and Keiley both remarked on as a beautiful sight, so much more for the fact that they were out of reach.

A strange echo of Barracks No. 3 lives on across town. Ten years after the war ended, a reformatory was opened within view of Woodlawn Cemetery, the site where the Rebels are interred. The Elmira Correctional Facility, as it is known today, resembles a crenellated Norman castle in imposing brick; it is literally hundreds of yards in length and is pierced with long, glaring Gothic windows. The building looks as though it has been, if not beheaded, then clum-

sily trimmed, its architectural details shorn off
when it became a maximum-security prison. Yet
another prison opened south of the river in recent years, creating a major source of employment for locals. Elmira decided that the "cor-
rections" business had a lot to offer after all.

Woodlawn became a national cemetery in
1874. The Confederates are buried "barracks
style," tightly fitted in narrow rows, head to toe.
The peaked marble headstones distinguish
them from the rounded stones nearby that mark
the graves of Union veterans and those of other
wars. The stones recite the depressing litany:
mortality number, name, date of death, and
unit, much as the bottles did when, stuffed with
a piece of paper, they were placed in the coffins
in the dead-house near Foster's Pond. The list
of the Confederate dead is thick enough to be a
small-town phone book.

At first glance, the stones seem all the same.
But some have been replaced with odd-shaped
slabs, the originals uprooted when family members found a name misspelled or a unit misiden-
tified. A few bodies were removed and reinterred
in the South by anxious relatives in the early
years (including, most likely, the remains of John
Rollins, son of John Jones's overseer). Jones himself, with a local housing project named after
him, is buried at the top of a hill in the adjacent
city cemetery. Since the old wooden headstones
were replaced with marble ones in 1907, none of
the Rebel dead has gone south.

The tally on Elmira is loaded. In dozens of memoirs and reminiscences, only the survivors are given voice. Should any of the 3,000 prisoners interred in Woodlawn stand up to recount their ordeals, the measure of Elmira would be far grimmer. That "dead men tell no tales" is perhaps the greatest fact—and blessing—of human memory. Only those who escaped a final reckoning in camp have any precise claim on us. Over them all broods the presence of that other Elmira, the one in the buried neighborhood at Woodlawn.

ENDNOTES

Prologue

For details on Petersburg during the war, particularly the skirmish on June 9, 1864, see James G. Scott and Edward Wyatt IV, *Petersburg's Story: A History* (Richmond, Va.: Dietz Press, 1960), 177–182; Sara Agnes Pryor, *Reminiscences of Peace and War* (Freeport, N.Y.: Books for Libraries, 1970), 264–291; and the Petersburg *Daily Express*, June 10, 1864 (original held by Virginia Historical Society).

All the available bell-metal. A. M. Keiley, *In Vinculis; or, The Prisoner of War* (New York: Blelock and Co., 1866), 15. All quotations from Keiley, unless otherwise noted, are from this text.

The usual discount. Keiley, *In Vinculis*, 15.

Replenish my commissariat. Keiley, *In Vinculis*, 16.

For the general facts of Keiley's life, see James H. Bailey, "Anthony Keiley and the 'Keiley Incident,'" *Virginia Magazine of History and Biography* 67 (January 1959): 65–81; and Joseph O'Grady, "Anthony Keiley (1832–1905), Virginia's Catholic Politician," *The Catholic Historical Review* 54, no. 4 (January 1969): 613–635. See also *Encyclopedia of Virginia Biography*, vol. 3 (1915); *The Cyclopaedia of American Biography*, vol. 13 (1906); William D. Henderson, *12th Virginia Infantry* (Lynchburg, Va.: H. E. Howard, 1984), 135; and Keiley's military service records, Roll 524, Microfilm No. 324, Record Group 109, National Archives, Washington (NAW).

Scattered the cavaliers like chaff. Keiley, 22.

The two nearest men to me. Keiley, *In Vinculis*, 23.

Hatchet-faced member. Keiley, *In Vinculis*, 24–25.

The North, in liberating four millions. Keiley, *In Vinculis*, 80.

I can use a saw and square. All quotes from King, unless otherwise noted, are from John R. King, *My Experience in the Confederate Army and in Northern Prisons* (Clarksburg, W.Va.: United Daughters of Confederacy, 1917), 5. Additional details of King's life can be gleaned from Wilbur C. Morrison, "Lewis County Boasts Only One Survivor of Confederate Army," *Clarksburg Exponent Telegram*, June 26, 1932. Facts of his military service can be gathered from Richard Armstrong, *25th Virginia Infantry and 9th Battalion Virginia Infantry* (Lynchburg, Va.: H. E. Howard, 1990), 189; and from his military service records, Roll 694, Microfilm No. 324, Record Group 109, NAW.

We were never safe at home. King, *My Experience*, 9.

I wish you could have seen me. King, *My Experience*, 11.

Men's heads were torn. King, *My Experience*, 13.

It is due to the hand of a Divine Providence. King, *My Experience*, 13–14.

I remember I did a fine job. King, *My Experience*, 13.

It seemed strange. King, *My Experience*, 14.

Was in the shape of a horseshoe. King, *My Experience*, 23.

"Boys, surrender." King, *My Experience*, 24.

And we saw him throw his arms. King, *My Experience*, 24.

A very young Yankee boy. King, *My Experience*, 25–26.

The main source for Marcus Toney is Marcus B. Toney, *The Privations of a Private* (Nashville, Tenn.: Author, 1905). All quotes from Toney derive from this source unless otherwise noted. Ancillary sources include Will Hale and Dixon Merritt, *A History of Tennessee and Tennesseans*, vol. 5 (Chicago: Lewis Publishing, 1913), 1507–1508; *Confederate Veteran* 34 (April 1931): 126–127; *Confederate Veteran* 3 (March 1895): 89–90; *Confederate Veteran* 14 (October 1906): 469; *Southern Historical Society Papers* 29, article 15 (1901): 193–197; and Kevin Ruffner, *44th Virginia Infantry* (Lynchburg, Va.: H. E. Howard, Inc., 1987), 110. Toney's service records can be found in Roll 105, Microfilm No. 268, RG 109, NAW; and Roll 882, Microfilm No. 324, Record Group 109.

Were living as one great family. Toney, *The Privations*, 10.

A libel upon the Southern people. Toney, *The Privations*, 9.

Our New England cousins. Toney, *The Privations*, 9.

The doleful dirge of the dead march. Toney, *The Privations*, 14.

As thick as pins in a pincushion. Toney, *The Privations*, 16.

We would have a battle in which. Toney, *The Privations*, 13.

We left Nashville with as good a lot. Toney, *The Privations*, 15.

I thought, probably, the war would end. Toney, *The Privations*, 19.

How many wiggletales and tadpoles. Toney, *The Privations*, 40.

We felt sorry for him. Toney, *The Privations*, 40.

I ran picket for four hours. Toney, *The Privations*, 31.

The fatalities of the campaign. Toney, *The Privations*, 34.

A large number of wagons. Toney, *The Privations*, 36.

Seen the monkey show. For excellent details regarding the life and times of Confederate soldiers during the war, including the language they used, see Bell Irvin Wiley, *The Life of Johnny Reb* (Baton Rouge: Louisiana State University Press, 1997), 33.

The dark and bloody ground. Toney, *The Privations*, 39.

We had ten men killed. Toney, *The Privations*, 43.

Our boys got so close to the battery. Toney, *The Privations*, 43.

Bivouack in the dust. Toney, *The Privations*, 58.

From the top of Lookout Mountain. Toney, *The Privations*, 62.

Showed the white feather. See Wiley, *The Life*, 224.

He had to erase the "dis." See *Confederate Veteran* 3 (February 1895): 52.

By the first of May. Toney, *The Privations*, 70.

Three days' rations. Toney, *The Privations*, 72.

As fine-looking a body of men. Toney, *The Privations*, 75–76.

With a black-jack tree for his headstone. Toney, *The Privations*, 76.

Why he did not shoot. Toney, *The Privations*, 80.

We were in a sorry plight. Toney, *The Privations*, 81.

They did not minister. Toney, *The Privations*, 83.

I do not believe that, in January. Toney, *The Privations*, 67.

Unless otherwise noted, quotes from Benson come from Clayton Holmes, *The Elmira Prison Camp* (New York: G. P. Putnam's, 1912), 209–253. Holmes prints verbatim Benson's own account of his escape, based on earlier notes and narratives the veteran compiled over the years. Excellent material on Benson's life during the war can be found in Susan Benson Williams, ed., *Berry Benson's Civil War Book: Memoirs of a Confederate Scout and Sharpshooter* (Athens: University of Georgia Press, 1962). Basic facts on Benson's military service come from his official war records: Roll 126, Microfilm No. 267, RG 109, NAW.

There we fought with them. Holmes, *The Elmira Prison*, 210.

Exchange myself. Much valuable information about Benson's capture and life as a whole can be found in an autobiography he penned in 1877, found in vol. 10 of the Berry Benson Papers, #2636, Southern Historical Collection (SHC), University of North Carolina at Chapel Hill (UNC). Hereafter cited as Benson, *Autobiography*. See Benson, *Autobiography*, 175.

I looked at everybody with suspicion. Benson, *Autobiography*, 181.

Chapter 1

In the summer of 1864, thousands of Confederate. For early history of Elmira, see Amy Wilson, *Chemung County: An Illustrated History* (Montgomery, Ala.: Community Communications, Inc., 1999), 8–25.

Pickpockets worked the busy Erie train station. The best source for daily life during the war period is the Elmira *Daily Advertiser* (Steele Memorial Library, Elmira, New York).

Barracks No. 3 fronted Water Street. A very good overall—and critical—account of the camp is to be found in Michael Horigan, *Elmira: Death Camp of the North* (Mechanicsburg, Pa.: Stackpole, 2002). A fine account of the camp's economic realities is Michael P. Gray's *The Business of Captivity: Elmira and Its Civil War Prison* (Kent, Ohio: Kent State University Press, 2001). For a brief history, including the camp's establishment, see James Robertson Jr., "The Scourge of Elmira," in William Hesseltine, ed., *Civil War Prisons* (Kent, Ohio: Kent State University Press, 1962), 80–97. See also Thomas Byrne, "Elmira's Prison Camp," in *Chemung Historical Journal* (September 1964): 1279–1300; and J. Michael Horigan, "Elmira Prison Camp—A Second Opinion," *Chemung Historical Journal* (March 1985): 3449–3457. For another, longer account of the camp, see Holmes, *The Elmira Prison*, an invaluable source replete with primary source materials, although marked by a strong polemical defense of the North and Holmes's hometown of Elmira. The most compelling single book on a POW camp during the war, to my knowledge, is William Marvel's *Andersonville: The Last Depot* (Chapel Hill: University of North Carolina Press, 1994).

A military report from 1862. See *War of the Rebellion: A Compilation of the Official Records of the Union and Confederate Armies* (hereafter referred to as OR, and all references to Series II). (Washington, D.C.: GPO, 1880–1901). Series II, vol. 4, 67–69.

There should be ample room between the fences and buildings. OR, vol. 7, 152.

Insufficient, incomplete, and filthy. OR, vol. 4, 68.

Three weeks later an official missive. OR, vol. 7, 505.

Like cattle . . . certain liquid comforts. See Keiley, *In Vinculis*, 28.

Despotism in his lowering eyebrow. Keiley, *In Vinculis*, 37.

Negro guard . . . in savory quarters. Keiley, *In Vinculis*, 50, 55.

Utterly innocent of tree, shrub, or any natural equivalent. Keiley, *In Vinculis*, 58.

Why this cape is so-called. Keiley, *In Vinculis*, 55.

Turning the contents of our pockets on the ground. Keiley, *In Vinculis*, 57.

A scum rises on the top of a vessel . . . half-pint of watery slop. Keiley, *In Vinculis*, 65, 67.

All the stupidity of a tread-mill. Keiley, *In Vinculis*, 83.

From disregard of the formalities of life. Keiley, *In Vinculis*, 62.

He conducts this establishment. Keiley, *In Vinculis*, 85.

Men became reckless. Keiley, *In Vinculis*, 62.

Another month here and I shall become. Keiley, *In Vinculis*, 115.

The sun melting pitch. Keiley, *In Vinculis*, 119.

American Venice . . . endless tide of wheel and foot. Keiley, *In Vinculis*, 121, 123.

A sort of fungus of the Erie Railroad . . . a pretty little city. Keiley, *In Vinculis*, 101, 126, 129.

Prisoner no. 766. Frame 0029, Roll 65, Microfilm 598, NAW. Keiley claimed he didn't arrive until July 12.

Nearer Hades than I thought any place could be. Confederate Veteran 20 (1912): 327.

In the hyperborean regions of New York. Keiley, *In Vinculis*, 129.

For a contemporary account of the Shohola mishap, see "Elmira Prison Camp," *New York Tribune,*

July 18, 1864, Chemung County Historical Society (CCHS), VF 500–320.

Many of [the injured] were in a horrible condition. Keiley, *In Vinculis*, 155.

The most elaborate account of Benson's stay at Point Lookout can be found in Benson, *Autobiography*. The major source for my reconstruction is Benson, *Berry Benson's Civil War Book*, 92–100.

With all my clothes on. Holmes, *The Elmira Prison*, 211.

Familiar taunt of Johnnies. My account of Benson's stay in Washington is based on Benson, *Autobiography*, 221–236.

I would occasionally turn. Benson, *Autobiography*, 236.

I ought to have escaped on the way. Holmes, *The Elmira Prison*, 211.

It is a matter, not only of regret. Benson, *Autobiography*, 237.

Clothing was of all sorts. Daily Advertiser, July 26, 1864.

For Benson's name in the Elmira camp registry, see Frame 0069, Roll 65, Microfilm 598, *Records Relating to Individual Prisons or Stations, Elmira, N.Y. Military Prison, General Register of Prisoners*, RG 109, NAW.

I liked to go over there. Holmes, *The Elmira Prison*, 212.

The prison by night was like a gaslit sidewalk. Benson, *Autobiography*, 241.

I stole a one-inch strip. Holmes, *The Elmira Prison*, 214.

To go into a prison of war. Quoted in Robert Doyle, *Voices from Captivity: Interpreting the American POW Narrative* (Lawrence: University Press of Kansas, 1994), 241.

Some 30,000 died in confinement. For POW numbers, see Hesseltine, *Civil War Prisons*, 6.

A member of John Hunt Morgan's cavalry. For Curtis Burke's story, see "Curtis Burke's Civil War Journal," *Indiana Magazine of History* 65, no. 4 (December 1969): 283–327; *Indiana Magazine of History* 66, no. 2 (June 1970): 110–172; and *Indiana Magazine of History* 67, no. 2 (June 1971): 129–170.

After his capture, Rebel infantryman John Copley. See John Copley, *A Sketch of the Battle of Franklin, Tennessee, with Reminiscences of Camp Douglas* (Austin, Tex.: E. Von Boeckmann, 1893), 68.

Lawrence Sangston of Baltimore. See Lawrence Sangston, *The Bastiles of the North* (Baltimore: Kelly, Hedian and Piet, 1863).

From his extreme bad English. See J. B. Stamp, "Ten Months Experience in Northern Prisons," *The Alabama Historical Quarterly* 18, no. 4 (winter 1956): 486.

This is the anniversary of the day. Sangston, *The Bastiles,* 9.

The Immortal Six Hundred. See Richard Current, ed., *Encyclopedia of the Confederacy,* vol. 3 (New York: Simon and Schuster, 1993), 1259.

For details on prison life at Camp Douglas, see the valuable study by George Levy, *To Die in Chicago: Confederate Prisoners at Camp Douglas* (Evanston, Ill.: Evanston Publishing Company, 1994), 82, 271.

They were administered by Lieutenant Colonel William H. Hoffman. See Current, *Encyclopedia,* 1256–1257; and Hesseltine, *Civil War Prisons,* 180–202.

As a result, prison operations during the Civil War came to hang. For details of the cartel, see Current, *Encyclopedia,* 1256–1258.

With superior numbers, the North could afford to have the cartel suspended. See Current, *Encyclopedia*, 1256–1263; Phillip Shriver and Donald Breen, "Ohio's Military Prisons in the Civil War," in *Ohio Civil War Centennial Commission*, no. 15 (Columbus: Ohio State University Press, 1964), 4–5; and the magisterial study of the war by James McPherson, *Battle Cry of Freedom: The Civil War Era* (New York: Ballantine, 1989), 566–567, 799–800.

The slaveholder is born to tyranny . . . essayed to bring starvation on the people. Quoted in William Hesseltine, *Civil War Prisons: A Study in War Psychology* (New York: Frederick Ungar, 1964), 195.

How different an example of humanity the North is setting. Quoted in Hesseltine, *Civil War Prisons: A Study*, 176.

We are killing them by treating them as southern gentlemen. Quoted in Hesseltine, *Civil War Prisons: A Study*, 193.

For the tour made by the Sanitary Commission, see Hesseltine, *Civil War Prisons: A Study*, 199–201.

The grand female dry-nurse of Yankee Doodle. Keiley, *In Vinculis*, 66.

Thousands passed through that gate. King, *My Experience*, 26.

Such was the prognosis for a quick victory. Shriver and Breen, "Ohio's Military Prisons," 29.

Elmire Prison—as I was informed. Stamp, "Ten Months," 494.

Some camps could not have been more poorly planned. See Current, *Encyclopedia*, 1259; and Robertson in Hesseltine, *Civil War Prisons*, 80–84.

Prisoners confined to Johnson's Island. See Shriver and Breen, "Ohio's Military Prisons"; and Edward T. Downer, "Johnson's Island," in Hesseltine, *Civil War Prisons*, 98–113.

When the weather got below zero. Henry Kyd Douglas, *I Rode with Stonewall* (Chapel Hill: University of North Carolina Press, 1940), 261.

We bury our own dead. Quoted in Doyle, *Voices from Captivity*, 149.

Whenever there was any news favorable to the Federal side. Toney, *The Privations*, 113.

I would attempt escape from a palace. Benson, File 32, Box 8, annotated copy of Holmes, *The Elmira Prison*, 167, Berry Benson Papers, #2636, SHC, UNC.

Chapter 2

In immaculate calligraphy. Keiley, *In Vinculis*, 150.

A free conversation on matters military. Keiley, *In Vinculis*, 151.

About four cents apiece—in greenbacks. Keiley, *In Vinculis*, 146.

I had the happiness of being the means. Keiley, *In Vinculis*, 153.

Barton was a good fellow. Keiley, *In Vinculis*, 133.

Rather fatal. Daily Advertiser, September 1, 1864.

Systematic inhumanity to the sick. Keiley, *In Vinculis*, 145.

I do not doubt that many . . . in a country where food was cheap. Keiley, *In Vinculis*, 140, 143.

Our curiosity has been excited for some days past. Keiley, *In Vinculis*, 157.

Living, moving panorama. Daily Advertiser, September 6, 1864.

Barnum has not taken the prisoners. Keiley, *In Vinculis*, 157–158.

Scrutinized the camp with much curiosity. Toney, *The Privations*, 105.

Elmira wasn't the only Yankee prison. See Levy, *To Die*, 251; and Shriver and Breen, "Ohio's Military Prisons," 39.

The potter's field where the prisoners are accorded. Keiley, *In Vinculis*, 170.

Practical and sensible. Keiley, *In Vinculis*, 159.

The clerical world in Puritan-dom has not changed. Keiley, *In Vinculis*, 166–167.

Obscene pictures . . . vulgarity of speech. Keiley, *In Vinculis*, 168–169.

At Point Lookout. See *Sketches from Prison: A Confederate Artist's Record of Life at Point Lookout* (Baltimore: Maryland State Park Foundation), pages unnumbered, undated.

Their conduct is as black as their skin. Keiley, *In Vinculis*, 96.

Dick had been importuned, time and again. Keiley, *In Vinculis*, 82.

The army had spoiled him pretty effectually. . . . His boots were as glossy. Keiley, *In Vinculis*, 171.

The Northern people, and I speak from long acquaintance. Keiley, *In Vinculis*, 179.

It is the free states which have made. Keiley, *In Vinculis*, 179–180.

Air pure, location healthy, no epidemic. Keiley, *In Vinculis*, 174.

Eleven more were added to the list. Keiley, *In Vinculis*, 175. For a modern and no less negative assessment of Sanger, see Andrew MacIsaac, "From Bangor to Elmira and Back Again: The Civil

War Career of Dr. Eugene Francis Sanger," *Maine History* 37, nos. 1–2 (summer–fall, 1997): 30–59. A balanced and thoughtful account of Sanger can be found in Horigan, *Elmira*, 127–142.

Walter Addison of Stewart's Horse. See folder 43, Thomas Jefferson Green Papers, #289, SHC, UNC.

To us the book of events was sealed . . . our little city. Keiley, *In Vinculis*, 175–176.

Infantile toy-books and dilapidated geographies. Keiley, *In Vinculis*, 176.

A fairer summer never blessed the eye. Keiley, *In Vinculis*, 176.

Profane devils. Keiley, *In Vinculis*, 27.

A more varied collection of heroes never blessed the eyes. Keiley, *In Vinculis*, 25.

Began to suffer severely. Keiley, *In Vinculis*, 177.

I went barefoot, both for comfort. Holmes, *The Elmira Prison*, 215. Valuable confirmation and additional details of Benson's escape related in Holmes can be found in Benson, *Autobiography*; Benson, *Berry Benson's Civil War Book*; and a narrative of Elmira written by Benson in 1866, shortly after his prison experience, File 1, Box 1, Berry Benson Papers, #2636, SHC, UNC.

The last night came, the night to finish the tunnel. Holmes, *The Elmira Prison*, 216.

I went under . . . men waiting, hungry for home. Holmes, *The Elmira Prison*, 216.

Now tonight there'll be a crowd here. Holmes, *The Elmira Prison*, 216–217.

Among the few gifts I have is intuition. Holmes, *The Elmira Prison*, 217.

Three days I looked everywhere. Holmes, *The Elmira Prison*, 217.

You'd better be careful. The conversation with the stranger by the pond can be found in Holmes, *The Elmira Prison*, 217–218.

The boys were all there. . . . In ten minutes I had got my shirt. Holmes, *The Elmira Prison*, 218.

For stories of the men and general details of the escape, including some of the accounts written by other escapees, see Holmes, *The Elmira Prison*, 168–208. There exists some confusion as to the name of one of the escapees. Maull (see Holmes, *The Elmira Prison*, 177) claims that Shelton never escaped, but Horigan, in *Elmira* (113), offers that Shelton absconded but then disappeared into thin air.

I never tried fish or vegetables, doubtful or undoubtful. Benson, *Autobiography*, 252.

I go into the tunnel. Holmes, *The Elmira Prison*, 220.

I felt that I wouldn't be able to look the boys. Benson, *Autobiography*, 247.

The incident with the Yankee officer is described in Benson, *Autobiography*, 249–250.

For the cell was to the guardhouse what the guardhouse. Benson, *Autobiography*, 279. For a good description of a sweatbox, see Gray, *The Business of Captivity*, 125.

It was only the enormous weight of the longing for freedom. Holmes, *The Elmira Prison*, 223.

We welcomed [Traweek] with open arms. Holmes, *The Elmira Prison*, 222.

As we lay on the left side, to have free use . . . now we had learned our lesson. Holmes, *The Elmira Prison*, 226.

It was next thing to death by suffocation. Benson, *Autobiography*, 263.

At midnight, as though in answer to an unspoken prayer. Holmes, *The Elmira Prison*, 227.

A button gives way, or something. Holmes, *The Elmira Prison*, 228.

I turn on my back. Holmes, *The Elmira Prison*, 228–229.

There is no more to do. Holmes, *The Elmira Prison*, 229.

Chapter 3

The account of Frank Wilkeson is from Frank Wilkeson, *Recollections of a Private Soldier in the Army of the Potomac* (New York: G. P. Putnam's Sons, 1887). Wilkeson's war memoirs, first published in 1886 and then reprinted in 1972 and 1997, have been used by many historians including James McPherson, but his account of Elmira and his stay in a Yankee lockup have been largely ignored. Wilkeson's service record can be found in File W440, CB 1867, Roll 382, Microfilm No. 1064, Record Group 94, NAW. His pension file is another valuable source of information—see Application 1.387.828, Certificate 1.159.993; and for his wife, Mary Crouse Wilkeson, application 1009.461, Certificate 762.623.

Most of this war history has been written. Wilkeson, *Recollections*, v.

Irreclaimable blackguards, thieves, and ruffians. Wilkeson, *Recollections*, 2.

A recruit's social standing . . . half a dozen cities, was assured. Wilkeson, *Recollections*, 2.

Almost to a man they were bullies and cowards. Wilkeson, *Recollections*, 3.

I saw the guards roughly haul straw-littered. Wilkeson, *Recollections*, 7.

The dead patriots lay by the roadside. Wilkeson, *Recollections*, 8.

Previous to my enlistment . . . people who saw us did not cheer. Wilkeson, *Recollections*, 8.

Bottles, flasks, canteens, full of whiskey. Wilkeson, *Recollections*, 10.

Promptly the hold was transformed. . . . Drunken men staggered to and fro. Wilkeson, *Recollections*, 14.

"Floating Heaven of American Patriots." Wilkeson, *Recollections*, 20.

And if they protested, their cries were silenced. Wilkeson, *Recollections*, 18.

Artillery humbug. . . . They taught us how to change. Wilkeson, *Recollections*, 22–23.

Ignorant of the power of a southern sun. Wilkeson, *Recollections*, 43.

"Get food, honestly if you can." Wilkeson, *Recollections*, 45.

To rob a soldier was to rob a man. Wilkeson, *Recollections*, 54.

The men who had fallen in that fierce fight. Wilkeson, *Recollections*, 49–50.

"That is what you are all coming to." Wilkeson, *Recollections*, 51.

By noon I was quite wild with curiosity. Wilkeson, *Recollections*, 58.

His pockets were turned inside out. Wilkeson, *Recollections*, 58.

It was not anywhere near as bloody. Wilkeson, *Recollections*, 63.

A swish of bullets and a fierce, exultant yell. . . . I feared the line would break. Wilkeson, *Recollections*, 71.

We fired and fired and fired. Wilkeson, *Recollections*, 73.

Had "turned up their toes." Wilkeson, *Recollections*, 74.

The stick that one picked up so cheerfully. Wilkeson, *Recollections*, 35–36.

Tied to the spare wheel. Graphic descriptions of typical military punishments can be found in Wilkeson, *Recollections*, 32–36.

Our troops caught the battle-exhausted Confederates. Wilkeson, *Recollections*, 86.

Grant looked tired. . . . None saluted him. Wilkeson, *Recollections*, 124.

Our cannon became silent. Wilkeson, *Recollections*, 131.

Not a man stirred from his place. Wilkeson, *Recollections*, 134–135.

I imagined myself prowling between the front and the rear. Wilkeson, *Recollections*, 141.

It was as though a huge pic-nic were going on. Wilkeson, *Recollections*, 167.

To call a soldier of the Army of the Potomac. Wilkeson, *Recollections*, 189.

They were the scum of the slums. Wilkeson, *Recollections*, 187.

A Mississippi slave-dealer was a refined. Wilkeson, *Recollections*, 188.

Had seen all manner of death and anguish. See Wilkeson, *Recollections*, 126, 149–150, 175–176.

His death ended the game. Wilkeson, *Recollections*, 120.

The unseen danger is the alarming one. Wilkeson, *Recollections*, 115–116.

Though a member of Battery H. Wilkeson's pension documents say he was a member of Battery K.

I use H in the narrative since he insists on it in his own book. As his book suggests, he was shifted around a good deal in the fall of 1864.

We marched to the railroad station. Wilkeson, *Recollections*, 220–221.

Grouped and photographed, very unfairly. Wilkeson, *Recollections*, 224.

A military prison, it matters not what people keep it. Wilkeson, *Recollections*, 224.

Nearly 200 at Rock Island alone died of disease. See T. R. Walker, "Rock Island Prison Barracks," in Hesseltine, *Civil War Prisons*, 50.

He behaved like a gentleman. King, *My Experience*, 43.

There were several hundred guards on duty at any given time. See "Helmira, 1864–1865," WSKG Public Television, 1993.

A member of the Alabama Third Infantry. See Stamp, "Ten Months," 495.

Whose whole intercourse with the prisoners was the essence of brutality. Keiley, *In Vinculis*, 134.

I met no Union soldier who had been confined. Wilkeson, *Recollections*, 224–225.

The prisoners, it was alleged, were allowed the same rations . . . as sheep with the rot. Wilkeson, *Recollections*, 225.

They stood motionless and gazed into one another's. Wilkeson, *Recollections*, 226.

Colt, some prisoners alleged, was ruthless. For another side of Colt, see G. W. D. Porter's remarks in *The Annals of the Army of Tennessee* 1, no. 4 (July 1878), 157–162.

Private Wilbur Grambling of the Fifth Florida. For Grambling's diary, see James Jones and Edward Keuchel, "A Rebel's Diary of Elmira Prison Camp," *Chemung Historical Journal* (August 1985): 2457–2463.

The discipline in the Confederate armies must have been. Wilkeson, *Recollections*, 226.

Digging ditches and trenches which were never used . . . over the frozen plain in menacing drill. Wilkeson, *Recollections*, 227.

A lack of discipline in the prison. . . . That night they gathered in mobs. Wilkeson, *Recollections*, 222.

One crowd of men followed us. Wilkeson, *Recollections*, 223.

"I am just up from the front where I have been." Wilkeson, *Recollections*, 223.

One night seven or eight Confederates escaped. Wilkeson, *Recollections*, 228.

"They are still in the tunnel!" Holmes, *The Elmira Prison*, 229.

Straightaway I was at the exit of the tunnel. Holmes, *The Elmira Prison*, 230.

I raised my head and looked out. Holmes, *The Elmira Prison*, 230.

At a quick pace, but not with haste. Holmes, *The Elmira Prison*, 230.

Silent and grim as a burying ground. Benson, *Autobiography*, 285.

In Elmira the next morning. See Toney, *The Privations*, 94–95; King, *My Experience*, 35; and Jones and Keuchel, "A Rebel's Diary," 2460.

There was a suspicion of their whereabouts. The Daily Advertiser, October 8, 1864.

Beautiful picture . . . get on my hands and knees and crawl zigzag. Holmes, *The Elmira Prison*, 231–232.

He knew the woods. See Benson, *Autobiography*, 4–6.

I hoped to find the half of a dinner. Holmes, *The Elmira Prison*, 232–233. In the Holmes narrative, published in 1912, Benson claims that he wrote the message; in Benson, *Autobiography*, he says that he was tempted, but decided not to so endanger himself. See Benson, *Autobiography*, 287–288.

The first tea I had tasted. Holmes, *The Elmira Prison*, 235.

I destroyed everything but the crockery. Benson, *Autobiography*, 293.

I walked all night, stopping but twice. . . . When a man has lived at a hotel. Holmes, *The Elmira Prison*, 236.

I now summed up that I had eleven pockets. Holmes, *The Elmira Prison*, 236.

Somewhere near Ralston, pains in my stomach. Holmes, *The Elmira Prison*, 237.

Why not enlist, get a thousand dollars. Holmes, *The Elmira Prison*, 238.

Some were as big as a dollar. Holmes, *The Elmira Prison*, 238.

There was not a man that enjoyed that night. Benson, *Autobiography*, 300.

Scattered them to the four winds. Holmes, *The Elmira Prison*, 240.

All was bustle. . . . I know he sees me. Holmes, *The Elmira Prison*, 241–242.

He remains silent a hundred years. Holmes, *The Elmira Prison*, 242.

Marching merrily, whistling Dixie. Holmes, *The Elmira Prison*, 243.

Burnt my mouth like pepper. Benson, *Autobiography*, 305.

Exuberance of negro fancy. Daily Advertiser, August 13, 1864.

People from the country are hardly willing to go home. Daily Advertiser, July 11, 1864.

The knowing ones are rubbing up their old complaints. Keiley, *In Vinculis*, 178.

Full rations of beef. Keiley, *In Vinculis*, 180.

Age, or sickness, or wounds. Keiley, *In Vinculis*, 181.

Four or five officers took the paroles. Keiley, *In Vinculis*, 181–182.

Hegira. Keiley, *In Vinculis*, 184.

Many a brawny fellow with the thews. Keiley, *In Vinculis*, 184–185.

Thus the poor ones had to rely on their wits. Keiley, *In Vinculis*, 186.

Eleven enterprising beavers. Keiley, *In Vinculis*, 177.

A knock at my door ten minutes after nine. Keiley, *In Vinculis*, 184.

His eyes filled as he bade me good-bye. Keiley, *In Vinculis*, 188.

Those unable to sit up. Daily Advertiser, October 12, 1864.

Fabulous quantities of crackers . . . guards robbed the nearest orchards. Keiley, *In Vinculis*, 190.

The first toll of the dread Reaper. Keiley, *In Vinculis*, 191.

Tearing a leaf from my note-book. Keiley, *In Vinculis*, 192.

Each of these sick cars was well provided. Daily Advertiser, October 12, 1864.

The condition of these men was pitiable. OR, vol. 7, 894.

Should not have been sent on such a journey. OR, vol. 7, 893.

Left a festering mass of corruption. OR, vol. 7, 1092.

A gangway plank was stretched from the side. Keiley, *In Vinculis*, 194.

As comfortable as possible. Keiley, *In Vinculis*, 196.

Administering hospital slops . . . the tedium of my cage. Keiley, *In Vinculis*, 203.

When called on by the doctor. Keiley, *In Vinculis*, 204.

Although Friar Peyton told Henry VIII. Keiley, *In Vinculis*, 205.

Boat-loads of soldiers are constantly passing. Keiley, *In Vinculis*, 209.

Every morning we saw coffins going over the side. Keiley, *In Vinculis*, 207–208.

Passing generations have not left a trace. Keiley, *In Vinculis*, 210.

Many of us lounged on deck. Keiley, *In Vinculis*, 213.

The most beautiful Atlantic city . . . all bipeds furnished with feathers. Keiley, *In Vinculis*, 214.

Sixty days are an aeon in these times. Keiley, *In Vinculis*, 214.

An imperial autumn moon . . . barricades of cotton-bales. Keiley, *In Vinculis*, 215.

In leaving prison, I found I had not come to peace. Keiley, *In Vinculis*, 216.

For escape totals during the war, see OR, vol. 8, 987–1003.

A Georgia sergeant nicknamed "Buttons." See Holmes, *The Elmira Prison*, 162–166, for various escapes; Benson later had his doubts about whether Buttons could really have accomplished this.

For the Orcutt and Womack escape stories, see Holmes, *The Elmira Prison*, 151–159, 163–169.

Chapter 4

"Men don't escape from prison every day." Holmes, *The Elmira Prison*, 248.

A very indifferent talker. Benson, *Autobiography*, 315.

"How are you, Hood?" Holmes, *The Elmira Prison*, 252.

"Dear Father, I am not dead, but alive and well." Holmes, *The Elmira Prison*, 252.

That night, when he thought I was asleep. Holmes, *The Elmira Prison*, 253.

Intensely dark . . . at the top of their voices. Wilkeson, *Recollections*, 228–229.

I saw the flash of his gun . . . as silent as death. Wilkeson, *Recollections*, 229–230.

"You will be court-martialed, sure." Wilkeson, *Recollections*, 230.

Shoulder-strapped office-holders. Wilkeson, *Recollections*, xvii.

I afterwards learned that a few. Wilkeson, *Recollections*, 230.

A crazy fool. File 40, Box 4, "The Military Prison at Elmira," Berry Benson Papers, #2636, SHC, UNC.

The military prison at Elmira was a place to be avoided. Wilkeson, *Recollections*, 225.

I saw hundreds of tall, gaunt, frouzy-headed. Wilkeson, *Recollections*, 233.

His girl's picture in his side pocket. King, *My Experience*, 25.

I am happy to say that your humble servant. King, *My Experience*, 32.

I will never forget. King, *My Experience*, 31.

There were hills on the east. King, *My Experience*, 33.

Prisoner no. 4403. King's camp registration can be found on Frame 0138, Roll 65, Microfilm 598, NAW.

Not healthful. King, *My Experience*, 33.

It mattered little to us. King, *My Experience*, 34.

Four beans to a gallon of water. Toney, *The Privations*, 98.

Those who could not carry it with them. King, *My Experience*, 35.

Old rags and strings and long unkept hair. King, *My Experience,* 36.

I was assured by the guard. Holmes, *The Elmira Prison,* 326.

Often we could see through the soup . . . we nearly starved. King, *My Experience,* 36–37.

Many men, once strong, would cry. King, *My Experience,* 46.

The official army meat ration. Daily Advertiser, July 6, 1864. For discussion of beef controversy, see Horigan, *Elmira,* 98–100. A brief discussion of the prison fund can be found in Holmes, *The Elmira Prison,* 21–22. Also see Horigan, *Elmira,* 86, 98–99; and Gray, *The Business of Captivity,* 161.

The prisoners ate every rat they could find. King, *My Experience,* 42.

I myself often watched for the bones. King, *My Experience,* 45.

The food as a general thing was very good. Holmes, *The Elmira Prison,* 337.

An excellent place for [prisoners] to find their graves. King, *My Experience,* 33.

The pants I had when arriving. King, *My Experience,* 38. For the cotton shipment, see Gray, *The Business of Captivity,* 65–69.

Should we have been out in the world. King, *My Experience,* 38.

Died rapidly, despondent, homesick, hungry. King, *My Experience,* 37, 40.

For figures on mortality in Rebel army, see Wiley, *The Life,* 244, 252.

So spongy and sore that portions. King, *My Experience,* 40. For more on scurvy and Civil War diseases in general, see Paul Steiner, *Disease in the Civil War* (Springfield, Ill.: Charles Thomas, 1968); and Keith Wilbur, *Civil War Medicine, 1861–1865* (Old Saybrook, Conn.: Globe Pequot Press, 1998).

Prisoner no. 4621. Toney's registration at the camp can be found on Frame 0144, Roll 67, Microfilm 598. NAW.

Point Lookout, with its army of ten thousand. Toney, *The Privations*, 87.

The sun's heat and reflection from the water. Toney, *The Privations*, 90.

The car windows were small. Toney, *The Privations*, 91.

A beautiful, clear, limpid mountain stream. Toney, *The Privations*, 93.

Two of them slept with their heads. Toney, *The Privations*, 103–104.

Nailed to the floor three feet. King, *My Experience*, 39.

With an open building. Toney, *The Privations*, 103.

Delirious for two days. Toney, *The Privations*, 110.

The second night one of our bedfellows died. Toney, *The Privations*, 111.

As there was very little currency in prison. Toney, *The Privations*, 100.

I have seen men go hungry a day. Toney, *The Privations*, 96. For a good discussion of the economics of daily prison life, see Gray, *The Business of Captivity*, 76–88.

James Marion Howard, a God-fearing Christian. See James Marion Howard, "A Short Sketch of My Early Life," VF 500–315, in Elmira Prison Camp Correspondence, CCHS.

A rude engine. King, *My Experience*, 42. Most men who spent any time at Elmira had detailed memories of the prisoner crafts there. See *Daily Advertiser,*

July 25, 1864. See also Michael Gray, "Uncovering a Ring Leader," *Chemung County Historical Journal* 43, no. 4 (June 1998): 4734–4739.

Finally the horses were about to lose their hair. Toney, *The Privations*, 108–109.

"Melancholia" (depression) was common. See Stanley Jackson, *Melancholia and Depression: From Hippocratic Times to Modern Times* (New Haven, Conn.: Yale University Press, 1986); for general practices, see Wiley, *The Life*, 244–269.

To write and receive letters not exceeding one page. Daily Advertiser, July 6, 1864.

The people at home never knew how we suffered. King, *My Experience*, 38.

Correspondents at Camp Douglas. For details concerning kites and camp life at Douglas in general, see Levy, *To Die*, 248–249; 235–236; 280–283; 238–243.

Woe be it to anyone who committed. The full range of punishments can only be gleaned through a review of dozens of narratives.

A prisoner carrying a barrel shirt. Toney, *The Privations*, 100.

As the prisoners had nothing to pay with. Toney, *The Privations*, 100.

The old measly pork barrel and I parted company. King, *My Experience*, 48.

Our wages would have been 5 and 10 cents. King, *My Experience*, 46.

Yankee justice could be vicious. For punishments in the Confederate army, see Wiley, *The Life*, 217–243.

King was proud he hadn't been tricked. See King, *My Experience*, 32–33; and Morrison, "Lewis County Boasts Only One."

G. W. D. Porter of the 44th Tennessee. See Porter, *Annals of the Army of Tennessee.*

These fellows looked like they had stolen something. See Copley, *A Sketch,* 153.

We had more respect for the men. Toney, *The Privations,* 115.

Voluntarily surrendered. Daily Advertiser, October 6, 1864.

J. L. Williams of the Ninth Alabama Infantry. Holmes, *The Elmira Prison,* 338.

While death began as a trickle. The monthly death toll at northern camps can be found in OR, vol. 8, 986–1003.

When a prisoner died, his name . . . the care of the dead. Toney, *The Privations,* 109–110.

Better housed, better clothed, better fed. Holmes, *The Elmira Prison,* 85.

Chapter 5

The water came into our prison higher and higher. King, *My Experience,* 46–47.

The south stockade wall washed away. Daily Advertiser, March 16–17, 1865.

As soon as we could with safety. King, *My Experience,* 47.

The walls were rebuilt and in a week or so. King, *My Experience,* 47.

There was great rejoicing and ringing bells. King, *My Experience,* 48.

This is a dark day for us. Toney, *The Privations,* 113.

The rebel prisoners are rejoicing with the rest. Daily Advertiser, April 11, 1865.

Framed as a sacred souvenir. Daily Advertiser, April 19, 1865.

"Old Abe ought to have been killed long ago." . . . *because he jeopardized so many lives.* Toney, *The Privations*, 116.

I do not believe we would have had the five years. Toney, *The Privations*, 116.

It was sad to hear the bells tolling in the city. King, *My Experience*, 46.

As the spring passed the number in our wards decreased. King, *My Experience*, 48. For the repatriation process from Elmira, see Horigan, *Elmira*, 170–171.

Highly pleased with the accommodations. Daily Advertiser, July 21, 1864.

The treatment of the rebels is exceedingly humane. Quoted in *Daily Advertiser,* August 19, 1864.

At this rate the entire command. OR, vol. 7, 1093.

Receiving all necessary care, and provision. OR, vol. 7, 1159.

Her only wish seemed to be that our prisoners. Daily Advertiser, November 21, 1864.

The prisoners are now well clothed. OR, vol. 7, 1213; see also OR, vol. 7, 1125.

They who visit them are universal. Quoted in *Daily Advertiser,* March 29, 1865.

Numbers have died both in quarters and hospital. OR, vol. 7, 878.

The mortality in this camp is so great. OR, vol. 7, 997.

Very bad health of the prisoners. OR, vol. 8, 209.

The first things that greeted our eyes on passing the gate. Daily Advertiser, April 26, 1865. See Gray, *The Business of Captivity,* 147, for a discussion of the circumstances of the visit.

Hale and hearty. Daily Advertiser, May 20, 1865.

A small Eden. Daily Advertiser, July 11, 1865.

The business of the prison camp. Daily Advertiser, July 12, 1865.

A farewell hop. Daily Advertiser, July 18, 1865.

"Helmira" became the burial place. See OR, vol. 8, 997–1003; Robertson, in Hesseltine, *Civil War Prisons*, 96; and Nat Daniel, "List of Confederate Soldiers Buried in Woodlawn National Cemetery (Chemung, N.Y.: Chemung County Historical Society, 1996). Some disagreement exists as to the actual number of Confederate dead at Elmira: Horigan, in *Elmira* (180), proposes 2,950; Gray, in *The Business of Captivity* (153), suggests 2,961; and the official OR count registers 2,933.

John Jones was born a slave. For Jones and the Underground Railroad in Elmira, see Holmes, *The Elmira Prison*, 140–150; Abner Wright, "The Underground Railroad," *Chemung Historical Journal* (August 1985): 1755–1758; and Jill McDonough, "Elmira's Underground Route to Freedom," *Chemung Historical Journal* (September 1974): 2421–2427. For economics of Jones's trade, see Gray, *The Business of Captivity*, 95–98.

Chapter 6

I believe Wanamaker would have made a better fit. King, *My Experience*, 50.

I will never forget the march from the cookhouse. King, *My Experience*, 50.

They cheered us as they passed . . . look at me kindly. King, *My Experience*, 51.

Timid to approach the house. King, *My Experience*, 51.

He was a good brother and I liked him. King, *Clarksburg Exponent Telegram*, June 26, 1932.

The days before the war were gone forever. For King's memories of childhood before the war, see regular columns he wrote for the *Weston* (West Virginia) *Independent*, entitled "Recollections of Other Days," December 10 and 17, 1918; January 7, 14, 21, and 28, 1919; February 18, 1919; and March 4, 11, 18, and 25, 1919.

It brings a sadness to my heart. King, *My Experience*, 50.

His grandfather Joshua Hedges King. Clarksburg Exponent Telegram, June 26, 1932. For obituaries of King, see *Weston Independent*, April 22, 1936, and *Weston Democrat*, April 24, 1936.

He said that he would send us to Dry Tortugas. Toney, *The Privations*, 119.

The effect of the prison diet can be seen. Toney, *The Privations*, 119.

Is supposed to be on the lookout. Toney, *The Privations*, 120.

We found change written upon everything. Toney, *The Privations*, 122.

I looked for the old homestead . . . got used to a bed. Toney, *The Privations*, 122–123.

Jim and his wife had to vamoose. Toney, *The Privations*, 123.

Auxiliaries of the police. Toney, *The Privations*, 125.

Our vessel commenced to burn and sink. Toney, *The Privations*, 127.

Mothers were calling for husbands and children. Toney, *The Privations*, 127.

We had been slaves to our own slaves. Toney, *The Privations*, 129.

A Southern soldier who deserted. Toney, *The Privations*, 130.

Our fallen heroes. See Marcus Toney, "Our Dead at Elmira," *Southern Historical Society Papers* 29 (1901): 194.

The old darky. Toney, "Our Dead at Elmira," 195.

In 1913, Toney came back. See "Tells of Days in Old Prison," from *Elmira Star Gazette*, June 16, 1913, in File 404B, CCHS.

Marcus Toney, husband of Sally Hill Claiborne. For Toney's obituary, see *Nashville Banner*, November 1–2, 1929.

For the crime of calling Clement C. Clay. Keiley, *In Vinculis*, 112.

The Elmira *Advertiser* ran extended excerpts. See *Elmira Advertiser*, July 1, 1865.

Certain to make [men] hogs, and very likely. Keiley, *In Vinculis*, 63. The best general sources for Keiley's life after the war are O'Grady, "Anthony M. Keiley: Virginia's Catholic Politician"; and Bailey, "Anthony M. Keiley and 'The Keiley Incident.'"

Not one in twenty of those who lie here. A. M. Keiley, "Our Fallen Heroes," *Southern Historical Society Papers* 7, no. 1 (January 1879): 377.

An act of "socialists and infidels." Quoted in Bailey, "Anthony M. Keiley," 74.

Reasons which in the nineteenth century are an affront. Quoted in Bailey, "Anthony M. Keiley," 79.

Providence . . . had preserved me unharmed. Keiley, *In Vinculis*, 215. For Keiley's obituary, see *Richmond Times-Dispatch*, January 31, 1905. Whether Keiley was driving a car or on foot seems unclear from the report.

Going up the Tennessee River. Wilkeson, *Recollections*, 244.

I had travelled on an order from Elmira. Wilkeson, *Recollections*, 245–246.

I had no interest in the regular army. Wilkeson, *Recollections*, 246. For more information on Wilkeson's postwar life, see *Gypsum Advocate*, April 25, 1913, and February 7, 1918; also see the memorial service program, Salina Public Library.

Berry Benson was given a much-deserved furlough. The best single source for Benson's exploits during the war after his return home from Elmira is in Benson, *Berry Benson's Civil War Book*, 174–203.

A black spot in the air. Berry Benson to Tom Murphy, undated, File 49, Box 6, Berry Benson Papers, #2636, SHC, UNC.

Ten years after the surrender. Holmes, *The Elmira Prison*, 372. See Benson copy of Holmes book with annotations: File 62, Box 8, Berry Benson Papers, #2636, SHC, UNC.

He wrote many a letter and placed. Berry Benson to M. M. Conklin, February 13, 1913, File 15, Box 2, Berry Benson Papers, #2636, SHC, UNC.

Your old comrade mole. Berry Benson to Washington Traweek, May 8, 1912, File 12, Box 1, Berry Benson Papers, #2636, SHC, UNC.

The police knew better than to start. Berry Benson to Blackwood Benson, July 1, 1917, File 20, Box 2, Berry Benson Papers, #2636, SHC, UNC.

A member of the Augusta Chronicle *staff.* Berry Benson to Blackwood Benson, July 1, 1917.

His querulous missives were made known. See "Controversy over Dictionary Unites Civil War Veterans," *Springfield* (Mass.) *Daily Republican*, May 17, 1922, File 37, Box 4, Berry Benson Papers, #2636, SHC, UNC.

And I am ashamed of neither. Berry Benson to John McElroy, March 27, 1913, File 16, Box 2, Berry Benson Papers, #2636, SHC, UNC.

Grandpapa in America. Berry Benson to Mrs. John Fox Maull, October 7, 1919, File 21, Box 2, Berry Benson Papers, #2636, SHC, UNC.

Unintelligible rot. Berry Benson to the *Chronicle.* Undated. File 24, Box 2, Berry Benson Papers, #2636, SHC, UNC.

Theosophist. Berry Benson to Arthur Conan Doyle, November 28, 1920, File 22, Box 2, Berry Benson Papers, #2636, SHC, UNC.

For an obituary of Benson, see the *Augusta Chronicle*, January 2–3, 1923.

BIBLIOGRAPHY

Manuscripts

National Archives, Washington, D.C. (NAW)
Southern Historical Collection, University of North
    Carolina at Chapel Hill (SHC)
Berry Benson Papers
Thomas Jefferson Green Papers
Virginia Historical Society, Richmond, Virginia
Anthony Keiley Family Papers

Newspapers

Augusta Chronicle, Augusta, Georgia
Clarksburg Exponent Telegram, Clarksburg, West
    Virginia
Confederate Veteran, Nashville, Tennessee
Daily Advertiser, Elmira, New York
Gypsum Advocate, Gypsum, Kansas
Nashville Banner, Nashville, Tennessee
Petersburg Daily Express, Petersburg, Virginia
Star Gazette, Elmira, New York
Richmond Times Dispatch, Richmond, Virginia
Weston Democrat, Weston, West Virginia
Weston Independent, Weston, West Virginia

Published Books and Articles

Adams, George Worthington. *Doctors in Blue: The
    Medical History of the Union Army in the Civil
    War.* New York: Henry Schuman, 1952.

Bailey, James. "Anthony M. Keiley and The Keiley Incident." *Virginia Magazine of History and Biography* 67 (January 1959): 65–81.

Benson, Susan Williams, editor. *Berry Benson's Civil War Book: Memoirs of a Confederate Scout and Sharpshooter.* Athens: University of Georgia Press, 1962.

Boyd, Joseph. "Shohola Train Wreck: Civil War Disaster." *Chemung Historical Journal* (June 1964; reprint 1985): 1253–1260.

Burke, Curtis. "Curtis Burke's Civil War Journal." *Indiana Magazine of History* 65 (December 1969): 283–327; *Indiana Magazine of History* 66 (June 1970): 100–172; *Indiana Magazine of History* 66 (December 1970): 318–361; and *Indiana Magazine of History* 67 (June 1971): 129–170.

Byrne, Thomas. "Elmira's Civil War Prison Camp: 1864–65." *Chemung Historical Journal* (September 1964; reprints 1985 and 1997): 1247–1252 (reprint 1985) and 1279–1300 (reprint 1997).

Copley, John. *A Sketch of the Battle of Franklin, Tennessee; with Reminiscences of Camp Douglas.* Austin, Tex.: E. Von Boeckmann, 1893.

Current, Richard, editor. *Encyclopedia of the Confederacy.* New York: Simon and Schuster, 1993.

Denney, Robert. *Civil War Prisons and Escapes.* New York: Sterling Publishing, 1993.

Douglas, Henry Kyd. *I Rode with Stonewall.* Chapel Hill: University of North Carolina Press, 1940.

Doyle, Robert. *Voices from Captivity: Interpreting the American POW Narrative.* Lawrence: University Press of Kansas, 1994.

Gallagher, Gary. *The American Civil War.* Chantilly, Va.: The Teaching Company, 1999.

Gray, Michael. *The Business of Captivity: Elmira and Its Civil War Prison.* Kent, Ohio: Kent State University Press, 2001.

———. "Uncovering a Ring Leader." *Chemung Historical Journal* (June 1998): 4734–4739.

Hemmerlein, Richard. *Prisons and Prisoners of the Civil War.* Boston: Christopher Publishing, 1934.

Hesseltine, William Best. *Civil War Prisons: A Study in War Psychology.* New York: Frederick Ungar, 1964.

Hesseltine, William Best, editor. *Civil War Prisons.* Kent, Ohio: Kent State University Press, 1972.

Holmes, Clay. *The Elmira Prison Camp: A History of the Military Prison at Elmira, New York.* New York: G. P. Putnam's Sons, 1912.

Horigan, Michael. *Elmira: Death Camp of the North.* Mechanicsburg, Pa.: Stackpole, 2002.

———. "Elmira Prison Camp—A Second Opinion." *Chemung Historical Journal* (March 1985): 3449–3457.

Howard, James Marion. "A Short Sketch of My Early Life." Chemung County Historical Society, 1917, 1–21.

Huffman, James. *Ups and Downs of a Confederate Soldier.* New York: William E. Rudge's Sons, 1940.

Jackson, Stanley. *Melancholia and Depression: From Hippocratic Times to Modern Times.* New Haven, Conn.: Yale University Press, 1986.

Jones, James, and Edward Keuchel. "A Rebel's Diary of Elmira Prison Camp." *Chemung Historical Journal* (March 1975, reprint 1985): 2457–2463.

Keiley, Anthony. "Our Fallen Heroes." *Southern Historical Society Papers* 7, no. 1 (January 1879): 373–384.

———. *In Vinculis; or, The Prisoner of War.* New York: Blelock, 1866.

King, John R. *My Experience in the Confederate Army and in Northern Prisons.* Clarksburg, W.Va.: United Daughters of Confederacy, 1917.

Leon, Louis. *Diary of a Tar Heel Confederate Soldier.* Charlotte, N.C.: Stone Publishing, 1913.

Levy, George. *To Die in Chicago: Confederate Prisoners at Camp Douglas, 1862–1865.* Evanston, Ill.: Evanston Publishing, 1994.

MacIsaac, Andrew. "From Bangor to Elmira and Back Again: The Civil War Career of Dr. Eugene Francis Sanger." *Maine History* 37, nos. 1–2 (summer-fall 1997): 30–59.

Marvel, William. *Andersonville: The Last Depot.* Chapel Hill: University of North Carolina Press, 1994.

McDonough, Jill. "Elmira's Underground Route to Freedom." *Chemung Historical Journal* (September 1974): 2421–2427.

McPherson, James. *Battle Cry of Freedom: The Civil War Era.* New York: Ballantine, 1989.

O'Grady, Joseph. "Anthony M. Keiley (1832–1905); Virginia's Catholic Politician." *Catholic Historical Review* 54, no. 4 (January 1969): 613–635.

———. "Politics and Diplomacy: The Appointment of Anthony M. Keiley to Rome in 1885." *Virginia Magazine of History and Biography* 76 (1968): 191–209.

Opie, John. *A Rebel Cavalryman with Lee, Stuart, and Jackson.* Chicago: W. B. Conkey, 1899.

Porter, G. W. D. "Nine Months in a Northern Prison." *Annals of the Army of Tennessee* 1, no. 4 (July 1878): 157–162.

Pryor, Sara Agnes. *Reminiscences of Peace and War.* Freeport, N.Y.: Books for Libraries, 1970.

Sangston, Lawrence. *The Bastiles of the North.* Baltimore: Kelly, Hedian, and Piet, 1863.

Scott, James, and Edward Wyatt IV. *Petersburg's Story: A History*. Richmond, Va.: Dietz Press, 1998.

Shriver, Phillip, and Donald Breen. "Ohio's Military Prisons in the Civil War." *Ohio Civil War Centennial Commission*, no. 15. Columbus: Ohio State University Press, 1964.

Sketches from Prison: A Confederate Artist's Record of Life at Point Lookout Prisoner-of-War Camp, 1863–1865. Baltimore: Maryland State Park Foundation, 1990.

Stamp, J. B. "Ten Months Experience in Northern Prisons." *Alabama Historical Quarterly* 18, no. 4 (winter 1956): 486–498. Courtesy Alabama Department of Archives and History, Montgomery, Alabama.

Steiner, Paul. *Disease in the Civil War: Natural Biological Warfare in 1861–1865*. Springfield, Ill.: Charles Thomas, 1968.

Toney, Marcus B. *The Privations of a Private*. Nashville, Tenn.: Author, 1905.

———. "Our Dead at Elmira." *Southern Historical Society Papers* 29, article 15 (1901): 194.

The War of the Rebellion: A Compilation of the Official Records of the Union and Confederate Armies, Series II, vols. 4, 6, and 8. Washington, D.C.: GPO, 1899.

Wilbur, C. Keith. *Civil War Medicine: 1861–1865*. Old Saybrook, Conn.: Globe Pequot Press, 1998.

Wiley, Bell Irvin. *The Life of Johnny Reb: The Common Soldier of the Confederacy*. Baton Rouge: Louisiana State University Press, 1997.

Wilkeson, Frank. *Recollections of a Private Soldier in the Army of the Potomac*. New York: G. P. Putnam's Sons, 1887.

INDEX

Jersey City, New Jersey, 202
Jessie's Scouts, 171
Johnson, Andrew, 56
Johnson, Bradley, 175
Johnson's Island (Ohio), 65,
 67, 77, 166
Johnston, Joseph, 235, 258
Johnstown, Pennsylvania,
 256
Jones, John, 232–34, 248,
 267
Jordan, William, 229

Kautz, Augustine
 Valentine, 38, 72
Keener, John, 13, 185–86
Keiley, Anthony, 5, 106–7,
 109, 134, 160, 180, 183,
 185, 188, 195–96, 200,
 204, 207, 209, 210, 218,
 220, 228, 232, 258, 266;
 attitude during
 imprisonment, 84–86;
 death of, 253–54; Elmira
 arrival, 44; Elmira jobs,
 72–73; Elmira journey,
 43–44; exchange,
 preparations for, 151–59;
 family background and
 education, 7–8; military
 background, 3–4;
 Negroes, opinions of,
 80–81; Petersburg life, 2;
 Point Lookout, journey

to and first residence at,
 37–43; Point Lookout,
 second visit, 160–62;
 political beliefs, 8–9;
 political career, post-war,
 251–53; post-war
 writings, 249–51;
 Richmond years, 250–52;
 Shohola train wreck,
 45–46; sickness, 74;
 southern homecoming,
 163–65; surrenders, 6
Kidder, John, 208
King, Cyrus, 9, 11, 237
King, John Rufus, 25, 121,
 128, 139, 157, 208, 211,
 216, 218, 226–27, 242, 253,
 266; army
 accommodations of,
 189–91; death of, 241;
 Elmira arrival, 188;
 Elmira departure,
 235–36; Elmira flood,
 221–23; Elmira food,
 191–94; Elmira winter,
 197–200; family
 background, 9;
 Gettysburg campaign,
 10–12; Lincoln
 assassination, opinions
 of, 224–26; Point
 Lookout residence, 64,
 186–88; post-war life,
 238–41; prison